THOSE BOYS ON THE HILL

Written By
ELLIOTT GLOVER

Edited by Leah Gallo

ELLIOTT GLOVER

Copyright © 2023

All Rights Reserved

ISBN: 978-1-963501-12-4

FOREWORD

Growing up, I knew of Elliott as the likable, and popular kid that my older sister was in theatre with. The word I associated with my memory of him most from high school is warm. He was friendly and effortlessly cool, and he had an inviting, positive energy that shone through, even in my very brief encounters with him, considering I was painfully shy, awkward, and three years younger. While I purposefully forgot most of high school, I remembered Elliott.

I was pretty oblivious to race and racism back then and had no idea Elliott was living in a group home (or even that one existed in our area) and certainly didn't know his backstory. So, I kinda marvel now, looking back, that my strongest memories of him are kindness and warmth when he was going through so much turmoil. I don't think my take is unique – many people who knew Elliott then would have similar recollections.

I reconnected with him, as a sign of the times, on social media. He posted about the concept for *Those Boys on The Hill*, intended to be a book about his experiences growing up, that would be a podcast first. I had been delving into anti-racism in the aftermath of George Floyd's murder. I had experience as a published author and editor and a background in photojournalism, and I have always loved books, reading, and storytelling. When I saw Elliott's post, it felt like fate – perhaps I could help edit in some way this project that reflected a story of where I grew up, one that I was too oblivious to know about when it was happening. I was finally gaining a deeper understanding of systemic racism and its sometimes subtle, sometimes glaringly obvious impact on the daily lives of Black, Indigenous, and People of Color. I knew nothing about foster care and its systemic problems that often heavily intersect with race. It seemed like such a necessary, vital story that should be told, so I reached out to Elliott to see if he would want help editing the book – and he and Iszel welcomed me with open arms.

It's been the best collaboration – both forming a friendship with Elliott and helping him in any small way to tell his truth. It's not easy to be vulnerable in the way Elliott and Iszel have been on the podcast, and Elliott is in this book. They share some of their darkest moments in a way that is not just illuminating and educational but also endearing and sometimes downright funny, finding humor and light woven amongst the grimmer circumstances of their childhood. The CHARISMA of those Glover boys is over the top, and it translates not just into the podcast but into Elliott's text.

This book is a necessary piece of the complicated and messy puzzle that is America. We need accounts like Elliott's out there, normalizing and bringing light to the Black experience in all its myriad forms. It's teaching through understanding on a deeply relatable level. But this biography goes so much beyond just race. It's the story of three brothers holding onto each other and holding each other up. It's the struggle for self-acceptance leading to self-discovery in the most difficult of circumstances. It's an insight into the complexities of love and unexpected friendships. It's an unflinching look at navigating and surviving abuse, emerging wounded but unbroken. It's about the tenacity and determination of the human spirit. It's brave and cathartic and healing. I could not be prouder to have contributed in some small way to the completion of this beautiful book. I hope you appreciate it and find it illuminating as much as I do.

Leah Gallo

Writer, Editor & Photographer

———————— ELLIOTT GLOVER ————————

Table of Contents

FOREWORD	4
AUTHOR'S NOTE	11
DEDICATION	12
CHAPTER 1: A Cold Start	13
CHAPTER 2: A Frosty Welcome	17
CHAPTER 3: Basketball Bonds	23
CHAPTER 4: A Life Shaped by Struggles	28
CHAPTER 5: First Day of School	34
CHAPTER 6: Iszel's Scars	45
CHAPTER 7: Culture Shock	54
CHAPTER 8: The Hills	60
CHAPTER 9: Home Visits	67
CHAPTER 10: Settling In	79
CHAPTER 11: Solitary	85
CHAPTER 12: Uncle Ricky	91
CHAPTER 13: Aunt Linda's Influence	110
CHAPTER 14: Dark Discovery	115
CHAPTER 15: Familial Violation	124
CHAPTER 16: Main Campus	128
CHAPTER 17: No Place Safe	138

CHAPTER 18: Early Dismissal	145
CHAPTER 19: Outdoor Ed	151
CHAPTER 20: Outdated	156
CHAPTER 21: Shoelaces and Showdowns	159
CHAPTER 22: The Soup Standoff	169
CHAPTER 23: Lights Out	176
CHAPTER 24: A New Day	184
CHAPTER 25: The Golden Age	191
CHAPTER 26: Counselling Sessions	198
CHAPTER 27: Behind Bars	201
CHAPTER 28: The Empty Seats	204
CHAPTER 29: Bonds & Breaks	206
CHAPTER 30: Childhood Nemesis	210
CHAPTER 31: Bonds in Transition	218
CHAPTER 32: Inevitable Clash of Paths	225
CHAPTER 33: One Last Visit	231
CHAPTER 34: Unraveling Harmony	235
CHAPTER 35: Those Boys	243
CHAPTER 36: Passing The Torch	246
CHAPTER 37: The Spencer Challenge	248
CHAPTER 38: An Early Second Chance	250
CHAPTER 39: The Weight of Aging Out	254
CHAPTER 40: Track and Triumphs	261

CHAPTER 41: A Standing Ovation	268
CHAPTER 42: The Brotherhood	270
CHAPTER 43: Leaving The House on the Hill	275
CHAPTER 44: Christmas 1994	278
EPILOGUE: Lost & Found	286
Two Sides to Every Story	291
MaryAnn's Account – December 2021	293
Against All Odds	295
About The Author	298
I Once	300
EDITOR'S NOTE	303
Fostering Understanding	303
BREAKING THE CYCLE	307
ACKNOWLEDGMENTS	310

AUTHOR'S NOTE

In sharing our family's story, I have chosen to use pseudonyms for some individuals. This decision was made to respect their privacy, maintain confidentiality, and ensure the comfort and anonymity of those whose accounts may be shared. While the events and experiences in this book are genuine, the names of certain individuals have been changed to protect their identities and safeguard their personal stories.

Thank you for understanding the considerations behind these changes, and I hope that the essence of our journey through this memoir remains as powerful and meaningful as intended.

Sincerely,

Elliott Glover

DEDICATION

To My Brothers who went through the Avondale Group Home for Boys,

You are not just my friends; you are my family. Through our ups and downs, we have grown together, supporting and inspiring each other in countless ways. This book is a testament to the strength and resilience that lives within each of us.

To All of Those Boys & Girls on the Hill,

May the hill we all climbed serve as a symbol of the challenges we faced and overcame. Our stories and experiences, though different, unite us as a community of survivors, dreamers, and achievers. This book is dedicated to each of you as a reminder that our lives and voices matter and our dreams are worth pursuing.

With love and gratitude,

Elliott Glover

CHAPTER 1

A Cold Start

I woke to the sound of screeching tires and the side-to-side veering of the Dodge Econoline van I was riding in. Disoriented, I grabbed the seat in front of me and gathered my bearings. My brother, Iszel, also snapped his eyes open. He sat next to me in the back of the tan ten-seater. Our older brother, Jacque, sat in the row in front of us, his 12-year-old arms spread across the back of his seat as if to create a physical barrier between us and the driver. He'd never let his guard down enough to sleep. Instead, his eyes were fixed on the white man who was trying to coax the shimmying van up a snowy hill.

I peered out the window at the churning mid-afternoon sky and saw that we were at the bottom of a long driveway, apparently in the middle of nowhere. The wind howled in different high and low tones past the van. My hammering heart began to slow as I switched my attention back to the driver, Henry Hill, the stiff and aloof man who had picked us up from Main Campus in Philly. We were informed that morning that he was the houseparent of a group home in Avondale, Pennsylvania, where my brothers and I had been placed. The house had five other guys living there and had openings for three more boys. None of us had heard of Avondale before and had no idea what to expect. It looked like the end of the world, populated by trees and little else. Just how long had I fallen asleep? It was my coping mechanism in stressful situations like this one, and I wondered how far from North Philly we had gone.

Henry took a long drag of his Newport in frustration. He let the smoke out in a noiseless whistle as he reached behind the steering wheel, cocked the gear stick, and put the van in reverse. Trying not to lose too much of his uphill progress, he pumped the van's brakes to avoid it gaining backward momentum. He shifted back to 'Drive' and gave it some gas. The van nudged forward a little bit but began fishtailing again in the accumulating snow on the driveway. He dropped the butt of his cigarette into a paper cup in the cupholder, the hot ash sizzling as it extinguished in the remnants of cold coffee. He reached into his shirt pocket, pulled another cigarette out of the pack, lit it, and took a long drag. I watched, disgusted, hating the smell and the whole situation. Henry considered his snowy nemesis, his unreadable eyes thickly bespectacled. He finally reached behind the steering wheel, jammed the gear stick to 'P,' turned the key, and peered through the rear-view mirror at us. Smoke escaped his lips as he spoke. "Boys, we're gonna hafta walk the rest of the way." His rough, country accent set me on edge.

Jacque gave us a nearly imperceptible nod to grab our stuff, which amounted to a couple of grocery bags of second-hand clothes each. Wearing a thin spring jacket with a t-shirt underneath, blue jeans, and a pair of Pro-Keds low-top black canvas shoes, he took a beat before shoving the door open and allowing the blast of icy air to invade the cabin of the vehicle. As he climbed out, the cold hit me like a ton of bricks. Instead of jumping out, I recoiled back into the van, using the bags as a shield.

"Elliott, Ikey, let's go!" Jacque called sternly. Resigned, we complied and climbed out into the wintry weather. I immediately began to shiver.

It was early January 1985. The thick layer of snow carpeting the ground suggested it had been snowing for days, and it wasn't showing any signs of letting up. I was nine years old. Iszel was eight. This would be the fifth alternative living situation for my brothers and me in the last year – if we survived the trek to the foreboding house overlooking the small development we had just driven through.

Henry didn't wait; instead, he plodded up the hill toward the house with his hands shoved deep in his pockets and the freshly lit Newport hanging from his mouth. His baseball cap was pulled low over his eyes, and his jacket collar was flipped up to protect his neck. He scrunched his shoulders as high as they could go, the tops of them nearly touching his exposed earlobes. His face was down, and he allowed the brim of the hat to take on the blustery, snowy gusts. Jacque gave him plenty of space before shuffling behind him, trying his best to shield us from the wintry onslaught while also keeping himself between Henry, Iszel, and me. Instead of following the long, arching driveway, Henry opted for the more direct path across the cornfield that ran alongside the driveway. His heavy boots crunched the remnants of last year's crop. Our sneakered footfalls were less effective. We trudged along, trying to lift our feet high enough to avoid the short, frozen stalks. I tripped and fell forward, spilling into the snow. Iszel, following closely behind, almost falling on top of me. The snow was numbingly cold on my bare hands, and I started crying.

Jacque grabbed my arm, pulling me. "Get up!" he ordered. He grabbed one of my bags and dusted the snow off my hands and knees. "You're fine. Stop crying."

We emerged from the cornfield onto the beginning of the large lawn in front of the house. Woods backed the dwelling like a thick, protective curtain. I also noted a weathered and dilapidated barn in the distance across the gravelly drive. Its white paint was peeling, its missing planks of wood exposing the inside to the elements. We still had a decent walk to go, but the grass was easier to negotiate than the cornfield. Henry was a good distance ahead of us, and Jacque picked up his pace. We followed suit, trying not to slip. Icy gusts blew the snow in billowy circles around us, battering our faces and settling in our hair.

With each step, my uneasiness grew. The house had a deep, red-brick exterior, dark windows, and white shutters. Its three stories towered ominously over the ten-house development below. It loomed tall and wide, like a thick-necked bully ready to take lunch money from a smaller, weaker classmate. Although there was a light dusting on its rooftop, the wintry mix pelting us seemed to avoid the overwhelming house, which swallowed the six acres of fields and woods around it.

It was eerily quiet as we finally made it to the front porch. Too quiet... for a house where five other boys were supposed to live. There was a coldness to it, and I had a feeling it would not be much warmer inside. We climbed the porch steps, kicking snow off our shoes as best we could before entering to discover what the house had in store for us.

CHAPTER 2

A Frosty Welcome

We stepped into the entryway of a well-lit kitchen. I was right. The house didn't feel much warmer inside. I patted my arms and shoulders, hoping it would help me thaw out a bit. I rubbed my hands together and, with chattering teeth, blew a staccato stream of air on them. Melting snow dripped from my hair onto the tops of my frost-bitten ears and neck, sending convulsive shivers down my spine. Water bubbled up and squished out of my shoes onto the light vinyl floor every time I shifted my weight.

Henry looked us over briefly when we entered but didn't offer us towels. He stood behind a grey Formica counter surround that encompassed the stove and dishwasher. It took up a decent part of the kitchen. There was a black, decorative wood-burning fireplace in the wall to our left with a small sitting area next to it.

With his back to us, he reached up, opened one of the white-painted cabinets on the back wall, grabbed a mug, and poured himself some coffee from an electric pot. I couldn't help but think that he must have horrible breath between the coffee and the cigarettes. I hoped I would never find out. He turned towards us, one hand on the handle of his coffee mug, the other cradling and drawing heat from the base, and blew into the cup as he edged his lips towards the rim, causing steam to fog his glasses.

He took a cautious sip from his cup and exhaled in satisfaction. "Ok. Let's get you boys settled."

He came from behind the counter, coffee in hand, and walked past us into the dining room on the right. A phone hung on the kitchen wall.

Its curly cord was stretched taut into the dining room. The room was filled with a large ten-person dining table that had a converted wagon-wheel chandelier hanging above it. At the end of the cord was a tall, dark-skinned, Black kid sitting in one of the ornate wooden chairs, talking to someone on the phone. He balanced precariously on the chair's two back legs against the flower-printed wall. He hushed his voice when Henry walked by.

"Sit on that chair properly or stand!" Henry barked in passing. The kid lowered the chair's front two legs to the floor, staring hard in Henry's direction. I watched the exchange warily. The boy gave the three of us a cursory nod and continued with his conversation.

Henry pointed towards a living room full of antiques that looked like a museum.

"You boys stay out of that there room."

At this, I pressed my foot deep into my shoe and left a little water on the hardwood floor. When we entered the main hallway, Henry stopped at the bottom of a staircase near an open door. He called someone named Janine to come out to meet us.

A pear-shaped, 50-something white woman appeared at the door next to the staircase wearing loose-fitting jeans with an elastic waist, a camisole tank top, and a long-sleeved jean overshirt. Her dyed platinum blond hair fell in tight coils to her shoulders. She crossed her arms, leaned her heft against the door jamb, and considered the three of us… waiting. We stood in awkward silence, staring up at her while her eyes shifted from one of us to the next for what felt like an eternity until her condescending soprano voice finally pierced the silence. "Well, don't you boys know to introduce yourselves when you meet somebody?" Her tone laced the question with annoyance and disdain, and the excess flesh at the base of her neck jiggled like a turkey gobbler when she spoke.

I assumed meeting us had interrupted whatever she had been doing, and she was not too happy about the distraction. Henry placed a heavy, booted foot on the third step of the staircase to watch the exchange, then pulled off his cap, exposing a salt and pepper military haircut. He rested his elbow on his knee, sipped at his coffee, and goaded us into the odd exchange. "Well, go on, boys, tell her your names."

Jacque took the lead. "I'm Jacque, this is Elliott and Iszel."

Janine silently chuckled a bit, taking a beat. She waved her finger pointedly toward Iszel and me. "Don't these other two have voices?" she finally asked.

"Yes," Jacque answered.

She stood, her middle-aged body now erect. The door jamb creaked softly, surely relieved it did not have to support her weight anymore. She recrossed her arms, looking annoyed; then she took a couple of steps towards Jacque. She lowered her voice, her southern drawl thickening.

"Then, if they have voices, you best start to let 'em' use 'em.' You ain't gonna be around every time they meet people." She pointed again towards Iszel and me. "They need to learn their own manners."

Jacque shrugged at her like the intensity of her last statement was overblown. *What's the big deal?*

"They know their manners. You know, 'speak when spoken to' and all. And I AM here now, so..." He let his voice fade off mid-sentence, allowing the rest of his point to be made in an uncomfortable, lingering silence. He smirked and shook his head slowly at her, looking to see that she got his point.

Janine's cheeks flushed bright red at Jacque's gall. "You best learn how to talk to people of authority, young man. We don't tolerate no such disrespect 'round here."

Janine directed her frustration towards her husband. "Henry, I don't have time for this." She shook her head at him as she spoke, causing her gobbler to jiggle vigorously. I couldn't stop looking at it. "Get these kids right and out of my sight until they know how to properly introduce themselves."

She turned and walked back into the apartment, driving her heels down hard onto the wooden floor.

What's it matter? I thought. *We're not going to be here long enough to learn how to address her anyway.*

Henry took his foot off the step and straightened upright. He tugged the brim of his baseball cap back on, tisked, and shook his head at us in disappointment. We had failed our first meeting with Janine, who I figured must be the lady of the house.

"You boys better not be any trouble 'round here," Henry grumbled. "You gotta do better than that. C'mon."

Instructing us to follow him, he walked up the large flight of stairs two at a time to a small landing, then up a smaller flight to the second floor. We followed behind in stony silence, still shivering and cold.

There were four bedrooms, each furnished simply with two beds and a pair of dressers. The rooms were all painted white, devoid of any warmth or personal touch. The one we walked past had a couple of posters of Run DMC and Whodini on the walls, a stark contrast to the otherwise sterile environment. We passed a fifth closed door, shrouded in mystery.

"Don't ever go in there," Henry instructed, his voice tinged with a stern warning. "That's not for any of the likes of y'all."

I shifted my weight to leave another extra wet footprint on the floor, my curiosity piqued by what lay behind that forbidden door.

Henry showed us which rooms were ours and instructed us to meet him in the kitchen to go over the house rules and chores. Iszel and I would be roommates, while Jacque would be bunking with someone we hadn't met yet.

For a few minutes, it was just Iszel and me. The encounter with Janine left a distinct impression on me. As I prepared to settle in, I turned to my brother Iszel, hoping to bring a bit of levity to our dire situation.

"Yo, how'd you like that turkey lady?" I joked, raising my eyebrows playfully, hoping he noticed what I noticed. It was another inside joke, a way for us to find solace in humor when everything else seemed grim. "I thought she was gonna gobble-gobble at us." I flapped my elbows like a bird.

It almost made him smile, but the weight of our situation overtook the levity of the joke, and the air grew thick and heavy again.

"Don't matter, none," he said, shrugging and dismissively waving both hands at the thought. "Dis gonna be three hots and a cot for a minute, just like dose other places." Iszel was missing his two front teeth, and it made his "THs" sound like "Ds."

I looked down at my three grocery bags, filled with the meager possessions I owned, and couldn't help but silently agree. We had spent the last year bouncing from the homes of aunts, uncles, our mother's friends, and state-run facilities. Nothing stuck longer than a couple of months. We fell silent as we readied ourselves. I pulled a fresh shirt from one of the bags, peeled off my wet one, and changed. There was no point in changing my socks since I only owned the wet shoes on my feet. Wet socks and shoes would have to do. Every part of me felt numb, cold, and tired. I tried not to shiver as I hung the wet shirt from a bedpost.

I opened the top drawer of a dresser and threw my plastic bags of possessions to the back, shoving it closed. Iszel had done much the same. We met Jacque in the hallway to go down to the kitchen together.

Henry directed us to a clipboard hanging from a nail on the wall holding a single sheet of paper. He tapped it. "This is the weekly chore list. I'll be adding you boys to it so you can earn your keep 'round here."

For this, Iszel and I would be paid a meager allowance of three dollars a week; Jacque would be paid five. Henry flashed an expectant smile towards us, but I couldn't get excited about it. I had been promised money for doing chores in the past and was mostly told, "I'll get you next week, kid," only to never receive the funds. Henry's smile slid from his face at our lack of enthusiasm.

"I'll give you envelopes with your allowance after school on Fridays," he said brusquely. "But," he added sternly, holding one finger up, "if you do the chores poorly, break any of my rules, or come home with poor reports or grades, then you forfeit a portion of your allowance."

"How much?" Jacque asked.

Henry shrugged with a wry smile. "It's at my discretion, depending on how badly you've messed up. So don't mess up."

I resisted the urge to roll my eyes. At nine years old, I already knew that the demerit system always had a catch and was never to the benefit of the one on the receiving end.

Henry left the kitchen with some further muttered warnings, and then, for the first time since we arrived, we were on our own to explore.

CHAPTER 3

Basketball Bonds

Our solitude didn't last long. As soon as Henry left, the porch door opened, and a lean, brown-skinned kid who looked to be the same age as Jacque walked in. He was dressed in a gray sweatsuit, a non-descript baseball cap, and black Chuck Taylor sneakers. He cradled a basketball under his arm.

"Sup, y'all? He done his 'earn your keep 'round here' chore speech yet?" the kid asked, changing his voice briefly to mimic Henry's nasal tone, and stomping around to mock him physically.

Jacque nodded, laughing.

"Y'alls from Philly?"

Jacque nodded again. "Yeah, you too?"

I could hear the hesitation in Jacque's voice and guessed that he was reluctant to say exactly what part of the city since being from the wrong part could give others a reason to start a turf war.

"E'erybody here's from Philly," the kid responded amiably. I read this to mean that at this group home, the solidarity of being from the city was more important than which part you were from.

"I'm Derek," he said. "What's y'alls names?"

Jacque introduced us, and Derek nodded at each of us in turn. He made a show of reaching to give each of us a proper handshake.

"Nice, strong shake, lil' man." He said to Iszel. I didn't get a compliment when he shook my hand. "Y'alls come through Main Campus? I hated that place."

"Yeah, they be fightin' all the time," I chimed in, trying to be part of the conversation.

This kid ain't too bad, I thought.

"Y'all tryna run some ball?" Derek asked. "Cuz we gotta court in the barn." He patted the basketball when he said this.

"Nah, I'm still cold from walking up that hill," I said. "Besides, my shoes are still wet." Though partially true, I was more concerned that I didn't know how to play basketball and did not want to embarrass myself in front of the new, cool housemate.

"Man, a lil cold ain't never stopped nobody from runnin' some ball. Plus, a good game will warm you up." He looked at my brothers. "Y'all comin'? We'll play a lil roughhouse."

"Might as well, don't see shit else to do out here in the sticks," Jacque said loudly.

Derek hushed his voice. "Yo, don't let Henry hear you cuss; he be trippin'." He shook his head in the general direction from which Henry had exited the room like he could see the old man standing in the doorway.

He smiled and shoved the ball into Iszel's mid-section like a quarterback handing a football off to a running back. "Here ya go, lil man, lemme see whatch'all got!" *A couple more 'Lil Mans' and Iszel is gonna have a new nickname,* I thought jealously.

"We call him Ikey," I corrected.

Iszel waved one hand in front of him and shook his head at this.

"Nah, only family calls me that, and they have to be older than me to do it."

Now he's correcting me, I thought crossly. Iszel hesitated a moment longer and followed with, "You can call me... Zel." He nodded his head approvingly at his own genius. I liked the new moniker for him. It made him seem older and more in control.

"Ok, then," Derek acquiesced. "Zel it is. No mo' 'Lil' man.'" He didn't ask for my nickname, which left me feeling socially deflated.

Derek pushed through the kitchen door and jogged towards the barn, expecting us to follow him. He left Iszel holding the ball. If nothing else, we had to get the ball back to him, so we headed toward the door. The tall, lanky kid that had been on the phone dropped the receiver back in its cradle on the wall, smiling broadly with a mouth full of teeth. "Yo y'all, I'm Anthony, but e'rybody 'round here calls me 'Jiggs.'"

We exchanged brief introductions.

"I'm coming too," he said, nodding at the door. We all trotted out into the frigid weather towards the barn.

The game played out like a nightmare for me. I stumbled and fumbled on the court, unable to dribble or shoot, and my attempts at handling the ball were anything but graceful. Iszel and Jacque had a natural knack for the game, which only served to highlight my inadequacies. Derek and Jiggs, on the other hand, were in a league of their own, effortlessly running layups and sinking shots from all over the court.

Derek's triumphant shout of "Magic, Baby!! My Ball!" after one of his shots caught me off guard. I had no idea what he meant or what the rules were. "What?!" I asked, clearly bewildered.

Derek looked at me in disbelief. "Come on, man! You gotta know who Magic Johnson is," he said, disappointment in his voice as he lowered his hands.

Jacque chimed in, trying to explain. "Yo, he's that guy on the 7-Up commercials who makes the basketballs disappear. And yeah, it's Derek's ball." He pointed towards Derek to emphasize the point.

"He's a magician?" I asked, still perplexed, as I tossed a wayward bounce pass toward Derek. He effortlessly caught the ball, cradling it to his hip as if my lack of knowledge needed immediate rectification.

"Naw, man! His name is Magic Johnson. He's the greatest basketball player of all time. His game's so good it's like magic," Derek explained incredulously.

I simply shrugged, uninterested in Derek's favorite player and the game's nuances. My indifference irked him, and he intensified his efforts to outplay me, taunting me with his "Magic, Baby!" jeers. The more Derek pressed the issue, the less I liked whoever this Magic Johnson was.

Frustration mounted as I took a hard foul from Derek, and my housemates, including my brothers, allowed it to pass without protest, accepting it as part of the game. Finally, unable to bear it any longer, I muttered, "I quit," and walked off the court. I had failed to fit in with the cool kids at the house, and my mood sank. I couldn't help but wonder why Derek couldn't be as cool with me as he was with Iszel.

As I watched from the sideline, Derek implored me to rejoin the game. "Com' on, man! Stop being a lil girl! It's just a lil roughhouse," he called out in frustration. But I stood my ground, avoiding the court while staying in the barn to avoid going back inside the house alone with the white house parents.

All but one of the boys from the house joined the game, and introductions were made all around. During that game, Iszel, Jacque, and I discovered that we were the youngest in the house. We were a diverse group. All boys of color but had family from the Caribbean, Africa, the south, and New York. The other boys' ages ranged from 12 to 17.

None of us dared to broach the topic of why we had ended up in this place. It was a silent agreement among us; our struggles were too burdensome to discuss. Instead, we engaged in light-hearted banter about cheesesteaks in Philly and which part of the city we hailed from. Such conversations were safe territory, fostering a sense of camaraderie among us. At Main Campus, differences in city origins could lead to fights, but here, they were a source of friendly rivalry.

The game continued, evolving into a chaotic scramble as six bodies hustled for the ball, with no clear teams in sight during this roughhouse game. As I stood on the sideline, I began to shiver in the cold, my thin t-shirt and jacket providing little warmth, my shoes still damp. They eventually decided to play three-on-three, a more manageable arrangement, and carried on until dinner. The intensity of the game caused steam to rise from the players' heads into the frigid air.

Later that night, I huddled under the covers of my bed, curled up to conserve heat, trying to warm the chill that had settled into my bones. I was exhausted, but my mind whirred, keeping me from sleeping. As I reflected on that first day of introductions, I couldn't help but think of my mother and extended family, even though I had never once mentioned them to the other boys. The memories of my past and the circumstances that had brought me to this place weighed heavily on my mind. I thought about my own difficult journey and my mom and her parents, all part of the path that had led me to this unfamiliar, lonely place.

CHAPTER 4

A Life Shaped by Struggles

My grandfather served in the Army, and unlike white Americans who returned to a hero's welcome and benefits, he and other Black Americans were denied what they were entitled to under the GI Bill.[1] At that time, it was widespread practice to forbid mortgages or rentals to Black Americans except in specific areas, and he and my grandmother were redlined into a neighborhood in North Philly.[2] They also struggled in the job market, as many Black Americans in their era did. Black Americans were often denied job opportunities given to white Americans and were paid less for the same jobs as their white coworkers.[3,4] Like Black people facing similar situations and economic circumstances, those neighborhoods became communities that took care of each other. Those who could afford it helped those who were struggling to keep everyone fed.[5]

When I was growing up, there was a Block Captain who ensured the neighborhood was kept clean and who arranged to have welfare lunches provided to those who were underprivileged. Each weekday, she would receive a large brown box early in the morning filled with cereal and cartons of milk for breakfast and one for lunch filled with sandwiches, fruit, and drinks. We used to take the thick slices of bologna, turkey, or salami out of the premade sandwiches and fry them up to give them some flavor before putting them back into the bread.

My grandparents and their kids, including my mom, were completely unaware of or didn't believe in using contraception. It wasn't taught in schools or families. Abstinence and luck were the only two unrealistic options to escape early parenthood. There was sex, and there were babies, and that was that. It was no surprise that my mom grew up lost among her ten brothers and sisters. For those like my mom, who grew up poor, opportunities to escape the cycle of poverty were both slim and grim, reinforced by American systems designed to keep segregation and an invisible caste system in place. [6]

My mother, MaryAnn, aspired to a better life for herself than the daily, incessant struggle to survive that she and most North Philly residents experienced. She studied culinary, sewing, and accounting vocations at Dobbins Technical High School with hopes of becoming a chef. But she was also young, insecure about her looks, and seeking love and connection in any way she could. She met an older man, and it wasn't long after that she was pregnant with Jacque. She hoped that she wouldn't give birth before her sixteenth birthday, and her prayers were answered by a mere two days' grace. Jacque's father remained in his life but provided little to no financial support.

MaryAnn's dreams were crushed before she could fully formulate them. In her era in inner-city neighborhoods, teens having kids were more common than teens graduating high school. Our grandparents made it clear that her baby was her responsibility, just as they had done with her older siblings.

Despite juggling her classes and providing for her newborn, my mother excelled in the culinary, sewing, and accounting programs. However, the responsibilities of motherhood became overwhelming, and she had to drop the culinary and sewing programs to focus solely on obtaining her accounting certification. She had always been good with numbers. She started hustling around the neighborhood, cleaning houses, working part-time hours as a cashier, and taking Jacque to babysitting jobs. She completed her accounting certification and dropped out of school shortly thereafter to join the workforce full-time.

She earned enough money to eventually put him in daycare, where she met my father. Shortly thereafter, I was on the way. My father was already married and had no interest in leaving his wife. My mother was five months shy of her nineteenth birthday when I was born. Nine months after she turned nineteen, Iszel came along. His father was an

R&B crooner she had known from around the neighborhood. He was interested in being a dad, but when Iszel was six months old, he was found guilty of being an accessory to murder and sentenced to life in prison.

My mother was struggling to make ends meet during the era of Mayor Frank Rizzo, a former commissioner of the Philadelphia police department. He was a supporter of Nixon; he opposed policies like public housing (then generally filled with African Americans) in majority-white neighborhoods[7], and he opposed desegregating schools.[8] His reign was characterized by police brutality, racism, and misconduct.[9] He presided over a city that was becoming increasingly racially divided. He was later ranked by historians and political scientists as one of the worst big-city mayors ever.[10]

Against this political backdrop, my mother now had three kids and no paternal financial support. With no high school diploma and no real skills to draw from, my mother's career prospects were slim. She applied for and was granted government benefits, welfare income, and food subsidies. Even with the aid, ends never met. She depended on the charity of friends and lovers or her ability to negotiate with acquaintances to house, feed, and clothe the three of us.

Our mother's struggle was one that many Black mothers faced then and now. Black families are three times more likely to be single-parent homes than white families.[11] Black children are also nearly five times more likely to experience foster care than their white counterparts.[12] When I was three, she had expended all her connections and was still not earning enough on minimum wage jobs and the welfare subsidies to make ends meet no matter how hard she worked. So, she voluntarily turned us over to a group home facility in West Philly named St. Vincent's.

Iszel learned how to walk and was potty trained there. I struggled to sleep. On bad nights, the group home aides placed a fold-out child's cot in the laundry room, turned on the dryers, and ran the washers. The rhythmic, ambient hum of the machines helped. I would peacefully wake up in that laundry room most mornings. It was less tranquil, perhaps, for the nurse who slept awkwardly and uncomfortably in a makeshift chair bed during my overnight struggles.

My mother decided the only way to earn enough money to save up so she could support all of us was to start hustling less legally. She aligned herself with a mail carrier, bartender, and beer distributor to cash social security checks of people who had passed away. Back then, the government might not realize someone had died for months, sometimes years, and would continue to send the checks if they were still being cashed. But after two years, when I was five years old, law enforcement had finally grown wise to my mom's involvement in this kiting scheme.

She collected us from the home and fled to Delaware to live off the grid while she figured out her next move. For a brief time, we lived in a trailer park in Smyrna, Delaware. I have very few memories from that time, but I loved the Smyrna Diner's pancakes whenever we went. We eventually ended up in a three-room shack on a dirt road with an outhouse. I went to kindergarten, which was a short walk from where we were living.

Mom's life was in constant turmoil, so ours was as well, and I didn't attend school all that often. She anesthetized her constant anxiety and worry with drugs and alcohol. When she finally grew tired of running after a year, she arranged for our grandparents to keep us while she served a plea-bargained sentence in jail. After she was released, we bounced around with her throughout the years before we landed back in the foster care system. And now, here we were, in a group home in the middle of rural, white Pennsylvania. I had no idea what was in store for us.

I lay in bed that first night at the House on the Hill, huddled, reflecting on the past. My thoughts were churning, a chaotic jumble of snippets of my life with my mother. My relationship with her had deteriorated over the years. She struggled to understand why I preferred the arts over basketball or football. In front of me, to her friends and family, she introduced and spoke of me as her "weird" son. Admittedly, I was different from my brothers, who gravitated towards sports instead of music and theatre. They were more socially adept than I was, and my introspective silence caused friends and family alike to feel uncomfortable. But "Weird"... "Weird"?! I didn't like the label. It felt like a scarlet letter, a giant "W" as a permanent mark of otherness, especially when compared to Jacque's "The Smart One" and Iszel's "The Golden Child." She preferred the company of my brothers over mine; and that capital "W" became a constant reminder of my perceived strangeness that would haunt me well into my teen years.

If my mother, the woman who had birthed me, thought I was "Weird," I expected every other woman to see me the same way. I didn't understand what was wrong with me, but I knew my mother wasn't completely comfortable with me. It was a chronic loneliness, a feeling of not belonging, that I couldn't shake.

It wasn't until I was older that I learned that "weird" for my mother meant possibly homosexual. She was clear about my brothers' sexuality but not mine. Singing, acting, dancing, and drawing were my outlets, and that meant gay to her. I wanted to be her son like my brothers were, but because of her misdiagnosed bias about my sexuality, we struggled to connect. It was okay for a friend of hers to be gay, but one of her sons?!! *Hell Naw!!*

My relationship with my mother was, at best, fraught as a result. I loved her, but she frustrated me. I felt demeaned by her. I was the different son. Less loved and less regarded than my brothers, like I had nothing to offer. It was hard to respect her authority. If I didn't like something, I told her so, and she didn't appreciate hearing that from me. Despite my frustrations, I loved her, but the divide between us was evident, like an unbridgeable chasm.

I shifted deeper into my pocket of heat under the covers. I felt a little guilty for thinking badly of my mom. After all, she was always scrambling to make something work for us. *No, for Them!* my brain contested resentfully. I just benefitted from her efforts for them. Middle

Child syndrome be damned! I was residual baggage, a reminder of her struggles. That thought left a hurtful lump in my throat that ached. I swallowed deeply, fighting the tears, but the hurt and anguish won out, and I cried hard. I wiped my tears with the heel of my hand and tried to regain my composure, but the weight of feeling unloved and different was overwhelming, exacerbated by how I'd felt unable to connect with the other kids all day in this cold, dreary place.

I sighed to myself, emotionally exhausted, contemplating some of my mother's good choices and her many short-sighted, bad ones. I thought about how, no matter what she did, she always seemed... stuck. And that sense of being stuck left us in this alien, quiet place, a stark contrast to the hustle and bustle of the city we once knew.

I closed my eyes and strained my ears but could hear nothing outside, no wind, no insects, no cars, no people. It was the kind of quiet you never had in the city. It was a stark reminder that this isolation had become our new reality. The only sound in the room was Iszel's deep, even breathing. I turned my head to look at him, though he was just an indistinct mound in the darkness, and I felt a little better. The two constants in my life were my brothers. Whatever was coming for us, whatever we had to face, we would do that together, as we always had. As we always would. Even if I didn't make a single friend, I still had them. I turned fully on my side to face him, pulled the covers up to my nose, and finally drifted to sleep, the bond with my brothers providing a flicker of warmth in the frosty, desolate night.

CHAPTER 5

First Day of School

Henry didn't waste time registering us for school. A few days after arriving at the House on the Hill, he opened a well-organized closet full of school supplies and selected a dark blue book bag. He filled it with two red composition books, a folder, and two unsharpened pencils.

"This should get you started for now," he said, handing me the loosely filled bookbag.

I didn't like the red-colored composition books. Every teacher of mine had marked every wrong answer in red. It seemed that anything I wrote in one of those books would be wrong, too. I inspected the notebooks closer, alarmed. *These aren't even red; they're closer to pink!!* I didn't want my classmates to question my masculinity because of the color of the notebooks chosen for me. I absolutely needed something different. These reddish-pink ones were starting me off on the wrong foot, and I needed all the help I could get.

"Can I have two black notebooks instead of the red ones?" I asked politely. I pointed to a stack of them in a box next to the red ones at the bottom of the closet.

Henry tapped the bookbag in my hands with his pointer finger. "No, you take what's given, and you will appreciate the gesture. Not every kid going to school this morning has the benefit of such charity."

Henry made a show of filling a second bookbag with equivalent items, except he included a blue and black composition book. He handed the bag to me. "Give that one to Iszel. Don't you go switching colors behind my back. I may not see you do it, but God will. He sees everything. He's always watching."

"If you gave me the colors I asked for, I wouldn't have to switch them in front of God," I said.

I turned and walked out of the room. He was pitting me against the heavenly Big Man, challenging me to abide by his arbitrary rules or be smote for my disobedience. I keenly felt like God was looking at me all the time, taking note of my every choice. Nevertheless, I switched the black one out for one of my red ones. I struggled with the idea for less than a millisecond. *God would understand and forgive me for this one*, I thought.

Iszel didn't even check on the contents of the bag when I handed it to him. He gave me a "Here we go again" smile and simply shrugged it onto his shoulder.

We walked down the hill to catch the school bus. It was just the two of us; Jacque was in middle school, so he had taken an earlier bus. A cluster of white kids who were familiar with each other stood on one side of the road. Iszel and I stopped on the opposite side and kept to ourselves. They stared at us, trying to figure out which house we had recently moved to in the neighborhood and how they missed our doing so. Not one to avoid a good stare-down, I returned their gazes with a hard look. I figured instilling fear in them was better than looking weak or like we could be taken advantage of out here in the sticks. Plus, we had to represent the streets of North Philly.

Bus 3 pulled up, and we had to cross the road to the 'white side' to board. The driver gave us a quick once over but was unfazed by her two new passengers. All the seats had at least one child in them, with a bookbag lying on the seat next to them. Some saw us coming and blocked the seat to indicate that we couldn't sit next to them. We were halfway down the bus, and I had grown frustrated with the game.

The driver was waiting for us to be seated before pulling off. I turned to see that she was watching everything play out through her large rear-view mirror, assessing whether to intervene. She was allowing the kids to figure out how we were going to relate before stepping in.

Ok, we'll play it your way, I thought.

I turned back around and gave the next meek-looking kid my hardest "North Philly" stare. It conveyed that I was willing to go further to make my point than he was to make his. *Move the bag or hurt, and still have one of us sitting next to you!*

He got the point, pulling his book bag up flush against his hip, creating a physical barrier for himself, and stared out the window.

God forbid our black skin touches your white skin on the way to school, I thought. I pointed to the now-empty seat for Iszel to sit in, then gave the same stare to the kid in the row directly behind them. He quickly moved his bag, and I took my seat. I wanted to be close to Iszel in case someone tried to start something. The social construct on the bus had been established. *Don't mess with the Glover brothers!* The driver pulled off.

The bus buzzed with chatter from the kids, primarily discussing what they received for Christmas or how they celebrated New Year's. I felt like the holidays had skipped us. There were no gifts, no fuss, not even a special meal to mark the season. We had missed many holidays and birthdays growing up. We had certainly never believed in Santa Claus. Santa was a myth only those with money could afford. This was one of the rare occasions I didn't mind being the new kid because no one asked me what I got for Christmas.

We checked into the office when we arrived at the school. Before long, an aide guided me through the halls of the school I would attend for fourth grade. Avon Grove Elementary was a small one-story, orange-brick building. The hallways were lined with a slate gray carpet that was meant to hide the dirt and stains of the students despite being cleaned daily. Whatever was in the cleaning solution left a warm fragrance behind throughout the whole building that calmed me. I noticed it on the first day and immediately liked the place.

I walked into Ms. Williams' fourth-grade class and scanned the room for a face like mine. I couldn't find one. The closest one was a Puerto Rican kid with big, thick glasses. The rest of them were white.

They all stared at me, taking stock of me, considering my oversized, second-hand clothes and uncut hair.

Ms. Williams took me to the front of the room and placed me in front of her immaculately kept desk. "Class, we have a new student that I want you all to welcome," she said. She looked down at me and smiled broadly and brightly, showing too many teeth. It looked forced.

"This is Elliott. Can we all say hi to him?"

A few murmured "Hi," but there wasn't much enthusiasm coming my way.

Ms. Williams tried again, adding more excitement to her voice by pitching it higher to transfer her energy to my new classmates. "Come on, everyone. We can do better than that!"

The second round of "Hi's" was a little stronger, but the room was still cold.

Having moved so much since kindergarten, I had grown accustomed to being the 'new student' and hated it when teachers put me on display like this. I just wanted to take my seat and let the norm of the day overtake the fact that I was there. At least I was the sole new kid today. A few other times, there had been another kid starting the same day. That second person always looked better, dressed better, came from a more interesting place, and was much smarter than I was. Being the new kid sucked.

"Elliott, why don't you tell everyone about yourself."

Here we go, I thought, mentally rolling my eyes.

"I just moved here from Philly," I said.

"He means the City of Philadelphia," Ms. Williams corrected, smiling brightly, nodding to the other students for understanding. She looked back at me, urging me to continue.

"I got two brothers, and we stayin' in Avondale."

"You HAVE two brothers, and you are LIVING in Avondale," she corrected again. I looked up at her and thought, *Lady, you makin' me sound stupid. Like I don't talk right.* She looked down at me, and I swear she could hear my thoughts and thought back, *You are, Sweety. You are stupid.*

She looked around the class.

"Well then, that's enough with the introductions," she said. "Who wants to be Elliott's friend?" Most of the white faces stared down at their desks. Others waited to see who would buddy up with the new Black kid. The Puerto Rican boy and a little girl with dirty blond hair on the opposite side of the room raised their hands.

"Sharon and Julio, that is so nice of you both," Ms. Williams enthused. She looked down at me. "You can take a seat next to Sharon. Julio, you can be friends with the next new student."

Julio sucked his teeth at this. I could almost hear him thinking, *Drat! Lost again.*

Sharon stood triumphantly, flagged me over, and tapped the empty desk next to hers.

The whitest bidder won, I thought glumly.

I took my place next to my new "friend" like a good boy should.

We were bound at the hip, and I became her project for the day. She grabbed my hand. "Come with me for your 'First-day' tour." She made a show of it as we passed Julio's desk.

He cupped his mouth and whispered to me. "Hey, New Kid, you breakdance? Some of us like to breakdance in the morning before class."

"Julio, he is my friend. I'll tell Ms. Williams you're talking," Sharon complained. Julio squinted at her in frustration behind his thick lenses.

We stopped in front of a door in the back of the room. "This is the bathroom. I've been told that kids in other schools get to leave the classroom to go. Not us. They don't think we're mature enough to leave class." She sucked her teeth at this.

We went into the cubby closet. "You can hang your coat in any one of the empty ones. Ms. Williams will assign one to you by tomorrow."

I walked over to the first empty one and hung up my coat.

"Whenever you bring lunch, you can keep it in here, too," she said brightly. She grabbed her lunch pail from her cubby and displayed the Cabbage Patch Kids on the front of it. I would have gone for He-Man or G.I. Joe if I had the choice, but I'd never owned a lunch box, and thinking about my new house parents, I thought I probably never would.

"I don't think I'll be bringing lunch to school," I said. "They gave me four lunch tickets for the rest of the week."

She gave me a sympathetic look. *Poor little New Kid.* "That's okay. A lot of kids have tickets. Even I eat some of the school lunches when they have something good to eat."

I didn't feel better when she said that. I felt looked down on.

We stepped out and walked around the perimeter of the desks to the front of the room to the hand crank pencil sharpener mounted on the wall next to Ms. Williams' desk. I sharpened the two pencils Henry gave me. "Try to sharpen your pencils before class. You don't wanna interrupt class with the grinding noise." She cut her eye towards Ms. Williams and said this in a hushed tone.

We went back to our seats just as Ms. Williams was about to start her lesson.

"Okay, class. Let's see what you remember since the holiday break."

Ms. Williams stood with a stack of pages in one arm, licked the tip of her finger to make it easier to count off pages for each student, and gave a stack of pages at the front of each row.

"Take one and pass the rest back. We'll do a small math quiz to warm up your brains."

Quiz?! She hasn't taught me a thing yet, and she's quizzing me already?

Her uncanny ability to hear my thoughts kicked in again.

"Elliott, you just do the best you can," she said brightly from the front of the room. This drew stares from the other students. Sharon supportively patted me on the arm as she placed the sheet face-side down in front of me. Confused, I grabbed it to turn it over. *How can anyone do a quiz without seeing the problems?* I wondered. She placed her open palm flush on its center and gave a slight shake of her head to indicate we were not to flip the page until we were told, her look conveying an obvious message—*No cheating.*

"You all will be given five minutes to complete as many problems as you can," Ms. Williams said.

I began to feel anxious about the level of arithmetic that was on the other side of the page. *Five minutes? For how many problems? What was the lady expecting us to complete?!* I wondered. *And please stop pointing me out because I am the stupid new kid!!* I hated the implied low expectation of my performance by her "Do your best" comment. *Besides, who races against the clock doing math problems? I'll show you!* I thought confidently.

She gazed up at the large white clock on the wall over the classroom door. We followed her eyes and were all now staring at the same spot above the door. Waiting. *What are we waiting for?* The clock's second hand swept smoothly past number seven. The stress level ramped up in the room, and there was a collective holding of breath in anticipation as the second hand drew closer to the top of the clock. When it reached twelve, everyone flipped their pages and began vigorously scribbling, not knowing that when the five minutes were going to start, I was a beat behind everyone else.

I scanned the page. *Addition, subtraction, and times tables.* I wasted time counting how many problems I had to complete, but I needed to know the count. *Fifty.* It would be a challenge, but I thought I could get through a lot of them. I wasn't too bad at math as long as I had my trusty fingers to get me through. I learned to do math in a class in Philly by tapping my chin or the table with my fingers to count.

My first-grade teacher, Mrs. Freeman, at Walton Elementary School in North Philly, figured out that the method helped me focus and encouraged me to use anything to get through a problem. When I got past the number ten, I would press my toes down in my shoes to continue counting. I thought I was clever for being able to add my toes to the "Best Abacus Ever!!" *Ms. Williams was going down.*

She paced the room during the quiz and caught me counting. "Uh, Uh, Elliott. Finger counting is not allowed. Do the problems properly... in your head."

In my head? I looked down at the page, and the numbers splash-scrambled in all directions. I was stuck. With my method taken away and the stress of the time limit, my numbers dyslexia went into hyperdrive. Mrs. Freeman's finger-counting method helped me manage my affliction. The numbers didn't flip but changed positions or order in my brain. I'd see 54321 as 53412. I'd finished the first five problems by the time Ms. Williams caught me "cheating." Without my fingers, the numbers made no sense to me. I tried using just my toes, but the quiz was broken for me. Of the 50 math problems on the page, I was only able to complete nine of them, and I had one answer wrong. Sharon completed 32. The other kids around me fared similarly to her. My performance confirmed what I thought Ms. Williams expected of me. *I was stupid...*

Around noon, a pair of kids with a student aide pulled a large lunch cart into the classroom. They called out the names of all the kids who were supposed to receive lunch for the day: nuggets, applesauce, and chocolate milk. My name wasn't called despite having a ticket. Ms. Williams addressed the oversight and asked that lunch be provided for me, too. The aide took my name, one of my tickets, and said she would come back with my lunch for the day. The other "privileged" kids, with packed lunches, rushed to the cubby room to collect their food in their designer lunch boxes. Some pulled out sandwiches and thermoses of hot soup and spaghetti. Others had whole meals in Tupperware.

When the lunch lady returned, she had a bagged lunch, which consisted of a sandwich made with a thick slice of processed turkey lunchmeat, a slice of cheese, and a mayo packet. It also had an apple and a carton of milk. It all looked last-minute slapped together and thrown in the bag. *No TLC here.* I had been looking forward to the chicken nuggets everyone else with tickets was eating. *I hate Ms. Williams' class!*

The rest of my day went without incident. I may have been giving off a vibe that caused "my new friend" to stand down a bit after my lunch disappointment. By the time the school bell rang, she didn't seem to notice me at all. I waited for Iszel just outside of the main entrance so we could walk to Bus 3 together. His mood told me everything I needed to know. His first day must have sucked too.

We were able to get a seat together on the bus ride back to the bottom of the hill. He slumped into the seat with his bookbag cradled in his arms and stared out of the window, deep in thought. The day had been a bad one. I waited to ask about it. He didn't want to get into it just then, so we rode in silence. The air was heavy with the unspoken frustrations of our day.

He opened up once it was just the two of us while we were walking up the hill.

"Yo, you good?" I asked him.

He shook his head.

"Teachers kept calling me Issle Glove-er. Hate that shit." It was a common problem that people who had never met Iszel pronounced his first name wrong instead of how it was supposed to be said, like Eye-zel. And we all dealt with people calling us Glove-er instead of Glow-ver.

"Man, that happens everywhere," I said. If that was the worst that had happened, then he was doing alright.

"Yeah, well, all dem white kids were also asking me about what happened to my face." He sucked his teeth in disappointment at this, the irritation clear in his expression.

I looked at him, and I had to really focus to "see" the scars I knew were there. I had become so used to them that they weren't noticeable any more than I would pick out a freckle on someone else's face. They were just part of what made my brother who he was. But when I forced myself to look at him the way a new person would, I could, once again, distinguish them, the most prominent a jagged line that ran diagonally on the top of the left side of his lip up to his left cheek along with thinner ones on his forehead, above his left eyebrow.

I spent the last four years fighting everyone about Iszel's scars. He was also missing his two front teeth, so he didn't smile but rather grinned close-lipped to avoid exposing the gap between his lateral incisors. Inside and out, I knew it weighed on him. I was there to protect him.

He got these questions with every new school he went to, five in the last year alone. I hated those nosey kids at Avon Grove immediately, as I hated anyone who questioned my brother about his scars. I felt my face go hot and clenched my fists together. I began thinking of ways to make them feel the way they made him feel. I wanted to hurt them. Iszel knew my temper would get the best of me and rested a calming hand briefly on my shoulder.

"Yo, don't worry 'bout it; I took care of it," he said while shaking his head at me, a mix of anger and relief in his eyes. "I'm good." He assured me. "One lil' honky with glasses kept askin' about my scars like we were good with each other like that. Like he was my boy and all. So, I asked him if he got a problem with the way I look?"

As soon as Iszel told me that, I knew that whatever happened next would involve violence. I waited for him to continue, but he stopped talking.

"And?" I prompted.

"He told me he was just curious, so I told him dat it was a knife fight and he better not mess with me. Den, I punched him right in da' face. It was a good one, too. You know, to make my point. Knocked his glasses clean off his face across da room."

I nodded with satisfaction. "They gonna kick you out?" I asked, wondering what that would mean for us. I had only *imagined* punching a few people that day; Iszel had done it. I was impressed and proud of my little brother. Jacque and I normally did the fighting. Outside of the "scars" issue, Iszel never really had to. His personality caused most people to fall in love with him almost immediately. Anyone else was looking to cause trouble or didn't know any better. Nonetheless, it felt good to hear that he stood up for himself.

"Nah," Iszel said, sounding surprised. "He didn't snitch. Nosy as hell, that honky, but he didn't tell no one." He was quiet for a beat and spoke. "Maybe not such a bad a dude as I initially thought, especially since he kept his mouth shut."

My temper cooled. That was high praise coming from Iszel. Maybe there was hope for at least one of us at this school after all. The camaraderie of brothers and the resilience in Iszel's spirit gave us a glimmer of hope amidst the chaos and prejudice that had marked our day.

CHAPTER 6

Iszel's Scars

I spent that evening thinking about how those scars came to be. I remember everything about that day. It was a warm spring evening in 1981. My mom was back with us for about a month after serving her time in jail, and we were all living at her parent's house on 24th & Oakdale Street in North Philly. I was 6, Iszel was 5. Between the cousins living at my grandparents' house with us and other neighborhood kids, there were a good 15-20 of us of all age ranges playing a game of hide-and-seek that evening.

Row homes lined both sides of the block in an array of red brick. Age had settled into the bones of the buildings, the scars of countless seasons visible in the scuffed paint, sagging awnings, weathered wood, and stained brick. Some had ivy creeping up their walls, adding a touch of greenery to the otherwise concrete and asphalt landscape. Grass sprang from the cracks in the uneven sidewalks, and the narrow strip of potholed and patched street barely left enough room with the line of parked vehicles for a single car to squeeze by. For this reason, cars rarely drove down the street, and if they did, it was slowly, as ours was a family neighborhood, with kids often playing outside. Sometimes, we would even chase the few cars that trundled down our block, running alongside them.

For all of the history of this city block written in its well-worn lines, the stretch of street was clean and well-kept, strictly monitored by the Block Captain. It was *our* space, and there was an air of generational camaraderie and community, which I remember keenly from that day. It was a lazy spring evening where everyone was enjoying themselves, and the street was filled with an ebullience, punctuated by bursts of laughter as the person who was "it" would find and race someone. Adults sat on the steps, chatting, drinking, and watching. The smell of burgers, hotdogs, and chicken on charcoal barbeque grills filled the air from some of the neighboring homes.

The north side of the street, where my grandparents' house was located, had covered porches. Traffic flowed east, and cars were parked on the south side.

We had decided that the home base would be the chipped and dented wooden electrical pole that doubled as a streetlight and was in the middle of the north side of the block. Conveniently, it was also in front of my grandparents' porch.

The light pole served several purposes. For us kids, it was primarily a timer, marking when we should be in the house or suffer the wrath of a parent for not being in "by the time the streetlights came on." If we donkey kicked the pole, the light flickered off for about 15 minutes, giving us a few more minutes to play or for an errant kid to make it home in time, so we kicked the pole nightly. That night, we didn't have to worry about that. It was a weekend, and most of the parents were out on their porches, enjoying the nice weather and each other's company.

There weren't many spaces to hide. Most of us crouched behind cars, waiting to make our move across the street to the base. Dusk had given way to evening, but the streetlights shone enough light to illuminate the whole block, reflecting a soft glow off the hoods of the cars. I crouched behind a Cutlass Sierra I had chosen as my hiding spot.

Our cousin, Jason, was "it," and I tracked him as he walked up and down the street, calling someone out to race them to the base. When he was distracted and looking the other way, I broke the telephone pole and tagged it before he even looked in my direction. "One two three! I got my base!!" I yelled in the air. Feeling satisfied that I would not be "it" during the next round of hiding, I grabbed the wooden banister railing of my grandparents' fenced-in porch, pulled myself up onto the edge, and hopped over.

My mom was seated on the top of the three steps leading to the porch, holding a Miller High Life in her right hand. Her left arm was propped on her knee, a Winston cigarette casually between the first two fingers, a steady stream of smoke emitting from the burning tip. She turned her head to smile at me.

"Hey, Baby," she said happily before turning back to watch the game. I settled on the porch's metal glider, using my feet to push off and swing. When her back was turned, I grimaced at the smell of her cigarette; I found the smoke revolting. But I didn't want to break her contented mood, so I made sure she didn't see. I turned my attention back to the game.

A neighbor tagged the pole successfully and did a little dance down the street to his porch. Jacque and Iszel were still out there somewhere, and my eyes flicked up and down the street to see if I could catch a glimpse of either of them. Surely, they didn't have much time left. Iszel must have realized that, too, because his head popped out between two cars just across the street from the base. Jason was a few cars further down.

Com' on Ikey, you can make it, I thought.

Everything happened at once. The creaking of the glider was loud in my ears as I rocked it back and forth. There was a blinding flash of headlights and yellow that appeared on the street, moving faster than any car should ever move down our tiny block. Iszel dashed at just this moment, his white Pac-Man t-shirt briefly illuminated by the vehicle barreling toward him. Then, his little body disappeared under the vehicle's carriage.

I don't remember the sound of the impact, but the confusion of his disappearing from view jarred me. He was running across the street one moment and gone the next. The boxy sedan continued forward another two car lengths and stopped to a halt, bringing it just past our porch. A whooshing of blood in my ears deafened me to all outside sounds. One moment, I was sitting, and the next, standing, my head buzzing as if someone had set off an explosion next to me.

I was at the porch rail, gripping it in horror as the car finally stopped, then backed up and went forward again. The driver was panicking and was trying to dislodge whatever was under her car by shifting from drive to reverse until it shook loose from under the carriage. All the while, Iszel's body was twisting like a rag doll underneath.

For a moment, everyone and everything on the block was frozen, silent. Quiet... So... quiet. I could only hear my heartbeat. It thudded loudly and rapidly in my chest and ears. And then, my mother's scream pierced my dazed silence. A group of people rushed towards the car, yelling at the driver through her closed car window to *"Just Stop!"* Someone beat on the hood of the car as it moved forward again. At the very moment, Iszel popped out of the back, the part of his shirt that had been snagged on the underside of the car finally ripped free.

My body felt numb and rubbery like none of my limbs worked anymore, and I stood there, elevated over everyone by the few feet of extra height the porch offered, as people crowded around his mangled body. My six-year-old mind was working to understand what had happened. I could see blood staining what remained of his white shirt, completely obliterating the Pac-Man logo on it.

Once the shirt became soaked, the blood began to pool, most of it seeping from his face. I thought how that was his favorite shirt and it would never be the same. Iszel's body was twisted at an awkward angle as he motioned towards the pole, only a few feet away, stretching out his now broken arms towards base and safety.

My mom was still screaming; other adults were shouting and scrambling.

"I'm calling 911!" shouted my grandmother from the screen door and began swiping her finger across the finger plate of the rotary phone.

The lady who had been driving the car clicked open her door and stumbled out. I recognized her as being the Catholic school crossing guard the next block over. She stared towards the back of the vehicle where Iszel lay. Her face paled at the sight of him, and she looked like she was going to throw up at the realization of what she had done.

"I thought it was cardboard!" she cried, her thin, high voice breaking. "I thought he was a piece of cardboard caught under my car!" She gripped the open door of the car as if she could not stand without it. A breeze was blowing, and the air had turned chilly. A neighbor, Mr. Johnson, who had been working on his car earlier in the day, pushed his way past the sobbing woman and others who had gathered at the back of the car where Iszel lay. He took off his oil-stained sweatshirt and gently laid it over my brother, trying his best to cover the scene from everyone until an ambulance arrived.

Iszel, who had been silent up until this point other than to continue to reach toward the base, suddenly started screaming. Whatever was on the shirt mixed with his wounds, and the pain became unbearable. His cries and my mother's joined together in a concert of agony.

Mr. Johnson quickly removed the shirt, and Iszel's screams settled into moans. My mother's cries trailed off as well, though she stood over him, wringing her hands, too afraid to touch him and hurt him further. Instead, with tears still flowing, she alternated between talking to Iszel and talking to the Almighty.

"Ikey, my baby, mommy's here, I love you." She pointed angrily to the sky, "God, don't you dare do me like this! Don't you take my baby from me!"

My body still tingled from head to toe, even my lips. Had anyone tried to speak to me, I don't think I could have responded. Instead, I stood, crushing the railing with my hands, pressing so hard the whites of my knuckles stood out against my darker skin. I strained to better see Iszel, through the crowd of people.

"Get these kids outta here. They shouldn't be seeing this," shouted Mr. Green, an elderly neighbor from the block, who then went around gently pulling kids back from the crowd, ushering them away. One of those kids was Jacque; I saw him being pulled reluctantly backward, away from Iszel.

"That's my lil brother, man," Jacque tearfully protested.

Mr. Green continued the gentle tug on his shoulder, and he eventually complied. But no one noticed me standing in the dim light of the porch. I just stood there, the wooden railing my lifeline, as I watched the blood slowly spread wider beneath Iszel's face. It looked bad. It looked really bad. His upper body and face were a mess. Deep facial gashes oozed blood. His upper lip was split wide open. His left ear was dangling off, hanging on by a small piece of flesh. His face was torn to shreds. Both of his arms were twisted the wrong shape, but he was alive. I clung to that.

Alive, I thought fiercely. It was minutes or hours later – time felt meaningless – when the blaring sirens and flashing lights of an ambulance stopped behind the accident.

I watched as the EMTs gently placed Iszel onto a stretcher. They loaded him into an ambulance, and my mom followed, still quietly lamenting, "Why, Lord? Why would you do this to me?"

The driver of the car was still inconsolable, sitting on the curb, with a neighbor patting her on the shoulder, trying to unsuccessfully calm her down. She was too hysterical to move her car, so Mr. Johnson slid into the driver's seat. The keys were still dangling in the ignition, and he restarted it and parked it in an open spot to allow the ambulance to pass down the street, blaring its emergency siren as they pulled off. It grew distant as they retreated further and further away.

And then they were gone. The cops came and went, too, a haze of red and blue lights. I kept watching, rooted to the spot, as neighbors with buckets of water began throwing them over the large pool of blood in the street, watching as the water and blood mixed, running to the nearest storm drain.

"I found a tooth!" I heard a neighbor declare to no one in particular. We would later find out that both of his adult front teeth had been knocked out during the accident.

My Aunt Bubbles came up the steps when she noticed me and put her hands on my shoulders. "Come on, Peanut, let's go inside. You feel cold." Peanut was the nickname she gave me at birth because of the shape of my head, I assumed.

Gently but firmly, she pulled me away from the railing. I had been clenching it so tightly I could not immediately let go. I had to pull my hands loose so that when I finally wrest them free, they remained claw-like at my side for many minutes until I could work movement back into them. She guided me into the house and away from the night. But the scene was burned into my eyelids so that when I closed them, I would see it all over again. It was a long time before I could step outside of my grandmother's house without seeing Iszel lying there, bloodied and broken. The whole block was quiet. My brother and best friend were gone for weeks. It felt like an eternity.

My mother spent every free moment at the hospital sitting beside him. Jacque and I were never allowed to visit. She didn't think we could handle seeing him that way. When Iszel came home, it was as if a wounded soldier had returned from the front lines of a brutal battle. The physical scars that adorned his face were a testament to the ordeal he had endured. More than 200 stitches had been meticulously woven together to pull his shattered features back into something resembling their former self. He bore the marks of a survivor, but they only hinted at the horrors he had faced.

Visitors began to trickle into our grandparents' quaint home, well-intentioned but visibly unsure of how to address the elephant in the room—Iszel's condition. They would awkwardly chat with him, around him, and about him as if skirting the subject would make it less real. Many struggled to find the right words, opting instead to steal cautious glances at his injuries. The room was often filled with palpable tension, the unspoken concern hanging heavy in the air.

Our care and Iszel's stubborn disposition didn't allow being run over by a car to get the better of him. He displayed an unyielding determination to recover, a resilience that inspired us all. In the face of adversity, we rallied around him, providing unwavering support. Our hearts ached for him, and we were determined to do whatever it took to help him heal.

To support his fragile body, the doctors had encased Iszel in a plastered, waist-to-neck body cast. His arms, both of which had been broken in the accident, were carefully secured in the cast and adjusted by the doctors to be as "normal" as possible to minimize discomfort. The whole thing was a massive, unwieldy contraption that seemed to weigh a ton on his already slight frame. This cumbersome cast sometimes caused him to topple over.

With Iszel's arms immobilized, the responsibility of caring for him fell heavily on Jacque and me when our mother was at work. We took on the roles of caregivers, assisting with the most basic daily tasks that Iszel could no longer manage on his own. We fed him, bathed him with gentle hands, and helped him with the most private and intimate tasks, never once making him feel his loss of independence.

Caring for his visible and invisible wounds became a daily routine. We would rub soothing cocoa butter on his facial scars, a bittersweet ritual that connected us as brothers, offering comfort in the face of adversity. We even employed a simple coat hanger to reach the itchy spots under the unforgiving cast, doing our best to alleviate his discomfort as he lay in bed, waiting for his body to heal.

Our days were a mixture of tender care, whispered words of encouragement, and the unspoken promise that we would stand by him through every step of his journey toward recovery. But it wasn't all warm and fuzzy between us. All of the doting gifts and constant attention got to Iszel's head, and he became a bit of a prima donna, ordering us around. People would show up with candy and treats like Tastykakes. Jacque and I would eye those sweets longingly. Being only five, Iszel wasn't too keen on sharing without prompting from our mother. He did, however, insist we feed him his treats, piece by delicious piece. Nonetheless, our brotherly bond deepened as we navigated the challenges of his rehabilitation together, proving that no matter how difficult the road was ahead, we would face it as a united family.

Our family became hypersensitive to the stares and questions of well-meaning visitors. Inquiries like, "What happened?" became an unwelcome intrusion into our daily lives, a constant reminder of the accident that had changed everything. And someone always did have the audacity to ask, despite our unspoken wish for them to understand how unwelcome the attention was. Just like the kid who Iszel had punched that first day at Avon Grove Elementary school, whose nickname was apparently "Weed."

"I might have scars, but at least I ain't got no drug as my nickname," Iszel said to me one day, and we both laughed.

It was almost inevitable then that he and Weed would become the best of friends.

CHAPTER 7
Culture Shock

Moving from the noisy streets of Philadelphia to the quiet town of Avondale was a dramatic shift. Avondale, a small corn and mushroom-farming town, was a world apart from the concrete jungle of Philly. It was a tranquil place with a single fire station at its heart. Yet, for all its charm, there were moments when its quirks grated on our nerves. The incessant alarm from the fire station, which could be triggered by anything from a raging fire to the need to coax a group of cows off the main road, disrupted the peace of this 320-square-acre haven. Volunteer firefighters would spring into action regardless of the time of day, answering the call with unwavering dedication.

Avondale was a town where holiday and summer parades and fairs were the highlights of the year. The aroma of funnel cakes, candied apples, and corndogs on a stick filled the air. The townsfolk gathered to watch bright, lime-green colored fire trucks slowly cruise past, horns blaring. These parades often featured volunteers in full firefighting gear, waving and smiling, while an 8-year-old fledgling ballet dancer awkwardly twirled a baton in a red, white, and blue tutu during holiday celebrations.

It was a stark contrast to the hustle and bustle of Philly, a different, slower way of life that I was gradually adjusting to. In Philly, the parades included the Mummers, five clubs of colorful string band performers, typically from South Philly. They performed on New Year's Day, competing for a small prize but mostly for bragging rights. Their notoriety was regional to the city and its immediate surroundings. It included a dance named after them called the Mummers Dance, where one would high step with an umbrella or cane in rhythm with the music.

Avondale, just an hour's drive from Philly, felt untouched by the tumult of my city. It was the epitome of a white-bread, wholesome rural slice of American life. The stuff of Beaver Cleaver, white picket fences, and edged lawns. The kind of life I had only seen on television.

I still vividly remember the first time Iszel and I saw a cow in real life. It was a spring afternoon, and we were out riding the bikes we had assembled from discarded parts found in a bicycle graveyard inside our barn. We learned to build bikes from my Uncle Ricky. Our mother had once surprised us with bikes for Christmas, but they came unassembled. Uncle Ricky, who was our great uncle, had come to the rescue, putting them together for us. The entire process had fascinated me, and it was one of the rare, positive memories I had of him.

As we pedaled toward Earl's Sub Shop, we passed Mr. Pusey's farm, where a black and white spotted cow stood at the edge of the enclosed pasture, calmly chewing its cud. It was our first encounter with a live cow, and we marveled at its size and girth.

The cow looked at us with curious eyes, nostrils flaring, a piece of grass dangling from its mouth as it chewed. I thought it would not have been happy to know that we were headed to Earl's for a double cheeseburger on a hoagie roll. It was the closest sandwich to something we would get in Philly for the few dollars we had burning a hole in our pockets. We kept our distance from the creature but stood there looking at it curiously.

Domesticated, it was not fazed by us. It simply stood at the fence and continued its methodical chews, its pink tongue occasionally peeking out, covered in gooey strands of spit. It was as though it was contemplating how it and its fellow cows could escape their pasture and disrupt traffic on State Road, Avondale's main thoroughfare.

We continued down State Road and over the train tracks to the heart of the small town, where Earl's squat, square brick exterior and hand-painted sign greeted us. We parked our bikes by the building, keeping a watchful eye on them through the large front window. In a town where everyone knew everyone, the store was not just a place to eat but also a hub of information. A few old white men, the town's unofficial historians, always huddled around the deli counter at the back, sharing stories, shooting the shit, and gossiping.

As we entered the store, the man behind the counter, who doubled as the cashier and fry cook, scolded us for leaning our bikes against the windows.

"Boys, you know better than to lean them bikes on my windows," he grumbled. "Ain't nobody gonna steal your Huffys out there. Next time, park 'em on the side of the building. They'll be there when you get back."

His confidence in the safety of our bikes clashed with my city-bred paranoia. In Philly, you kept your eyes on your belongings or risked losing them.

The men in the store, one in particular, made no effort to hide their disdain for us. He rested one elbow on the deli case and held a half-gallon jug of iced tea in his other hand, which he allowed to simply rest on top of his large gut. The drink was so cold that condensation formed on the outside, dampening his unbuttoned, collared company shirt. The embroidered, iron-on name patch said "Frank" in some curly font. Under the shirt was a sweat-stained, white crew neck that was tucked deep into his jeans, accentuating his gut-turned-table, which itself was amply draped over his overtight belt.

Complimenting his outfit was a pair of well-worn, dark work boots. The hand holding the jug was dirty, rough, and calloused, and I thought he must do manual labor of some kind. His eyes bagged, and the skin around them was darker than the rest of his face. His hair didn't have a style but instead was disheveled and pulled in every direction.

He had a day's worth of facial and neck stubble already, and it was only lunchtime. He looked to be younger than the rest of the men standing around. They seemed rested and jovial for 60+ year-olds. He, on the other hand, was still grinding through his workdays. He looked tired and frustrated. Iszel's and my presence at the store was just the excuse he needed to unload.

He took a deep swallow of the beverage he held and wiped the moisture from his mouth with the back of his hand. He used the jug to point as he turned his attention to us. "I see you let all kinds come in here," he remarked to the fry cook, not bothering to veil his prejudice.

The fry cook, however, retorted calmly, "Their money folds just like yours, Frank. When that stops happening, we can have a different conversation."

Frank scowled at him. "Before you know it, the whole town's gonna be filled with em'." He shook his head disapprovingly at his friend and stormed out of the store, glaring at us as he brushed past.

I had the brief urge to be a smart ass and ask the fry cook, "So, I see you let all kinds in here?" Instead, I held my silence. I mostly just wanted to get my burger and leave.

The fry cook looked at us and asked, "Now, what can I getchu boys?"

It was a routine encounter with racism, something my brothers and I had become accustomed to in Avondale. Initially shocking, it had gradually become expected as time went on. The casual cruelty of it was something we could never fully get used to, no matter how many times we faced it.

Living in Avondale was a far cry from our previous life in Philadelphia, where we had been exposed to diverse cultures and races. Now, walking into the local sub shop meant being met with stares and hushed comments. We were just 15 miles from Rising Sun, Maryland. Its acreage was just north of the Mason-Dixon line, and the town was infamous for its active Ku Klux Klan presence. Flyers and applications to join the Knights of the KKK regularly made their way into our town. The palpable racism extended to Avondale, and it forever altered my perception of the world. Some people were more overt with their disdain than others, but the feeling was always there. Moving here, I swapped one problem for another, and my brain didn't know how to rank them. They were both bad.

I regularly considered which was worse: not always having enough food to eat three square meals a day versus the disdain for my mere existence. The instability of life with my mother was less than desirable. But here, in this white-bread town, my presence at the fairs and parades was met with parents hurrying their kids along while glaring at me with contemptuous stares. They made it clear I had ruined the familial moment or day for them by my mere presence. It all weighed on my self-existence. A mother who couldn't get it together enough to keep us versus living somewhere feeling so unwelcome because I was Black.

Those feelings could sometimes be cut like a knife. My young brain knew there were places like this, but until I moved to Avondale, I didn't realize it existed so close to Philly. I had seen movies about the KKK, but they always referenced some deep southern town I never wanted to visit. I heard stories from my grandfather, who grew up in South Carolina in the 1930s and 40s, about racism and how it played a part in his decision to move north with his brothers and sister.

I expected it to be so much further South than Avondale. And though I had witnessed the occasional ugliness of people who lacked acceptance of other races while living in the city, this was vastly different, more frequent, and proximal.

Avondale was divided along an imaginary line, segregating the town into different areas for white and Black families. The group home was situated separately from the Black families, creating a hierarchy within the town; White, then Black, and last, the group home kids. Any journey outside of the house to hang with kids who looked like me took me through the white part of town, where I encountered overt racism.

The disparity between the wholesome image of American life I had seen on TV and the reality of my existence in Avondale emphasized the idea that Beave's life was never meant for someone who looked like me. That realization left me with a sense of loss. My imagined slice of

Americana was tainted by comparison, and I became hyperaware of the people around me. Racism seeped into every aspect of my life outside the home, from schoolteachers and faculty to my classmates. I was not welcomed with open arms in Avondale. I was viewed with suspicion, disdain, and even hostility simply because of the color of my skin. It was a harsh reality to face, one that tested my resilience every day.

CHAPTER 8

The Hills

Iszel's prediction that our stay at the House on the Hill would be quick stretched into weeks and then months. I turned 10 in February and Iszel 9 in March, both of our birthdays occurring with little fanfare. We ignored such milestones in favor of day-to-day survival. We began getting our hair cut with the rest of the boys at the House at a Black barber in a nearby town, thanks to Jiggs, who had convinced Henry the boys needed a Black barber long before we arrived at the House. Henry likely acquiesced because he was cheap. We were just happy to have our hair cut by someone who understood it.

Living with the Hills was also an adjustment from the life I had known before. Food became a defining point of difference between what we had known and what the Hills provided. Although it was offered more consistently than some of the times when my mom had been too poor to afford it, there was never any love or care at mealtime. I had lived in the homes of some of the greatest cooks I knew. Their hands were influenced by the well-seasoned Negro kitchens of the South. Soul Food was a transcendent experience; you felt something when you ate it. It fed your body and spirit, leaving a nostalgic imprint on you. It connected you to everyone else sharing the meal and to your ancestral past. Soul Food was love.

Henry, by comparison, cooked like he didn't care for anyone. In fact, he and Janine didn't eat what they served us. Instead, Janine's losing battle with her post-menopausal, slowing metabolism led her to calorie-restrictive, portioned, pre-packaged, microwavable meals. Henry would show up at the table with replated Hungry Man Frozen Dinners.

Meals for the rest of us were bland if we were lucky and downright gross if we weren't. His choice of meals was particularly confounding for young kids. Some of his favorites were oyster stew, French onion soup, and dry fish that always tasted like it was on the cusp of spoiling. He had a fondness for Brussel sprouts and cornbread so dry it was hard to swallow. We would all sit at the dining room table while he'd bring our plates or bowls of whatever dubious dinner he'd made, and I'd always catch a whiff of his breath, as foul as I feared on that first day. I started holding my breath whenever he leaned over me.

When we first arrived at the house, Iszel and I would eat around what we didn't like, then stand up and take our plates to the kitchen. Within a few minutes of leaving the table, we were outside playing, much to Henry's chagrin. He allowed this to go on for a few months, but one evening, when Iszel and I stood with our plates in hand to leave the table, Henry stopped us short. "Uh, where do you two think you're goin'?"

"I'm finished," I said. "I'm taking my plate to the kitchen."

"Both of you sit back down," he ordered. "Janine and I haven't finished our meals. And you didn't ask to be excused."

"Us leavin' don't stop you and Janine from finishing your dinner," I said. "You're eatin' it, not us."

Janine snapped, "Excuse me, lil boy! You best watch ya tone! Where are your manners?!"

Iszel chimed in. "My manners are where everyone else's are. In the barn playing basketball." He looked pointedly at the nearly empty table. "No one else asked to be excused. No one else is sitting here watchin' you two eat. They just got up and left. Why do we hafta?"

"It's called having manners!" Janine shot back. "And you haven't touched a thing on your plates. There are starving kids who don't have the blessing of a meal today like you do. You two are being ungrateful."

It was ironic for her to aim such a statement at kids who had actually gone hungry, something she had probably never experienced. The three of us never took being fed consistent meals for granted. Living with our mother, we had so little that we resorted to syrup or mayonnaise sandwiches or recycling milk from each other's cereal bowls to ensure we each had some in the morning. But it would have been impossible to explain to Janine and Henry the distinction between our appreciation for being fed and our resentment and humiliation at being forced to eat the gruel that they served. It was a callous and manipulative tactic to use other's misfortune to guilt us into eating something that repulsed us, but it seemed impossible to explain to Janine and people like her who often used such tropes that even if we were just poor foster kids, we also deserved basic human dignity.

"You can give them this if you want," I offered. "I don't like it."

Iszel started toward the kitchen. "I guess I got the same manners as everyone else."

I followed behind, leaving them sitting red-faced at our perceived disrespect.

After that encounter, Henry insisted that we ask to be excused from the table going forward. He couldn't come up with reasons for making us stay at the table while he and Janine finished their dinner, as we never engaged in conversation during the meal. After a few days of him attempting to do so, which involved us glaring silently at them as they ate, he finally relented and allowed us to leave when we were done, as long as we asked permission first.

Another adjustment was the strange family dynamic between the Hills. Their relationship was a place of quiet tension and hidden disappointments. At its center was Dave, their 25-year-old openly homosexual son, who lived on the third floor of the house. His parents' disappointed expectations cast a shadow over his presence. It was clear that his life choices were a source of their constant consternation. His sexuality must have seemed a big slap in the face of their strong religious beliefs, and they never failed to make that known.

Contrasting Dave's tumultuous journey, his older sister Helene had taken a markedly different path. She had married a successful man and embraced her role as a stay-at-home mother to two little girls. The Hills considered her more traditional life choices worthy of praise. Helene would occasionally visit the group home, along with her husband and children, staying in the RV they owned since there were no extra rooms for guests at the House on the Hill. Her presence was a stark contrast to Dave's solitary existence on the third floor.

Janine never openly doted on Dave in front of others, her disapproval of him always simmering just below the surface. In contrast, she openly celebrated Helene's accomplishments as a mother and wife. The warmth and enthusiasm Janine showed when Helene and her family arrived were absent at any other time, and it did not go unnoticed by Dave or the rest of us.

It was difficult to watch as Henry regularly berated Dave. Whether it was about work, school, or his plans, Henry didn't hold back. Their confrontations were a regular occurrence, and they always played out in the same way. Dave would eventually lose his temper, shouting, "Get off my back, Dad!" before stomping away to the solitude of the third floor or making a swift exit through the front door. To add insult to injury, Henry often praised Helene's husband and welcomed him with open arms. The tension that filled the house during Dave's conflicts with his father was replaced by a sense of harmony and unity when Helene and her family were present.

Dave's life was a complex and enigmatic puzzle, marked by uncertainty and a constant search for something elusive, perhaps a sense of fulfillment or acceptance that he'd never received from his parents. He was in a state of perpetual uncertainty, characterized by a lack of stability and ever-changing aspirations. He floated in and out of the house, trying his hand at various jobs and educational pursuits. One day, he might arrive with a stack of schoolbooks committed to his studies. But the very next day, he would be on the verge of tossing those books out. Meanwhile, Helene's life was marked by the stability and consistency of her role as a mother, with her dedication to her family never wavering.

It was unclear whether Dave was officially allowed to live in the house, and the involvement of Baptist Children Services (BCS) suggested a precarious living situation. When officials from the agency came to visit, Dave would disappear, either leaving the house or locking himself away on the third floor, a place BCS never ventured. His interactions with the boys at the house were cordial but distant. He would occasionally go out, meet someone, and bring them home, doing his best to keep his overnight guests hidden from the scrutiny of his parents. In contrast, Helene's visits were seamless, with no need for secrecy or concealed interactions.

It wasn't easy to watch Dave's constant struggles with his parents compared to the way they treated his sister. He seemed like a good guy, much more likable than his parents. The Hills' consistent neglect and indifferent treatment towards their son reaffirmed my perception of the Hills as callous individuals we should minimize contact with. Unfortunately, this wasn't always possible, especially when they sought to display us as embodiments of their Christian charity.

Occasionally, the Hills would pack us into the van, a motley crew of brown faces, and take us to their all-white Presbyterian church. It was always a production to find seating that could accommodate most of us in one place, and the parishioners, with their polite but strained smiles, would willingly shift around to make room for us. I couldn't help but feel like they didn't want us sitting too close to them. Our Black faces stood out like pepper specks in a large saltshaker amidst the sea of white.

This was nothing like the churches I had attended with my aunts back in Philly. In those vibrant houses of worship, people would get themselves so riled up that someone might "catch the Holy Ghost," tumbling out of the pews and requiring the assistance of ushers. The fiery orators of the Baptist tradition could rouse an entire congregation to their feet, and the music from the choirs energized me to move in rhythm with the spirit.

I had witnessed a decent spectrum of how people practiced their faith—from the gentle humming, praying, and swaying to the soul-stirring funeral wailings of women and the fervent faith healings during revivals. I had even seen devout individuals smack disease and demons out of people's bodies, causing them to miraculously walk again. The Hills' church, by comparison, felt stoic and lifeless. The sermons were quiet and monotonous, and there was little energy in the room. I sat in the pew, staring down at an unopened Bible on my lap, feeling disconnected from the God I had once believed in.

I couldn't bring myself to pray to the God that had given me this broken life. A mother trapped in a cycle of poverty and addiction, with no paternal figure to lean on and no stability to speak of. I had been abused and neglected by both family and foster care, and life felt like I was walking on shaky, cracked ground, waiting for it to crumble and swallow me whole. It had all soured me towards God. My earlier understanding of Him and His influence on my life had fractured.

The Hills, with their façade of piety, were the final straw for me when it came to my crisis of faith. When people gathered around them to praise their work of saving our lost souls, it pushed me further away from the God they claimed to glorify. I couldn't reconcile a God who would create a life like mine and not intervene in any meaningful way. I didn't see my trials and tribulations as preparation for some grander purpose; I wanted a God who would smite those who caused me harm. But God remained distant, silent, and unproven.

It all began to seem like snake oil to me, a tool people used to manipulate others, isolate and alienate them, or control their behavior. Just like the Hills, who told me I wasn't worthy of the kingdom of heaven because of the color of my skin – my melanated skin, as they put it, as if too much melanin damned me to hell. The harshness of my life experiences had hardened me, and I stopped communicating with God altogether.

It would take two decades and a journey through music ministry for me to understand the difference between faith and the religion that had been used to control, isolate, and alienate me. It would take 20 years for me to start talking to God again, to begin healing the wounds that had led me to abandon my faith in the first place. The scars of my past, the doubts about religion, and the search for a higher purpose would be a long and arduous journey, one that would test my faith and my resilience and bring me back to the concept of a God whose love transcends human constraints and embraces all with boundless compassion.

But long before that journey of faith, I had to find my way through a group home run by authoritarian, racist houseparents with a fractured family in a town that mistrusted Black people, attending a school I felt ill-prepared for. My brothers and I had a long and uncertain road ahead of us.

CHAPTER 9

Home Visits

As the months rolled on and it seemed we were in it for the long haul at the House on the Hill, BCS and the Department of Human Services (DHS) encouraged home visits to keep us connected to our families. These were allowed every other weekend, on holidays, and in exceptional circumstances, like funerals. They required rigorous home inspections and background checks.

Our Aunt Angel was one of the few people we knew who maintained a stable enough living situation and was also willing to jump through the bureaucratic hoops so my brothers and I had a place to visit our family. Staying with our mother was theoretically possible, but they scrutinized her more than Angel. She would have to work closely with our family social worker to prove she was fit enough to get us back or visit: no drugs, a home that had enough space for us all, and a solid job to support us properly, either on its own or with the help of welfare. Unfortunately, over the months we had been living at BCS's Main Campus and the House on the Hill while waiting for DHS to approve visits to Angel, our mother had, once again, fallen out of our family's good graces. No longer allowed to live with or borrow from them, she stayed on the streets, at friends' homes, or with boyfriends. There was no way she would pass the DHS requirements.

Angel's youngest son, our cousin Jason, still lived at home. He was a couple of years older than Jacque. He was cool, street-smart, easy-going, and funny. We were all crazy about him. Their home was our first alternative living situation at the beginning of 1984. When Iszel and I moved to Uncle Ricky's house, Jacque remained with Angel and Jason. During that time, Jacque and Jason became extremely close. For Jacque, it was the best possible outcome to have our home visits where Jason lived. He was more than a cousin; he was the fourth Glover brother.

Our first visit was approved in late spring of 1985. Henry gave us Septa tokens and bus transfer money and loaded the van with everyone going away for the weekend. He dropped us at the bus depot in West Chester and left after he watched us climb onto the 104 Bus to Philly. We traveled with overnight bags on our laps; my arms crossed through the straps as the easy jostling of the large bus lulled me to sleep for the hour-long ride. Jacque nudged me awake as we approached our stop in Upper Darby at 69th Street Terminal, adjacent to the city.

From there, we went our separate ways from the other guys to ride or walk to our respective parts of the city. It didn't feel odd to be so young traveling on public transportation without an adult. Jacque handled the money, told us where to sit, and kept a watchful eye on us despite having some of the older guys from the House on the Hill on the initial bus with us.

Jason met us at the Upper Darby terminal, eagerly awaiting our arrival. Despite being only 14, he had traveled an hour on multiple buses and trains to meet us there, coming from North Philly. As soon as we stepped off the bus for that first visit, he wasted no time greeting us in his normal fashion and wrapped Jacque in a playful headlock.

"Damn, y'all, I've been waitin' here for a minute! Where'd they move y'all asses to? Timbuktu?" Jason grunted, struggling to maintain his grip on Jacque's neck. He wore a mock wrestling grimace, biting his lower lip in exaggeration.

Jacque managed to pull away from Jason's hold and retaliated by returning a headlock himself. "Hell yeah, I told you on the phone we live in the sticks now. We were on that bus fo' a hot minute," Jacque retorted playfully.

Jason easily broke free from Jacque's hold and stood beside me, taking a moment to assess my height by saluting from his forehead over the gap between us. He nodded approvingly and said, "Y'all actin' like y'all tryna get tall." Then he playfully jabbed my stomach, and I couldn't react quickly enough to block it.

Iszel received a similar jab and teasing comment about his height. "Ikey's still short as shit, though. Damn! Look at his stomach. They must be feedin' y'all good," Jason laughed.

Jacque chimed in, sharing our challenges with Henry's cooking. "Naw, Henry can't cook for shit. Then he gets mad if you don't eat what he makes."

"Yeah, he be puttin' cheese on everything," Iszel added, scrunching his face in distaste.

"Yo, it be a battle sometimes," Jacque agreed, sharing the sentiment.

With Jason's presence, Jacque let go of some of the responsibility of looking out for us and relaxed a bit. He appeared lighter, as if he were able to relinquish the burden of being the oldest brother, at least temporarily.

From 69th Street, we huddled in a corner of the Market-Frankford subway line. The train began above ground before descending underground after a few stops. The rhythmic clacking of the wheels against the rails had a soothing effect on me. Just like sailors had to earn their sea legs, we had to adapt to the movements of the train—learning to stand steadily as it jostled and rocked. Jacque and Jason had mastered it, but Iszel and I had not, often getting knocked off our feet at stops. The flickering train lights between stations didn't bother anyone.

Our journey took us to the 15th & Market terminal, where we made a free interchange to the Broad Street Line, eventually reaching Lehigh Avenue. From there, a short ride on the 54 Bus brought us to 22nd & Lehigh in North Philly—our neighborhood.

We were back in our beloved city—Philadelphia. The sounds of car horns, the ambient buzz of streetlights, and the diverse aromas of delis, corner stores, food carts, and homes filled the air. Nothing compared to the enticing scent of a cheesesteak with fried onions sizzling on a grill—it made my stomach growl every time I caught a whiff of it. It felt like home.

Despite our young ages ranging from 9 to 14, we didn't fear the city. We were family, moving around our familiar urban landscape, poking fun at each other along the way.

This familiar commute became a regular part of our lives during home visits. Even as Angel moved around, she stayed in the same neighborhood, and the comfort of returning to our familiar surroundings was indescribable.

On our first visit, we disembarked near a corner diner where Angel had rented an apartment and moonlighted as a server. Jason strode in as if he owned the place, the small bell above the door jingling when he entered. He created a makeshift megaphone with his hand and called out, "Ang-gel?!" Jason had always referred to his mother by her first name rather than calling her "Mom." When we were younger, Jacque did the same to our mom until one of our aunts corrected him. He had referred to her as "My MaryAnn."

Jason called again, his voice bellowing over the background music, much to the annoyance of some patrons and the fry cook, who I assumed managed the diner. We followed behind Jason, each of us with bags and backpacks, resembling a group of young wanderers. The air inside was thick with the scents of fried food, coffee, and hot grease—a combination I relished. It reminded me of the Smyrna Diner back when we lived in Delaware. A row of eight booths with white tabletops and red vinyl cushioned seats lined the windows facing 22nd Street. To the left, there was a counter with an opening for waitstaff to serve and bus tables. High-top stools with backless red vinyl cushions matched the booth seats. Those sitting at the counter faced the open kitchen, separated by a serving area. A rectangular opening behind the service area allowed the cook to pass out prepared orders. The floor was tiled with brown carpeted, no-slip runners, and dim, brownish-yellow overhead lights cast a warm golden hue over everything.

Angel emerged from the kitchen with a coffee pot in hand. She was tall and slender, sporting a low, natural afro cut. Her movements were unhurried, as if she had never rushed anywhere. She wore glasses but still squinted when she looked at us. A stained, white, and red striped apron covered her pristine white server uniform, and she had on a pair of flats.

"Look who's here," Jason announced as if introducing us as royalty.

"Hey, boys," Angel greeted us. Her voice was low, husky, and scratchy, reminiscent of the actor Esther Rolle, but with a smoker's rasp. She scanned us briefly. "I see y'all made it here in one piece," she said appreciatively.

From her expression, it was clear she had missed us. She set the coffee pot down and opened her arms wide. "Come on, give your auntie some hugs." Although her arms were long enough to wrap around all three of us at once, we each took turns embracing her. When I leaned in, I caught a medley of scents—fried food and coffee, a fading hint of perfume, cigarettes, and a subtle whiff of the weed she occasionally smoked.

"Boy, I done tole' you to stop coming in here screaming for me like you ain't got no sense. Like I ain't taught you no better. I done tole' you about that before," she chided Jason, who dismissed her scolding with a wave of his hand.

She let that slide and returned her focus to us. "Let me look at y'all." She peered over her glasses, her expression disapproving. "Are they feeding y'all anything?! Jacque, you thin as a rail." She clicked her tongue in disapproval. "Y'all want something to eat?" Without waiting for our response, she continued, "Sit down in one of the booths. I'll take care of anything you want. Take a look at the menu."

I was overjoyed at the prospect of ordering from the menu, especially after months of Henry's group home food. I ordered a large cheesesteak, even though it was too much for my 10-year-old appetite. People often said we had "eyes bigger than our stomachs," but it was a survival instinct for us. Angel didn't object to our choices; she simply placed the oversized platters of food in front of us to sort out. She understood where our food-hoarding mentality came from.

My upbringing had taught me that my next meal was never guaranteed. The timing of the next meal depended on when the means became available or when someone offered charity. I had no intention of eating the entire cheesesteak in one sitting; I ate until I was content and planned to save the rest for later. The sandwich would be there, even if I had to eat it cold. We all did it despite knowing that there would be plenty to eat at Angel's throughout the weekend. She always kept something in the refrigerator for us, and if all else failed, she would send us down to the restaurant to eat.

The restaurant door swung open, and the bell rang wildly. Our mother stood in the doorway, scanning the room for us. Jacque and Jason immediately caught her eye. Jacque exclaimed with excitement, "Ma!" and Jason gave a knowing smile while casually calling, "Hey Mer," the family's nickname for her. She rushed over to our booth, and we could tell she was both thrilled and intoxicated. Angel had tracked her down by phone and let her know we were at the restaurant.

Mom joyfully showered us with hugs and kisses as we sat in the booth. She didn't wait for us to get out of the booth to embrace her; instead, she leaned across Iszel to reach me and did the same over Jason to hug Jacque. We were all thrilled to see her. It had been over a year since we'd spent any real amount of time with her other than the brief car rides to Uncle Ricky's from Aunt Angel's in the spring of 1984 and to our Aunt Linda's house later that fall. Living with Angel began a series of alternate living situations that year.

Mom squeezed in next to Iszel in the booth as Angel returned to the dining area. Holding the coffee pot again, Angel placed a hand on her hip and shook her head in concern after assessing her sister. She said, "Mer, you look like you could use a good meal yourself. Girl, you're wasting away out there in the streets. Grab a menu and get something to eat. I've got you on the food. And don't you dare try to tell me 'No' in front of these babies," She added. Mom had always been petite, but she looked even more frail and skeletal than the last time I saw her. Her hug had felt bony against me.

Mom's eyes briefly narrowed with a hint of disdain. She didn't appreciate being told what to do. Reluctantly, she picked up a menu and replied, "Girl, you always trying to be the boss over somebody." After a quick scan of the menu, she pointed and said, "I'll have some coffee and a large ham and cheese hoagie with mayo, oil, vinegar, and everything on it since you're offering." She glanced around the room, then back at Angel, and whispered through gritted teeth, "And don't be putting my business out here for everyone to know about."

"Mer, ain't nobody said nothing about you that nobody don't already know," Angel replied matter-of-factly. She was one of the few people I'd seen speak to my mother so bluntly and get away with it. I had witnessed her do so more since she had taken us in. Angel checking my mom made us all anxious. Our mother had a short temper, and saying the wrong thing could set her off, making her unpredictable and sometimes even violent. I didn't want our reunion to be ruined so quickly. I could feel the tension escalating between them.

Angel stared at my mom for a moment before saying, "Girl, get over yourself. Haven't you figured out that nobody cares what you're doing to yourself except the people who love you? You haven't seen these babies in over a year. They need to be your focus right now." Angel looked over her glasses, sizing her up once more. "And you need to eat something before you disappear into nothing." She played the big sister card before my mother could say much more, or worse, leave out of spite. The tightness in my mom's shoulders eased, and I knew she was going to let it slide this time.

Angel poured a cup of coffee and went back to the kitchen with the sandwich order. We all caught up while our mother sipped her coffee and nibbled on her sandwich. We talked over each other, sharing details about Avondale, the House on the Hill, the other boys, our schools, and all the white people we encountered. I mostly skirted around the details about the Hills, fearing they would upset my mother, who could do nothing but rant angrily at us about them anyway. There was no point in provoking her when there was nothing she could do about it.

We kept the conversation light, focusing on how much we missed her and being home. Angel kept our drinks refreshed and didn't rush us back to the apartment. We all needed this time together, and Jason was just as interested in our stories as our mother was. He asked a lot of questions about life in the rural area, school, and being surrounded by cornfields. He had watched the movie *Children of the Corn*, and the thought of it still made him uneasy.

Our talk eventually tapered off. Our mother promised to get her life together so we could be a family again. Sitting in that booth together filled me with hopeful optimism that she would keep her promise.

Angel carefully packed up our leftovers, and when she returned, our mother looked at her longingly, and they shared a moment. It ended with Angel pursing her lips and shaking her head no. Mom nodded in understanding and said, "Come here, babies." Her tone was tinged with regret, and her eyes began to well up. She wiped away the tears with the back of her hand and sniffled, as her nose had started running, too. "Mommy has to go for the night." She reached across Iszel and hugged both him and me in one big embrace.

Jacque got up to hug her and asked, "You're not staying at Angel's with us this weekend? What's up with that?"

She hugged Jacque where he stood and grabbed her wrapped sandwich. "No, baby," she replied. "But I'll be around to see y'all tomorrow and before y'all leave."

Even under the special circumstances of our first visit, Angel would not allow our mother to stay. Whatever had happened between my mother and our family included Angel. We gathered our leftovers from the restaurant and made our way upstairs to the apartment to settle in for the night. The apartment was a large, rectangular space that mirrored the size and shape of the restaurant below. It had hardwood floors, wooden walls, and a wooden ceiling, appearing to have served as a storage area for the business that once occupied the space before the restaurant. The apartment was divided into two bedrooms, a full bathroom, and a makeshift kitchen in the main area. Jason's room was sparsely furnished with a king mattress on the floor, a tall steel pedestal lamp, and a portable wardrobe for his clothes. Angel's room was similarly furnished, with her bed resting on cinderblocks and a small TV with a cable box on top of two milk crates. It was the only television they had.

We dropped our bags in Jason's room, and he put a pot of water on the stove to warm up for Angel. She liked to soak her feet after a long day of work, adding a little Epsom salt and green rubbing alcohol to the water.

Once settled, we sprawled out on Angel's bed and the floor while Jason flipped through the Friday night TV programs. He gravitated toward the latest hip-hop music videos. "Yo, man, what y'all wanna watch? You know I can watch videos all night," he said, clicking the remote to the 'Video Jukebox Network' channel.

"Are they playing Cosby right now?" I asked.

"Naw, it's too late for Cosby, but they should be playing some rap soon on this station," Jason replied. He gave Jacque a playful shove, causing him to fall off the bed, and they began wrestling. Iszel joined in by grabbing Jason from behind. While I was happy to see them playing, I knew Angel would walk in at any moment, and we would all be in trouble for roughhousing in her room. I stayed out of it.

Angel's shift ended shortly after we got settled. She washed away the day's work, sat in a chair, and pulled out a foldable dining tray in front of her. Jason grabbed her a beer and prepared her basin to soak her feet. She slid her feet into the warm water and sighed with relief. Then, she reached into her purse, retrieved a joint, and lit it. She took a kissing drag, blowing the smoke into the air.

"Y'all okay staying out there in that house? Keeping an eye out for each other?" she asked.

"Mostly white folks, but yeah, we're good," Jacque replied without taking his eyes off the TV. "Nobody messes with us, and you know we've got each other's backs."

"It's good that y'all are together. That makes me happy," Angel said with a touch of sadness.

She took another drag of her joint and held the smoke in her lungs before exhaling. She considered the joint, "Reefer ain't all that bad," she conceded.

I disliked drugs and resented them for the trouble they had caused my family. However, Angel's casual attitude toward it made it seem less menacing than the smell of cigarettes, which I detested even more.

"Yeah, we're luckier than a lot of dudes up there. Their brothers and sisters are all over the place," Jacque continued.

"Well, y'all can stay here as often as they allow. Y'all know that, right? We're going to sort out getting y'all back home again for good. Kids are supposed to be with family," Angel assured us. Her shoulders slumped a bit with guilt.

"I just wasn't in a position to keep y'all with me last year," she added softly as if we weren't in the room. My brothers and I had lived with Aunt Angel for two months before it became too many kids for her to handle. She had kept Jacque while Iszel and I had moved to our Uncle Ricky's. It was the only time the three of us had been split up. "And when MaryAnn came and took Jacque..." Her voice turned sharp with anger and then trailed off. She never finished her statement but took another deep drag of the joint and a large gulp of beer.

"It's all good. We know you woulda if you could. Can't say that about everyone in the fam, but we know you got us," Jacque reassured her.

Angel accepted the placation. Coupled with the weed and beer, it soothed her mood.

Feeling tired, I walked down to Jason's room and changed into a pair of shorts and a T-shirt. Although Jason's bed was available and prime real estate for a good night's rest, I opted to create a makeshift bed on the floor near the window. I didn't want to be crowded on the bed with the other guys, and the floor was surprisingly comfortable. Jason kept his window cracked to allow fresh air in, regardless of how cold it was. The cool breeze felt refreshing. The radiators in each room kept the whole apartment warm, and I enjoyed having my own space. The city's ambient noise was just right to lull me to sleep. I wrapped myself in the covers, poked one foot out, and drifted off to sleep.

The weekend passed too quickly. We spent it visiting with family and friends who lived nearby. Most of them were shocked at how much we had grown. Our mother never returned to see us that first weekend, but she managed to catch us on the phone before we boarded the bus back to West Chester. While I had a wonderful time seeing everyone and being away from the House, a bit of the hope my mother had instilled in me on Friday began to wither away during the bus ride back to the House on the Hill.

Bi-monthly trips to visit Aunt Angel's would become our routine for years. As the trips became a habit, I began to appreciate seeing our family so often. It felt like we saw them more now than when we had lived in Philly.

Despite our initial fears, BCS didn't follow us during our home visits. Their lack of oversight became glaringly apparent, as they didn't even bother calling Aunt Angel to verify our whereabouts while we were away from the group home. At first, we were diligent rule followers, determined to adhere to the strict guidelines that governed our lives, ensuring we never stayed overnight anywhere else. The weight of our responsibilities loomed large, a constant reminder of the precariousness of our situation.

Yet, as time passed, we began to realize the lax nature of their check-in system. We took a few calculated risks, the most daring of which was spending nights at our mother's boyfriend's. It was a gamble we were willing to take, especially when her boyfriend, Mr. Jim, was around. The allure of reconnecting with our family, even if it meant breaking the rules, proved irresistible in the face of our desire for a semblance of normalcy.

Mr. Jim had seamlessly woven himself into my mother's life, becoming a steadfast presence. Her excitement for us to meet him was evident. He struck me as a pillar of strength and reliability, a man who treated my mother with unwavering respect and kindness. Jim, despite his imposing size, was quiet by nature but inherently good-hearted. In stark contrast, my mother buzzed around him with her characteristic energy and enthusiasm. They were an odd couple, differing in many ways, but somehow, their differences complemented each other perfectly.

During our visits, we met Jim's daughter, Kumi. She was my age, and I couldn't help but find her to be the sweetest and prettiest girl I'd ever met. She might have been my very first crush. Kumi's presence during our visits added an extra layer of warmth and familiarity to the already comforting environment of Jim's home. Even though our visits were infrequent, I cherished those moments when we spent time together.

What set Mr. Jim apart from other men our mother had dated was his consistency. He never displayed any red flags or behavior that caused me to fear for my mother's safety, contrary to some of the tumultuous relationships she had been in. Jim's unwavering support, both emotional and practical, was a welcome respite from the chaos of our lives. His presence brought a sense of stability and calm that had been conspicuously absent from our chaotic world, and for that, I was truly grateful. It was as though he had become a beacon of hope for her, settling the stormy seas of her often-troubled life.

CHAPTER 10

Settling In

Adherence to Avondale's white Standard English was expected at school and the group home. The language spoken in Avondale felt foreign compared to the regional dialect in North Philly, and using Ebonics (now known as African-American Vernacular English or AAVE) seemed like speaking another language. We were often corrected by teachers like Ms. Williams and the Hills, while white peers frequently commented on our speech. To assimilate and avoid drawing attention, we adapted by gradually adopting Avondale's English—this involved monitoring our speech, avoiding slang, and maintaining impeccable grammar and pronunciation.

Visiting Philly felt like stepping back into our distinct world, where lively streets echoed with the vibrant cadence of AAVE. In this environment, Avondale's English stood out starkly, sounding noticeably white and formal. During our home visits, we effortlessly reverted to Ebonics, embracing the familiar rhythm of our city and reconnecting with our roots. This shift provided a profound sense of belonging that was undeniable.

As our language evolved, the seamless meshing of Ebonics and Avondale's English became more apparent, especially during our visits to Philly. Our family members, once familiar with the distinct rhythm of our original language, began to take notice. Their criticism emerged as they observed the interplay of these two linguistic worlds, expressing dissatisfaction with our fluid linguistic transition. The blending that once felt like a bridge between two worlds became a point of contention, and the pressure to conform to either end of the language spectrum increased. In the eyes of our family, adopting the "White Man's" language was perceived as selling out, and this scrutiny from our kin amplified the exhaustion we felt from the constant toggling between two linguistic identities, reinforcing our yearning for a day when we could simply be ourselves without judgment or expectation.

Over time, we recognized the power of language and how it shaped perception and influenced how others saw us. Our ability to switch between languages connected us to different communities and worlds. Our journey to bilingualism wasn't just about learning two languages; it was about finding our voice amid a chorus of expectations on every side. We evolved, shedding layers of dialect and slang until our speech reflected a blend of our roots and aspirations.

Ultimately, our language symbolized resilience, highlighting our adaptability, survival skills, and unique ability to thrive in different environments. It emphasized that being different was not a weakness but a remarkable strength, proving that we were defined by who we chose to be rather than where we came from or where we now lived.

***

While we learned how to navigate language that first year in Avondale, we also began to establish a routine at both the House on the Hill and at school. My initial fears and apprehension about Ms. Williams were alleviated. She lacked the nuance to understand my particular struggles as a Black kid in a white class, but it became clear that she genuinely cared about her students, including me, showing a level of dedication that surprised me. Her warm, encouraging words and willingness to help, especially in areas like math, slowly eased the anxieties that had been building within me. Stress exacerbated the problem I had with numbers switching places, so as I became more confident in my abilities and understanding, it became less of an issue.

Sharon and I formed a real friendship beyond her assignment as such by Ms. Williams, and she played a pivotal role in my transition. She also patiently helped me catch up in math. Our first-day "friendship" wasn't a point of contention between Julio and her anymore. I soon came to realize that their rivalry extended to everything in their playful banter; they would compete in academics, sports, and even who could crack the funniest jokes during lunch break.

Julio and I bonded quickly over our shared passion for breakdancing. Our love for this art form was more than just a hobby; it was a form of self-expression that allowed us to escape the realities of our lives, if only for a little while. Our spare moments in the back of the classroom were dedicated to practicing our moves, refining our routines, and pushing the boundaries of our creativity. It was during these times that we truly felt free, and the rhythmic beats of our music transported us to a different world, one where our worries were momentarily forgotten.

This developing talent set me apart from my peers. With each dynamic move, I realized that I had something unique, something that made me stand out in a crowd. People were impressed with my skills, and I quickly became known as the street gymnast from Philly. I had never received formal training, but I was daring enough to try gravity-defying stunts that left my classmates in awe. It became a source of pride for me, my realm of excellence, a domain that Jacque and Iszel couldn't follow. I was carving my path, creating an identity beyond the shadows of my brothers.

During recess, Julio and I would mesmerize our classmates with our flips and spins. The schoolyard became our stage, where we choreographed acrobatic displays that captivated everyone who watched. It was exhilarating to be recognized and celebrated for something I had worked so hard to perfect.

The school decided to host a talent show, and I eagerly embraced the opportunity to display my skills. Julio and I took center stage, our performance a dazzling display of precision and agility. The audience was captivated by our routine, but it was the grand finale that left a lasting impression. With a fearless leap, I somersaulted over a group of five kids from the audience, landing gracefully on the other side. The cheers and chants of "Glover! Glover! Glover!" filled the auditorium, and I felt a rush of pride and elation that I had never experienced before.

However, as the school year drew to a close, a sense of melancholy began to settle in. I couldn't escape the reality that the approaching summer months meant not having a break from the House on the Hill and being away from the adoration of my classmates. The prospect of becoming invisible once again during those long summer months brought tears to my eyes. I couldn't help but mourn the spotlight that had briefly illuminated my life, and I clung to those moments of recognition as the days at school grew shorter.

Despite the friendships I was forming, I continued to struggle with connecting with people on a deeper level, and I felt this most keenly when I was at the House, without the admiration of classmates impressed with my physical prowess. While I had learned to adapt to the daily life of the group home's environment, there was an emotional distance that I couldn't bridge with the other housemates. Jacque and Iszel, on the other hand, had no trouble breaking the ice and forming connections. They had an innate ability to connect with people, excelling both academically and athletically. Their confident and outgoing personalities allowed them to more easily navigate the complexities of social interactions.

I found closer kinship with the animals in the house, one of the silver linings of our stay there. There were two cats – Mr. Martin and the Hills' cat, who we affectionately referred to as "Fatty" due to her generous girth. Fatty was too large to leap onto furniture or beds but was incredibly affectionate and would reciprocate with love bites when she was particularly pleased with the petting she received.

Mr. Martin was an old and wise indoor/outdoor cat who roamed the surrounding grounds and woods, ever on the hunt. On occasion, he would return with half-eaten prey as if offering a gift of appreciation for letting him come in on cold or hot days. He seemed to possess an uncanny ability to sense when one of the boys needed his comforting presence, and I often found him entering my room and brightening my day when I was feeling low. What set him apart was that he was polydactyl, a unique feature of having extra toes on every paw. Mr.

THOSE BOYS ON THE HILL

Martin had seven toes on each paw, which allowed him to grasp and manipulate objects, even turning doorknobs, granting him an astonishing level of autonomy.

In addition to the feline companions, the house was also home to three dogs. Lady, a Labrador Retriever mix, had been a part of the house before the Hills' tenure. She was a loving and calming presence, offering service-like qualities to the boys in the house, including myself.

Beatrice, an amiable small Shepherd mix, was another furry resident. She enjoyed being around the guys, basking in the attention and affection lavished upon her. A significant portion of her time was spent with Dave, the Hills' son. She mirrored his disposition: friendly but easily nervous. She would roll over and show her belly if she thought you were mad at her, similar to how quickly David would shrink under the weight of his father's criticisms. The two were a comfort to each other.

The Hills also brought Wimpy, an Airedale mix whose disposition mirrored that of the Hills themselves. She was rather temperamental and never fully acclimated to the bustling atmosphere of the House, occasionally snapping at the boys. We soon discovered that she had a peculiar fear of water spray bottles, so we kept them handy as a means of gentle persuasion.

Except for Wimpy, I formed a bond with all the animals, and they helped ease my loneliness a bit. Before Avondale, I had never spent much time around pets, my only previous experience being my Uncle Ricky's terrifying Doberman. Now, they provided comfort and constancy that surprised me.

I also sought escape in the familiar solitude of the barn. It became my refuge, a place where I could let my imagination run wild as I explored its nooks and crannies. The dusty corners held secrets and stories, providing a respite from the complexities of life in the group home. Iszel and I often stayed close together when he wasn't busy with his passion for basketball, finding solace in each other's company and avoiding interactions with the Hills as much as we could.

As summer started, I focused on surviving day-to-day life. I relied on my brothers, on the support and friendships that were slowly forming, and on the comfort of the animals, all while carrying the weight of my circumstances for being at the group home. My journey of self-discovery was just beginning, and the road ahead was long and uncertain.

CHAPTER 11

Solitary

As we spent more time at the House on the Hill, it became clear that Henry's demerit system was a finely tuned instrument, one that was easily triggered, much as I had suspected. He had a knack for finding infractions in even the most mundane actions, and our promised allowances often bore the brunt of his scrutiny.

The envelopes that held our meager allowances regularly fell short of the promised amounts, often without any warning. When we confronted Henry about the discrepancies, he would rattle off a laundry list of transgressions that, in his view, warranted withholding the few dollars we were supposed to receive. Some of these infractions were downright ridiculous, like not reaching his standards for how we made our beds or folded our clothes during his daily room inspections or leaving our bedroom light on for too long after being told to go to bed. It felt like traversing a minefield just to keep hold of our hard-earned allowances.

"Iszel," I whispered one evening as we huddled in our room. "I can't believe he's taking even more money from our allowances this week. We barely have anything left."

Iszel's face scrunched up; frustration was evident in his voice. "Yeah, it's ridiculous. I swear, he finds any excuse to dock our funds. We work too hard for those few bucks for him to keep snatching them away."

The following day, I mustered the courage to approach Henry. "Henry, why did you take away our allowance again? We did everything you asked this week."

Henry looked down at me with an almost condescending smile. "Well, boys, you need to learn that life isn't easy. These deductions are for your own good, to teach you discipline and responsibility."

"But it feels like you're just being unfair," I protested. "We never get a break."

But Henry's tactics didn't stop there. When he exhausted the full amount of deductions for one week, he didn't hesitate to dip into the funds for the following week, ensuring that we were constantly on edge about our financial prospects.

For Iszel and me, it wasn't just about the money. Henry coupled these deductions with in-room confinement as punishment. We found ourselves restricted to our room for various reasons, all dependent on the kind of day Henry and Janine were having. It was a sentence that was never imposed on the older boys, primarily because he couldn't make them stay in their rooms. They were beyond the reach of that particular disciplinary tactic.

During one of our room confinements, I sat with Iszel, sharing an unhappy silence. He finally broke the quiet, frustration clear in his voice. "Yo, this is ridiculous, man! We've been stuck in here for days, and I can't even remember what got us into trouble this time."

I sighed, my voice weary. "I know, man. It's like he just wants to make our lives miserable."

Henry enforced these punishments with a capricious hand, often adding days to our confinement on a whim. If we received a poor grade at school, instead of sitting down with us to help us understand the lesson better, he would ensure we suffered for the bad grade. We would serve our time, but it was never enough for Henry. He would tack on additional days, determined to ensure that we learned his intended lesson, no matter the cost. Before the year was out, he began ramping up the length of these incarcerations.

The July day began innocently enough, with the warm sun casting a golden glow over our small town. Iszel and I decided to take our bikes to explore the familiar streets and eventually found ourselves at a place known as Box Canyon, a secluded spot in a rock quarry often frequented by local kids on wheels. This hidden gem featured natural half-pipes and winding wooded trails away from the construction company's usual attention.

We spent some exhilarating moments riding the half-pipes and biking the forested paths, but our adventures took an unexpected turn when we ventured onto the adjacent grounds of a mulching and manure company. Avondale was known for its mushroom farming, and the pungent smell of fertilizer often lingered in the air, a reminder of the town's agricultural roots.

We spotted a few of our classmates in the area, some presumably collecting mulch for their families. With a surplus of the smelly stuff lying around, I guessed the owner didn't mind if a few kids took a wheelbarrow's worth on occasion.

Iszel and I began riding our bikes on the undulating mounds of mulch. I took the lead and pushed my luck, almost colliding with a kid who was using a pitchfork to load a wheelbarrow.

"Hey, Neeger, watch where you're riding," he spat out, and I couldn't tolerate the town's overt racism anymore. I walked up to the wheelbarrow and kicked it over, spilling its contents onto the kid's legs and feet. Satisfied, I walked away to retrieve my bike, feeling a sudden impact on my left shoulder. He had hurled the pitchfork at me, and it caught me as I bent down to grab the handlebars. I suffered a deep, bleeding gash on my shoulder before I felt the sharp sting.

Enraged, I charged at him, and a brawl ensued. Though he managed to land a few punches, I connected with a solid blow to his nose, causing him to yelp in pain and clutch his bleeding face. Iszel, who had been watching, shouted at me. "Yo, we better get outta here!"

I hopped on my bike, and we rode back into town, adrenaline pumping through our veins. Suddenly, we heard a police siren blaring behind us, and a town police cruiser pulled up just as we were passing Earl's Sub Shop.

"Boys, get off your bikes," the officer commanded over the car's speaker. We obeyed, and he stepped out of the car. "Were you two just at the quarry fighting?"

"Yes," I replied. "That kid called me a bad name and cut me with a pitchfork." I showed him my bleeding shoulder.

Ignoring my injury, the officer asked, "Are you boys from the group home up the hill? Does Henry know you two are downtown starting fights?"

Frustration bubbled inside me. "That kid shouldn't be calling people out their name and hitting people with pitchforks."

The officer seemed taken aback by my retort; his eyes narrowed as if measuring my defiance. He instructed us to ride our bikes back to the House on the Hill. He followed closely as if he expected us to try and flee on our bikes.

As we arrived back at the group home with the officer, my nerves were on edge. The officer and Henry exchanged pleasantries like old friends.

"Hey, Henry," The officer greeted with a friendly nod. "We just had a little situation down at the quarry."

I exchanged a worried glance with Iszel, who stood beside me, and Henry crossed his arms, giving us a stern look. "Well, what happened?"

The officer puffed up his chest. "You see, these two troublemakers were down at Box Canyon, and they confronted some other kids. There was some name-calling, and it escalated into a scuffle. Unfortunately, they may have provoked it."

I couldn't believe what I was hearing. That wasn't how it happened at all—no mention of the racial slur or me being attacked with a pitchfork. I was seething with frustration.

Henry seemed satisfied with the officer's account of events. "Thanks for keeping a lookout, John. I'll take care of it and make sure they understand the rules."

"John's not telling the whole story," I protested.

"That's Officer Schmidt to you, boy!" Henry corrected, dripping with disdain, my defiance hitting a nerve.

Unfazed, I continued, "I don't know his name. I just called him what you called him."

"He is a person of authority, and you will respect his position by addressing him properly," Henry insisted.

"Then why don't you hafta call him Officer John too?" Iszel asked.

Henry's face reddened, and he eyed Iszel contemptuously but said nothing, his silence thick with unspoken animosity. I shrugged and displayed my bleeding shoulder again.

"That other kid called me a bad name and hit me with a pitchfork. I may need stitches and a shot! That thing was shoveling manure. I could be infected."

Henry's response was swift and harsh. "Thirty days! The both of you!"

"I didn't even do nothing," Iszel chimed in.

I echoed his sentiment. "Yeah, Iszel didn't fight no one."

Henry pointed a finger toward the house. "You want to make it for the rest of the summer?!"

He was putting on a show for his officer friend. I glanced at them both, silently challenging their authority.

After the officer left, Henry grabbed my arm, his grip firm and unyielding. He marched me inside, dug out a bandage from the medicine cabinet in the bathroom, and ordered me to wash off the wound on my shoulder. He didn't take me to the doctor for antibiotics or stitches. Miraculously, it didn't become infected, though it did leave a permanent scar.

Henry must have realized that confining us together would allow us to bond, so he separated us. During the week, I was placed in the weekend house parents' bunk, a small room with a bed and a card table. Meals were delivered to the room with a knock at the door, and I had to shout down the hall for permission to leave for the bathroom.

Confinements were always harder during the summer when school couldn't provide a welcome escape from our rooms. To pass the time, I was allowed jigsaw puzzles, which I would assemble, disassemble, and reassemble repeatedly.

Sometimes, I would watch out the window, straining for any sight of the older kids, having fun in the sunlight while I was stuck in a 9' x 12' prison. Sometimes, I lay on the bed with my arms behind my head, staring at the ceiling, stewing about our current situation, and thinking about my past. My thoughts kept returning to my Uncle Ricky and his version of solitary. I tried to console myself with the thought that no punishment in this group home could ever match the horrors my Uncle Ricky had put me through.

CHAPTER 12

Uncle Ricky

In the summer of 1984, after having stayed with my Aunt Angel for two months, my mom came to collect us and took Iszel and me to live with our Uncle Ricky and his family. While technically he was our grandmother's brother, we never thought of him that way. An uncle was an uncle, the same way that a brother was a brother, whether half or whole. First, second, or third cousins – it didn't matter; they were all cousins. In many Black communities, the concept of "family" was much more bound together and all-encompassing than in white communities. It held a fundamental importance, providing us with crucial social support through the vast networks that helped us navigate a world that sometimes appeared to overlook or neglect our presence.

This arrangement was the second of five alternative living situations that year, and it left me feeling disjointed, especially without Jacque by my side, who was still at our Aunt Angel's. Uncle Ricky and his wife, Roxanne, were known for their love of partying. Roxanne enjoyed the good times with him, but there was a point where the atmosphere would turn volatile. It happened like clockwork every few weeks, and Roxanne would lock Uncle Ricky out of their bedroom. We'd overhear their exchanges through the thin walls, his slurred pleas and her unwavering refusal.

"Come on, Rox," Uncle Ricky would begin, desperation creeping into his voice. "Come on, baby. We havin' a good time," he'd singsong.

"Ricky, I don't want no more parts of you tonight," Roxanne's soft but firm voice would respond. "Go on down there with the boys."

"Rox, come on. Open this door. You got me out here like I don't pay any bills around here!" Anger would start to poison his words.

"Ricky, go on down there with the boys and leave me be." Roxanne's resolve remained unshaken.

Uncle Ricky would hit the door hard with his fist. The sound would echo down the hallway and into our room. The boom caused a cold chill of fear to run down my spine. I was scared that he would break the door down and hurt her. I feared he would then turn his drunken and drugged-up anger on us. "Rox, I ain't playin' no mo'!" Uncle Ricky would shout. "Open the fuckin' door! Got me out here askin' to sleep in my own bed like I'm some nigga from the streets!" Roxanne wouldn't answer. She'd become stone silent when he got like that. She would simply wait him out. "Rox? Rox?! Come on, baby," he'd wheedle.

We'd hold our breath, hoping she would relent, but usually, silence was her only response. Eventually, exhaustion and inebriation would triumph, and Uncle Ricky would stumble his way down the dark hallway to our room. In our small bedroom, a king-size mattress nearly filled the space. As he entered, he'd fall upon us like a felled tree in the woods, leading with knees, elbows, or head, driving them into our small bodies. It hurt, and I'd almost hear an imaginary voice saying, "Timber!" as he landed on us.

He'd rest his weight on us, the scent of alcohol and something else oozing from his sweaty pores. It smelled like decay, and his moisture felt like a stain that would never wash off. I'd rush to the bathroom as soon as he left, eager to rid myself of that clinging smell and feeling. Some nights, he'd vomit or urinate on us as he slept off his drugged-up inebriation. The next morning, he'd demand that we clean up his mess, threatening that we'd have to sleep in it if we didn't. It was a never-ending cycle of fear, discomfort, and dread.

***

That summer with Uncle Ricky and Roxanne was just another stop on our tumultuous journey, but it was a chapter filled with memories that would haunt me for years to come, including the worst beating I've ever endured. It happened suddenly and unexpectedly. He and Roxanne had cooked a huge boil of crab, shrimp, and fixins. We ate well, and

THOSE BOYS ON THE HILL

Uncle Ricky seemed happy. He had Stevie Wonder's "Hotter than July" and Jackson's latest album "Victory" on repeat. He also threw in some Marvin Gaye's "What's Going On" and Michael Jackson's "Thriller" for good measure. With the music playing in the background and the food flowing, everyone was getting along and having a good time.

When dinner ended, everyone was in an upbeat mood. Uncle Ricky and Roxanne decided to continue partying elsewhere. They left the kitchen full of dirty dishes and instructed our cousin, Donald, to have the place clean by the time they got back. But Donald played, watched TV, and forgot about these instructions.

It was approaching 11 pm. Donald was upstairs in the bedroom, and Iszel and I were still chatting drowsily in the living room, opting for the floor rather than the sticky, clear plastic that snugly fit on the tan and brown striped couch. My back was to the door when I heard it click open and turned to see that Uncle Ricky and Roxanne were back from partying. Roxanne smiled at us, but Uncle Ricky blew past with a grunt, moving towards the dining room. He stopped cold when he saw the kitchen.

"Donald, bring yo' ass down here to this kitchen!" he roared. He turned to us. "Y'all too!" His voice was ugly, and my heart started thumping loudly in my chest. Iszel and I scrambled to obey him, traveling the distance from the living room to the kitchen in a nanosecond, hoping to calm his anger through obedience. I was moving so fast that I had an uncharacteristically clumsy moment, almost tripping on the kitchen floor's buckling linoleum and crashing into the farmer's sink against the opposite wall. I edged away from it, wanting to put some distance between myself and the offending dirty dishes. Uncle Ricky just sneered. Donald hastily joined us a moment later, and because Iszel was to my left, he skulked over to the only spot left near the sink.

We stood lined up in a row in the middle of the small kitchen, our backs to the stove. The smell of Old Bay and seafood lingered heavily in the air. The door to the basement was on the same side of the wall as the entrance to the kitchen. I thought briefly about trying to make my escape there, even though they kept Zeus, their mean-looking Doberman, locked down there in the dark. Instead, I stared past Uncle Ricky, looming in front of us, trying not to make eye contact, my gaze landing on the fridge behind him.

"Yes, Dad?" Donald asked, his voice high and thin with fear.

Ricky slowly circled us, past Iszel, who shrank away from him involuntarily, past the basement door, coming behind us as he trailed his hand along the oil-stained, four-burner stove. He turned again, edging between Donald and the sink, stopped briefly and pointedly, hip-checking Donald so he stumbled a bit. He then rounded the corner again, past the fridge, until his pacing brought him in front of us, standing directly opposite me.

"Why the hell ain't these dishes done?" he asked calmly now, with no hint of the former violence in his voice. His breath reeked of booze. His level demeanor scared me more than his yelling had done. The three of us stood in a row, shoulder to shoulder. Unsure how to answer without getting the beating that was about to ensue, we remained silent. This frustrated him.

He stared up at the ceiling, looking for the will to control himself. Anger crept back into his voice. He poked Donald hard in his chest, causing him to take an unbalanced step back, and asked, "Why the hell ain't these dishes done?!"

Roxanne poked her head into the room, smiling, still feeling the night. "Ricky, leave dem boys alone and come on upstairs. They gonna get to 'em.'"

"Naw, Rox, don't try to save 'em now," Ricky retorted. "They got dis ass whoopin' comin' to 'em. I told dem to have this place cleaned up when we got back."

Roxanne considered him with a stare, gave an apologetic shrug in our direction, shook her head, and faded out of the room. He turned his attention towards me and leaned to within an inch of my face.

He took a beat between each word. "Why. Ain't. These. Dishes. Done?"

The smell of alcohol on his breath turned my stomach. His face was full of malice, but his eyes were wide with excitement as he waited for my answer. I knew I was going to be hit regardless of what I said, and a dread grew in me that pushed tears into the corners of my eyes. So, I assigned the blame to my cousin.

"You told Donald to wash 'em'," I replied, tears now blurring my vision.

"Boy, yo' gon' stop that crying or I'm gon' give yo' something to cry about!"

I couldn't hold the tears in, and one began rolling down my face. Seeing it fall set Uncle Ricky off. He instantly punched me hard in my solar plexus. It knocked the air out of my lungs and sent me hurling back, off my feet, across the room. My back slammed into the stove, and I crumpled to the floor in a small heap. My lungs felt collapsed. I grabbed at my chest and gasped for breath.

"We gon make a man outta yo'!" Uncle Ricky yelled.

He turned to Donald and got to within an inch of his face. "Why, ain't these fuckin' dishes done, boy?!" he asked through gritted teeth.

Donald gave an inaudible whimper, and Uncle Ricky unleashed a sledgehammer-sized fist on his ribcage. It sent Donald flying into the sink full of dishes and dropped him to his knees. Uncle Ricky didn't waste time asking Iszel the question, instead circling him as Iszel rotated in fear, then crushed him with a blow to the chest that threw Iszel into the refrigerator. It rocked so hard that the opened box of Corn Flakes on top of it fell to the floor, spilling its contents. Uncle Ricky stood triumphantly in the middle of the kitchen. He raised his fists over his head like a prize-winning boxer and began bouncing on his toes. He dropped back to a defensive stance, bobbed, and weaved around our fallen bodies, stepping on the cereal.

"I still got it!" Uncle Ricky shouted. "I STILL got it! Knocked these three lil niggas OUT!"

He completed a full circle around the kitchen as if it were an imaginary boxing ring, finally dancing his way out of the room and up the stairs, repeating his chant.

We each sat in silence near our appliances for a minute, collecting ourselves. Iszel stood and grabbed the broom and dustpan. Donald began filling the sink with soap and water. I took to drying whatever he passed me. My chest and back ached, and my anger swelled up in me with each dish I dried. The feeling knotted my stomach.

I don't know when. I don't know how, but I'm gonna get you back when I'm big enough when my size matches yours. We gonna see if you STILL got it THEN.

***

A few days later, just after dinner, Uncle Ricky grabbed me by my shoulders and steered me to the basement door. He handed me a worn, black flashlight and a rusty snow shovel. "Basement floor needs cleaning. Zeus has been shittin' down there for a week."

He shoved me to the first step despite my protests and locked me in the dark. I heard growling and fumbled with the flashlight, finding the switch to emit a weak beam of light that illuminated the snout of the Doberman at the bottom of the steps, fangs pulled back into a snarl. I waved the shovel and shouted, and Zeus began pacing in a circle. When he was far enough away, I raced to the bottom of the steps and wedged the shovel towards the base of the stairs diagonally across, hoping to create a discouraging barrier. Then I ran back to the top of the stairs, banging on the door, screaming for all I was worth, hoping someone would let me out.

"Yo' better stop that shit!" Ricky yelled from the other side. The smell from the basement caused me to dry heave. Piss and shit and dirty, hungry dog all mixed into an overwhelming fug. I could hear the plop of the dog's pads hitting the sticky, excrement-covered floors as he paced in the dark. The sound of his breathing filled the hollow room. I banged harder on the door. Uncle Ricky opened it, and the kitchen light behind him silhouetted his broad figure.

"Boy, I'm bout tired of yo' shit. Yo' better not touch this damn door again. Stop that crying, get off these fuckin' steps, and go clean that shit up!"

He slammed the door, and I slumped back down on the top step. The dog settled at the base of the staircase. The light that crept under the door went off. I began to cry. When he wasn't at the bottom of the steps, he trotted in large circles around the room. He hadn't been walked in for over a week, and no one came down to engage with him. He never tried to climb the steps. Armed with the flashlight, I leaned against the wall and eventually fell into a broken sleep. I was roused awake by the sound of Zeus lapping from his water bucket and an urgent need to pee. When he wasn't at the bottom of the steps, he trotted in large circles around the room. In desperation, flashlight and shovel held out like weapons, I shouted at Zeus to "Stay!" I quickly edged around him to a corner of the basement to relieve myself. The circle of the flashlight reflected off his eyes so that he appeared devilish as he watched me curiously. But he never attacked, and I quickly resumed my spot on the top step.

I doze. Daylight soon showed in a strip under the base of the door until it was broken by someone's shadow. Iszel's welcome voice whispered from the other side of the door. "Elliott, you good in there?"

I leaned my back against the door, trying to get closer to him. "Yeah, just sitting on the step."

"Zeus messin' witcha?"

"Nah, he walkin' in circles down here. Why even have a dog you gonna leave him like dis?"

I heard a floorboard creak followed by Uncle Ricky's voice. "Boy, get yo' ass away from that do' before I put yo' down there wid eem." He shouted through the door. "Yo' clean that shit up?!"

"No," I responded weakly.

"Yo' ain't comin' outta there til yo' do. Gets ta shovelin'!"

I shined the light on Zeus, who had stopped pacing when he heard his owner's voice. When he sensed that Uncle Ricky had moved away from the door, he whimpered and resumed his trot.

A few hours later, Roxanne opened the door with a turkey and cheese sandwich and a glass of water in her hand. Based on the meal, I figured it was around lunchtime. I began to push through her to get out of the basement to the first floor, but she stopped me. "Baby, I can't let you back up here. Not until you do what he says, or we'll all be in trouble."

I looked over my shoulder into the dark basement. "Zeus is down there waiting for me."

I could hear him trotting and breathing. He didn't respond to Roxanne's voice like he did to Uncle Ricky's.

"He ain't gonna bother you none," she said reassuringly. "But you gotta do what your Uncle Ricky says. Now stand here and eat this."

I thought of the one reason I could warrant freedom from the basement. "But I gotta go to the bathroom," I pleaded.

She took a beat, held her breath to listen, and looked towards the other room. She exhaled and turned back towards me. "You're gonna hafta clean up that mess down there before he lets you back up. Now hurry up and eat this food."

I took a bite of the sandwich and a swallow of the water. "I can't see nothin."

"Use the flashlight he gave you."

She must have heard him moving about the house.

"Hurry up!" she whispered.

I stuffed large bites in my mouth and washed them down. I had almost finished the water when she grabbed the plastic cup from me and closed the door. She left the last bite of the sandwich in my hand. I heard the lock engage, and I was back in the dark again.

I crept down the steps into the darker recesses of the room, stopping every third step or so until I was sitting on the bottom with the shovel in hand in case Zeus lunged at me. He paid me little mind.

I held the flashlight down the shaft of the shovel and began pushing the blade across the floor towards the small garage door, collecting as much of the feces in my path as I could. Flies were having a smorgasbord on the piles. My passing shovel disturbed their feast, and they scattered in all directions. I came close to bashing my face in with the flashlight when one landed on me. I could only think of the last place its little legs had been, and it skeeved me out.

The room was warm and moist, the ideal conditions for the maggots that had made their home in the many piles I pushed to the garage door. I worked while trying to avoid Zeus as best I could, but the dog would occasionally circle me. When he did, I would shine my light on him and command him to "Stay!" or "Sit!" anything to stop him from biting me.

The crack of light under the door had gone dark again. I finished the shoveling, climbed the stairs, and knocked on the door. Uncle Ricky's voice eventually came from the other side. "Yo' clean that shit up?"

"Ain't no place to put it. I pushed it to the door."

"Yo' gon' hafta finish with the hose and some bleach tomorrow."

"Can I come out now?"

"Naw boy, I said yo' come up when that shit is cleaned up. Yo' still got work to do. Yo' keep Zeus company again tonight. I think he startin' to like yo,'" he singsonged.

The knot in my stomach tightened. My eyes began to water in anger. I pressed my forehead hard against the door in frustration and began squeezing the flashlight in my hands as though I was choking Uncle Ricky.

Zeus and I slept better the second night. Me, at the top of the stairs; him at the bottom near his water bucket and food. The hours spent shoveling as he circled the room had established a little more trust that he was no longer looking to eat me.

I woke when a bit of light began creeping under the door. The house started to rouse, and I heard the other kids' voices. The lock to the garage door where I shoveled the excrement turned. The rusty casters and tumblers on the ceiling creaked as Uncle Ricky heaved the door open with more strength than was needed.

Zeus darted towards the door like he was ready to escape his captivity. I understood his desire to breathe fresh air and free himself of Uncle Ricky. Iszel and Donald were standing outside the door with buckets, a push broom, a hose, and a large container of bleach. They both backed away at the sight of Zeus in full stride. Uncle Ricky stood in the middle of the doorway and bellowed, "Sit!"

Zeus immediately ceased his advance, dropping his rear to the floor, muscles tensed and body almost motionless with his face staring up at his master. Uncle Ricky grabbed his collar, attached a leash to it, and yanked on it hard. The dog's front two feet were barely touching the floor.

"Where tha fuck yo' think yo' going?!" Ricky asked Zeus between gritted, snaggled teeth that nearly matched the dog's snarl. He stood like that for a moment, like he expected the dog to answer. Zeus could only squeeze out a high-pitched whimper, which I think was a cry for air or for one of us to help.

I would rather be dead than have that dog's life, I thought to myself, all too aware that I had been locked in the basement with him and *had* just lived his life for the last two days. Uncle Ricky looked around at the three of us with a malicious smile on his face. He drew out the moment to emphasize his control over us.

"Y'all see?" he asked finally. "I run this shit!" He gave Zeus a heavy, broad-handed swat across the ribs that seemed meant to cause pain rather than a warm, endearing exchange from owner to pet. "Now y'all clean this shit up and rinse this floor good! I'm gonna take Zeus for a walk." They began walking down the alley.

Donald called to him. "Where should we put it?"

"In the buckets," Uncle Ricky shouted back. "Carry it down to the sewer on the corner and dump it. Use the hose, bleach, and broom to brush that flo' clean. There better not be any shit in there when y'all done. Less y'all wanna nother ass whoopin'." He said the last sentence in a taunting singsong, alluding to the "Appliance Beating," as Iszel, Donald, and I had dubbed it.

We spent the better part of the day flushing out the room. We even refreshed Zeus' water bucket and put out fresh food. When Uncle Ricky returned with Zeus, he closed the garage and gave the room a smell test. His broad nostrils took in as much bleachy air as his lungs could inhale, trying to find any hint of the smell of poop. Luckily for us, he didn't find any.

Uncle Ricky sent us upstairs to the first floor. He wasn't far behind as he left Zeus downstairs in the dark, where I imagined him starting his lonely, circular trotting again.

Ricky and Roxanne went out that evening to party. I'd had my fill of the abuse and decided that I needed to find my mother or Jacque to get away from Uncle Ricky or from being locked in the basement again. I waited for what I thought to be a solid amount of time and tried the front door, but it had a dual lock that required a key to open it. The windows on the first floor were all locked, and I couldn't figure out how to unlock them. Although I was no longer terrified of Zeus, I wasn't sure how to unlock and open the garage from the inside. So, I opted for the second floor.

I tested one window after another, finally finding one that was unlatched in the bathroom. I was able to raise the window and pull the screen inside. I looked out the window at the two-story drop to Uncle Ricky's cherry red Corvette that he had been nursing back to health. The narrow window was over the basin of the toilet. I could just fit through if I angled my shoulders correctly. I laid my body across it to go out backward, feet first through the small opening, thinking I could pull myself back up if I changed my mind about dropping out of the window. I wriggled myself through until I was hanging onto the edge of the windowpane, dangling over the Corvette.

Uncle Ricky is going to kill me if I stay or if I try to leave. I'll at least have a chance on the run. That realization gave me the will to let go and drop two stories. It felt like I was falling through the air forever. The impact of my weight jarred my knees and created two large dents in the hood where I landed. If Uncle Ricky wasn't going to kill me before, those dents guaranteed he would now.

I jumped off the vehicle and sprinted down the alleyway to the street as fast as I could. I didn't think about where I was going. I only knew I had to get as far away from Uncle Ricky's house as possible. I was in an unfamiliar neighborhood and had no idea how to find Jacque or my mother. I simply ran. I had made it six blocks when I heard Donald's voice yelling from behind me.

"Elliott! Elliott!"

He was faster than I was, getting louder as he neared, even though I was running away from his pleas. He finally caught up to me, but I didn't stop running. He simply kept up with me.

"Get away from me, Donald," I said, jogging breathlessly.

"Cuz, you gotta come back before my dad gets home. He's gonna kill us all if you ain't there."

I stopped and rested my hands on my knees to catch my breath.

"How'd you get outta the house?" I asked suspiciously.

Donald reached into the neck of his t-shirt and pulled a necklace out from under it. At the end of it was a house key. "I have a key in case of an emergency."

THOSE BOYS ON THE HILL

Thinking about the damage to Uncle Ricky's Corvette, I wanted to snatch the key off the chain. "You had this the whole time they've been locking us in the house?!" I asked incredulously.

Donald's eyes glazed over. "You gotta come home, cuz," he pleaded.

I envisioned the abusive future he was trying to avoid. I'd been so frantic to escape that I'd left Iszel behind. His future would be the same as Donald's. That realization made me feel like shit. I needed to get him out, too. Donald must have seen the change in my demeanor. He placed an arm across my shoulder and turned me back towards the house. "C'mon man, please. We gotta get back. I'm already in trouble for unlocking the door."

We started a slow walk back to the house. "They gonna be able to tell?" I asked. "And what about Uncle Ricky's car? He's gonna kill me anyway."

"He hasn't messed with that car for months. We'll figure something out or take that ass whoopin' too. For now, we don't say shit about it."

His calm resignation about these inevitable future beatings almost caused me to turn around and start running again. If it weren't for Iszel, I might have given it a go, but instead, I continued back towards the house. I hoped to see my mother soon, wherever she was. Living on the streets homeless was better than staying at Uncle Ricky's.

Uncle Ricky and Roxanne returned happy and thoroughly buzzed. Everyone kept my runaway attempt quiet, as much for their sakes as for mine. I spent some hellish days worrying about him discovering the dents, but he never did, at least not while I was there.

A few days later, the phone rang. Uncle Ricky spoke to the person on the other end for a minute. He became agitated and animated. *Somebody was getting the business from Uncle Ricky on the other end of the line.* He called Iszel over to the phone. "Come 'ere boy. It's yo' mama."

Hearing this, I jumped from the living room couch and ran towards the kitchen, where the phone was hanging on the wall. Uncle Ricky shoved me back. "Did I call yo' black ass?" Seeing this as one of the few chances to get my mom to come to rescue us before Uncle Ricky killed me, I stood back up and walked toward the phone.

"I wanna talk to my mom," I said, as commanding as possible, staring up at the big man.

Uncle Ricky smiled proudly. "Oh, this lil nigga starting to get a lil heart," he said.

His eyes gleamed, and he tensed as though he was about to punch me. I cowardly turned away to avoid the blow, but he stopped short of hitting me. He was simply making the point that I was still afraid of him. He pointed towards the couch.

"Yo' sit yo black ass down and wait til Ikey's done," he said. "And don't yo be telling my biznez. What happens in da house, stays in da house."

I assumed he meant the "Appliance Beating" and my time with Zeus. "I won't," I lied. I intended to tell her enough to get us out of here.

Iszel finished talking and passed me the phone.

"Hey Babee," my mom brightly slurred out, "Do ya mish mommy?"

She was drunk and high. She also sounded like she had been crying. Slurring was common for her. The pitch of her voice told me she had more than just a few drinks in her. It was higher than her normal speaking tone. I'd heard her sound like that before when she had been partying. The crying was new. At least this amount of crying. She seemed to cry every time we spoke to her. She was in a bad state and a bad place. Her cheerful tone did not convince me that everything was ok. She was trying to cover it, but there were more important things to talk about.

I stared in Uncle Ricky's general direction and hoped he was not within earshot. "Ma, you gotta come get us. I don't like it here," I whispered. "And where are you?" I added since I wasn't sure if I would need to run away again.

"I'm gonna come to get you as soon as I figure some shtuff out." Her voice quivered on the other end.

She didn't understand. Shaking my head into the phone, trying to project my fear, I said the words I knew might set her off most.

"Ma, he hits us when he's angry. Me, Iszel, and Donald. You gotta come get us."

Silence...

Did I lose her?

"Ma?" I asked. "Ma, did you hear me?"

Nothing...then: "Put Uncle Ricky on the phone," she said soberly.

I pointed the phone towards him.

"She wants to talk to you again," I said. He walked over, grabbed the receiver, and cocked his head to the side to cradle it between his broad shoulder and ear. Hands-free, he crossed his arms and spoke into the phone.

"Yeah?" he asked like he was conducting a business call.

I could hear my mother talking loudly. "I don't give a damn what you do to your kids, but don't you lay another hand on mine, or I swear fo' God, I'll cut you!"

His body stiffened. He pulled the receiver off his shoulder and faced it towards himself. "Who tha fuck yo' think yo' talkin' to?!" he yelled. He put it back up to his ear to hear her response, but she had already hung up.

Uncle Ricky glowered at me, slammed the phone back into the cradle, and grabbed me by the top of my shirt, driving his knuckles into my throat as he pulled me off the ground.

"Boy, tha fuck yo' say to yo' mama? I told yo' ass to keep yo' mouff shut! House biznez stays in tha house!"

He threw my small frame to the ground and stomped up the stairs. Relieved that I had probably seen the worst of it for the night, I went up to pack. I figured my mom was on her way to retrieve us.

That night lasted forever. I stayed up waiting for her, but she never came. Every day, I stayed up late and woke up early, spending most of my days staring out the front window. A long week passed, and my hopes began to diminish. *She's not coming. It was all for show. At least he hasn't hit me. Yeah, but no telling how long that would last…*

A week and a half after the phone exchange, my mother showed up riding in a friend's matte grey, suped-up muscle car to collect us from Uncle Ricky's house. I was so happy to see her, I couldn't contain myself. I didn't want to. I nearly tackled her off her feet with my embrace.

"Ma, are we leavin'? We don't hafta stay here no more, right?" I stared up at her with my arms still wrapped around both her legs, pleading. She nearly tripped.

"Y'all don't hafta stay here no mo' baby. Go get your stuff." She worked herself out of my grasp to avoid toppling over.

"Iszel, ma said to get our stuff!" I shouted towards the upstairs. "We leavin'!"

Uncle Ricky heard my shouts and sauntered into the living room while I raced past him. I heard my mom and him start arguing about how he had treated us as soon as he appeared.

"Ricky, how you gonna be beatin' on my babies?" she started.

He raised his hands in innocent defense. "Aww, I ain't hurt dem none," he protested. "Besides, yo' raisin' some bitch ass boys. Elliott always be cryin' and shit. Gotta man dem up."

Anger crept into his voice. "And who yo' talkin' to on the phone like dat? My ass is doin' yo' ass a favor with yo' kids."

My mom put her hands on her hips. "That's why I didn't even wanna go here witchu Ricky. I knew it was gonna be about some shit you'd throw back in my face as soon as you had a chance. You shouldn't be hitting nobody's kids as big as you are. Always tryna prove something. It's cool. It's the last time you ever lay a hand on my babies."

I darted up the stairs two at a time. Iszel was already packing by the time I arrived in our shared room, and I took what little I hadn't already packed in long anticipation of this very moment and shoved it in my bag.

"Let's get in the car and go!" I urged Iszel, whose pace of packing was just a beat slower than mine. It had been three months too long and we couldn't get out of there fast enough. We hustled down the steps, past the arguing adults, and out the front door without saying goodbye to anyone. But my mom would not allow such blatant disrespect.

"Elliott, Ikey!" The sharp reprimand in her voice stopped us short. "Come back in here and say goodbye to folks. Y'all know I taught y'all better than that."

Grudgingly, we turned and mumbled our goodbyes, my heart aching for my cousin Donald, who had to stay with his father. I could only imagine what life had in store for him. Jacque was waiting in the car. Aunt Angel's had been Mom's first stop to collect him. Iszel and I jumped on him in the back seat. He took his time fighting us off, mostly repeating, "Get off me!" I think he had missed us as much as we'd missed him. The Glover brothers were back together again. Everything was gonna be ok. It didn't matter where we were going next as long as we stayed together.

I noted the dark-skinned, stocky man in the driver's seat, someone I didn't recognize. He had a toothpick hanging out of the corner of his mouth and was twirling it between his thumb and pointer finger. He glanced back at us with a raised eyebrow when we hopped in the car but didn't bother speaking to us. Even though he wasn't smoking, the cloth seats and loose-hanging headliner exuded the essence of weed and cigarette smoke. I didn't care. I was beyond elated that I was leaving Uncle Ricky's. But the feeling was short-lived. Our mom gave him directions to our Aunt Linda's house. When we got there, she gave him a light tap on his forearm and pointed for him to pull over. She got out, but he left the car running. She ushered us all out of the car to the steps.

"Y'all got your bags?" she asked, and before we could answer, she started giving us hugs.

The joy that had buoyed me only moments before instantly drained away. "Ma, ain't you comin'?" I asked.

"Baby, I really want to, but I've gotta go somewhere..." she trailed off for a moment, with a haunted look in her eyes. She stared into the cool October breeze and pulled her thin coat tight around her small frame. "Gotta do... something." I could tell she was taking stock of her situation and bracing herself, and it dawned on me that my mother was making compromises for this ride around town, doing whatever was necessary to keep us safe as best as she could. My stomach churned, and I glanced at the toothpick man, who was looking straight ahead.

"Ma," Iszel pleaded.

At this, her eyes began to fill with tears. She blinked hard a few times, trying to hold them back.

"Don't worry, baby." Her voice quavered. She wiped her face with the base of her sleeve and turned away. She walked around to the passenger side door, reaching for the car handle. "Aunt Linda's expectin' y'all. It's gonna be alright as long as y'all stick together. Jacque, you look out for your brothers. Elliott, Ikey, y'all listen to Jacque. You hear me?"

Jacque's face remained stoic, a mask of both determination and sadness. His brow furrowed slightly, and there was a tightness around his lips that revealed the weight of the moment. He didn't utter a word, but his silent resolve spoke volumes. He simply nodded at her, like he knew hearing his voice would only break her more.

She didn't wait for him to say anything. She hopped in the car, slammed the door, and cupped her face in her hands as she sobbed, a wash of emotion finally bubbling over. They pulled away, and she never looked back. I figured she couldn't take the sight of the three of us standing there on the sidewalk like that. We watched the car quietly. Its brake lights illuminated red as it slowed at the stop sign on the corner. The car turned right and disappeared. She was gone again, and I didn't believe she would be back anytime soon.

Jacque picked up his plastic bags and urged us to do the same. "Let's go, y'all." Silently, we walked up the three steps to Aunt Linda's porch and waited as Jacque knocked on her door. Having my brother lead us cheered me up a bit. At least he was with us again, and we didn't have to fear Uncle Ricky anymore.

Aunt Linda opened the door to see just the three of us standing there. She was brown-skinned and petite at 5'1". Her soft but high voice always carried a soothing tone, and her warm smile could light up a room. Her hair, still vibrant, framed her face beautifully. She stepped past us and peered down the street for our mother. She took a beat when she didn't see her and shook her head in disbelief. She gently corralled the three of us into her arms and ushered us into the warmth of her house. "It's gonna be alright, boys," she said softly. "It's gonna be alright."

CHAPTER 13

Aunt Linda's Influence

During the third week of that first 30-day confinement at the House on the Hill, my young mind was getting the best of me. I had begun pacing the small room like a caged tiger, back and forth, back and forth, wondering if Aunt Linda would still think it was "gonna be alright." I was also questioning if the basement confinement at Uncle Ricky's had been worse than this endless stretch at the House on the Hill. Sure, I had been convinced I'd be eaten by a deranged Doberman at any moment, had no access to a bathroom or food, and had to shovel shit filled with maggots and flies in the dark. But it had only been three days, whereas 30 was dragging on and on. With each passing day, the walls of that house seemed to close in on me. My world had shrunk to the oppressive confines of the room of the creaky old mansion; its eerie silence was interrupted only by the haunting sounds of the wind whistling through the windows. The house mocked me. It was as if the very structure of the place conspired to keep me in, to keep me from the freedom I longed for.

Aunt Linda's words, "It's gonna be alright," echoed in my mind, but their reassuring charm had faded like an old photograph. I began to question whether she had genuinely believed it or had merely said it to comfort us because our mother was so unpredictable.

My mind turned to our time with Aunt Linda again. Though short, I had loved living with her. She had been so much better than Uncle Ricky. She was one of the most grounded of my mother's family. To me, Aunt Linda was a beacon of stability. She was unwavering in her commitment to her job and deeply immersed in her faith. Her active involvement in the church wasn't just a testament to her spirituality; it was a conscious effort to try to shield her sons from the perils of the streets. She seemed to hope that church offered a set of morals and values amid the turbulent surroundings and dangerous allure of the Philly streets.

Aunt Linda's house, a modest yet welcoming three-bedroom row home, bore the indelible mark of her caring heart. It was a place where warmth enveloped you the moment you stepped through the door, a refuge from the harsh realities that often raged just outside. For a fleeting five weeks, we had found solace and security in her care. It was the happiest I had been in a long time. She had two sons, but I gelled best with my cousin Matilda, her youngest and only daughter. She enrolled us in schools, set up lunch tickets, and provided books and clothing.

However, our respite was short-lived, and the circumstances surrounding our departure were a poignant reflection of the intricate dynamics within our family. Aunt Linda, driven by love and a profound sense of responsibility, had opened her home to us. But the weight of our presence bore heavily on her budget.

Aunt Linda needed the welfare benefits and government assistance that my mother had been collecting to adequately provide for her now expanded family. Her three children shared the same roof and extending her care to include me and my brothers strained her already stretched finances. In a desperate plea for support, she turned to our mother, beseeching her for the financial assistance she was still receiving for all of us to ensure that we could continue living together under Aunt Linda's guardianship.

Regrettably, our mother, grappling with her own challenges and constraints, was either unable or unwilling to provide the financial help that Aunt Linda so desperately needed. The situation devolved into a tense standoff, a silent battle for the resources needed to support our fragile stability.

Unable to sustain six kids on her salary, Aunt Linda decided to involve Social Services, seeking their intervention to transfer welfare benefits in support of us living with her. She tried to establish legal foster status for my brothers and me, hoping to secure the much-needed resources to ensure our well-being. Unfortunately, the bureaucratic wheels turn slowly or not at all for those in need, and despite Aunt Linda's earnest efforts, her plea to transfer benefits fell on deaf ears. Her verbal agreement with our mother became her undoing. She provided our food, clothing, and shelter as agreed, but the legal framework did not recognize us as her official foster children, leaving our family's situation in limbo.

The harsh reality was that Aunt Linda's battle with the government for support, and foster recognition was a common problem among those caring for extended family members. Later, in 2000, the American Civil Liberties Union successfully sued child welfare agencies in six Pennsylvania counties (including Philadelphia) for withholding tens of millions of dollars in federal benefit payments to relatives, like my aunt, caring for fostered children.[13][14] However, that victory would come years too late for Aunt Linda, adding another layer of tragedy to her courageous struggle.

As the days turned into weeks, marked by the conspicuous absence of any communication from our mother, Aunt Linda faced an agonizing dilemma. The weight of responsibility pressed upon her shoulders, and it became clear that she could no longer bear the financial burden alone. With tears in her eyes, Aunt Linda made the most crushing decision of all. She reached out to Social Services. Since they would not provide her with funding to care for us, she implored them to intervene and arrange for our removal from her home. We hadn't seen our mother since the day she dropped us off on Aunt Linda's doorstep, and the void left by her absence weighed heavily on me. I grew more emotionally removed from her.

As the caseworker from a private child welfare agency named Baptist Children's Services (BCS) arrived to escort us away from Aunt

Linda's warm and inviting home, we clung to each other, bewildered. It was a sad truth that the State was willing to pay a stranger to care for us but not our aunt. Jacque led us out of her house just as he had led us in a little over a month earlier, resolute and accepting. He allowed Iszel and me to climb into the large van with window guards and a cage separating the rear passengers from the driver and caseworker in the front seats. It was spec'd out for unruly kids or prisoners, not kids like us.

In that poignant moment, we faced an uncertain future leaving Aunt Linda's house, our family bonds tested by the relentless forces of circumstance. The fragile threads that had briefly woven us together were fraying, and we were left to navigate the turbulent waters of our lives without the steadfast presence of anyone familiar to us. Our winding path would eventually land us at the Avondale Group home under Henry's dictatorship, where 30-day confinements could be handed out for any or no reason at all.

By the time my 30 days were up, I nearly burst out into song. I hardly knew what to do with my freedom. I couldn't stand living inside my head so much, remembering what could have been, what should have been, what was. I could finally pee when I needed to without screaming my head off and hoping someone heard me. I surely experienced some of the same emotions as a prisoner being released from solitary. I could see the same relief on Iszel's face on that 31st day.

The silver lining of it all was that being confined for a month meant we couldn't break any rules to warrant docking our allowance. We each received envelopes with $12 in them. There was only one place to go with a pocket full of money.

We grabbed our bikes and rode down to Earl's Sub Shop, enjoying the feeling of the sun on our faces and the wind across our skin as we pedaled through green, open spaces. We parked our bikes on the side of the store and went inside to grab a couple of double burgers on hoagie rolls. I had cheese on mine. Much to our relief, our bikes were still out there when we returned to them.

We slowly rode back to the house to eat our sandwiches in the barn. Most of the older guys were out at work or out with friends, so there wasn't a basketball game going on. We sat on the floor and grabbed our food and drinks.

"Yo, man, I can't believe we made it through that mess," Iszel said, his voice filled with relief as we unwrapped the burgers.

"Yeah, man," I replied with a grin. "We're free now. No more lockdown." I looked towards the house, even though the weekend house parents were there and the Hills had left for the weekend.

"You know," Iszel continued, "Henry's punishments are just unfair. He ain't right. He be trippin'." He shook his head, thinking about the man.

I nodded in agreement, my anger at Henry still simmering beneath the surface. "Yeah, man, that punishment was straight-up messed up."

Iszel laughed, a carefree sound that lifted my spirits. "Yo, he really thought he was gonna break us though."

"Man, I'm glad to be out, though," I said, my voice filled with gratitude. I took a bite out of my sandwich. I held it up appreciatively. "Earl's don't be playin' with these burgers."

It was the best meal we'd had all month since we couldn't supplement Henry's bad cooking with tastier food during the confinement. Iszel shook his head, his mouth too full to respond. We hung like that for the rest of the day, reveling in the simple joys of our freedom.

CHAPTER 14

Dark Discovery

Life with the Hills was a series of ups and downs, pros and cons. We experienced daily racism living around so many white people, but we had a form of stability we'd never had before – and we still had each other. Henry was often cruel, but we met several caring adults, including one of the weekend house parents, Dave Lichter. Dave was a solid caregiver who improved our weekends with his unwavering support. He not only provided us with a safe and welcoming environment but also took the time to listen, mentor, and guide us through the challenges we faced. His presence as a dependable and caring house parent added to the support system that helped us manage the complexities of life in that environment, and he was a welcome respite from the Hills.

One of the positives of being at the group home was access to healthcare. Thankfully, we were not sickly children when we lived with our mother because we didn't see a doctor regularly. They were too expensive and for real emergencies only. My mom would seek home remedies or the advice of friends for our medical needs. Her most important concern was that we had our shots and could go to school.

When I was six, I cut my face, falling onto the jagged edge of a car's rusty bumper while playing outside. When I found her at her boyfriend's house partying, she held the gash closed with ice, sealed it with a bit of crazy glue, and sent me back out to play. Her partying could not be interrupted. I needed stitches to heal properly. My mother's haphazard medical effort left a large scar across my small face.

Once I moved to the House on the Hill, I started having annual checkups with a pediatrician named Dr. Morris. He was easygoing and took good care of us. He diagnosed me with tonsillitis during a routine check-up. He was so concerned about the size of my tonsils that he referred us immediately to an ear, nose, and throat specialist in West Chester.

"Looks like two grapefruits fighting for space back there," Dr. Morris said with concern in his voice. "They have to be obstructing his breathing." He handed Henry a paper with the address of an ear, nose, and throat specialist in West Chester scribbled on it.

"I think they're going to have to remove his tonsils. Drive to the office now. Dr. Smith will be waiting for you."

Henry called Janine from Dr. Morris's office, and we headed to West Chester.

During the drive, I asked, "What does he mean by 'remove my tonsils?'"

"Looks like you may have to have them cut out so you can breathe better," Henry answered. "They're in the way, so you may have to spend a night in the hospital."

The idea gave me chills. I feared an overnight in the hospital more than the surgery.

When Iszel was hit by a car, he was housed in a unit with other patients who had experienced similar serious injuries. My fear about hospital stays started when he came home. Not because of the way he looked but the stories he told me about his time there. He spoke of dark nights, shadows, and noises. He described in detail the trauma of his roommates. The one that stood out to me was a kid hit by a train. They had to nearly mummify him, suspend him over the bed, and keep him in a bubble of some kind to avoid infection. This was the image that came to mind when Henry mentioned I'd be staying overnight, and I was terrified.

"Are they gonna put me in a room with a kid that got hit by a train?" I asked.

Henry laughed a bit but could hardly understand where the question came from. "No, you'll most likely be in a room with another kid who is getting their tonsils out. Don't worry. We don't even know if they need to come out yet. If they do, they give you a lot of ice cream."

His reassurance and the prospect of ice cream didn't ease my fears. We drove the rest of the way in silence as I tossed around the idea of a hospital stay in my ten-year-old mind.

Dr. Smith made his preliminary evaluation and, with the tongue depressor still in my mouth, said to Henry, "Yep, it's good you came right over, sir. We're gonna have to remove them soon. When he has his surgery, we'll monitor him for a night. That work for you?"

No, that does not work for me!! I thought.

Henry nodded, gave me a shrug, and said, "Welp, it looks like ice cream for you." Then he asked the doctor, "When's the earliest we can get this done?"

The surgery was scheduled two weeks later, Friday, November 15th. I lost a lot of sleep as the day approached, worrying about a night in the hospital. I drove Iszel crazy with questions about his memory from his stay.

When the day finally came, I was a wreck. That lasted until the pre-anesthesia shot, which leveled me. By the time they came in with a transport bed for the surgery, I was unable to move without assistance. I remember the passing overhead lights as they wheeled me down the hallway and into the bright lights of the operating room. There was a table full of shiny, sharp instruments, and everything was brightly polished chrome and white.

The recovery was nothing like I had imagined.

Instead of a shadowy and menacing space with mummified roommates, I lay in a colorful children's ward with similar patients and would not see half the things Iszel described.

There were ambient nightlights to wash out scary shadows and calming sounds like ocean waves played during the nighttime hours. The low chatter and hourly rounds of the nurses helped, too. The prescribed medication kept me sleepy for the most part, and Henry was right; they gave me a few small cups of flavored sherbet. It wasn't ice cream, but it was a close second.

I did get a roommate. He was wheeled in after his surgery. I don't recall what he was there for, but I found out during breakfast the next morning that it was not for a tonsillectomy. Our serving platters came in, and when they opened his, he had pancakes, sausage, milk, and orange juice. I was served barely set jello because my throat couldn't take anything rough. I wasn't happy about that at all. To add to my jealousy, when they brought me a small cup of sherbet, he was offered one, too, which he happily accepted. Lunch was another disappointing entree of warm rice pudding with raisins. He was eating like a king with his beef hotdog and fries. I was eating a step up from baby food.

Shortly after lunch, the doctor made his rounds with his post-op patients and told me everything looked good and I would be discharged to my house parent soon. I thought to myself, *Yeah, get me back to the house with Dave and the guys where I can get some real food.* Our weekend house parent, Dave Lichter, made some of the best tacos, and he was at the house, probably setting some aside for me.

To my disappointment, it was Henry who walked into the room to pick me up and collect my things. He sat in the chair next to my bed, opened a newspaper, and asked through a knowing smile, "Did they give you ice cream like I told you they would?"

Taking the opportunity to undercut his attempt to know something, I simply said, "No."

He never took his eyes off the paper. "You must not have been good here last night if they didn't." His matter-of-fact tone hinted at a possible punishment for placing his reputation in a bad light among the hospital staff.

THOSE BOYS ON THE HILL

Realizing the flaw in poking the bear that Henry could be, I added, "They gave me sherbet instead." That pacified him.

Henry sat next to me on the bed when the discharge nurse came with a page of instructions, a list of acceptable menu items, a bag of meds filled by the hospital pharmacy, and a wheelchair. She explained that the meds would keep me sleepy. Henry listened intently, nodding and smiling appreciably in a concerned, fatherly way as she spoke. He put on the full act.

He gingerly helped me into the wheelchair. The nurse wheeled me towards the exit, chatting with Henry behind me. When we arrived at the front of the hospital, Henry left to retrieve the van, but instead of pulling up in the Dodge, he drove up in Helene's RV. Janine was in the front seat, feigning a happy smile. Henry looked down at me in the wheelchair and explained that we were going camping for the weekend. He played up the trip to be something exciting and new. I had never been camping before but didn't understand why it made sense to go right after my surgery. He helped me up into the vehicle, which was empty except for the three of us. I figured the rest of the guys would be there when we arrived.

I hadn't been in the RV before. It was spec'd out with a kitchenette, a bathroom with a small one-person hosed shower, and four bunk beds. The windows allowed plenty of natural light into the cabin when they were open. There was seating for four towards the front, but Henry insisted I lay down on one of the bunks. I didn't mind. I was still working off the effects of the surgery, and I always slept well on the road. He took his place in the driver's seat, and I was out within a few minutes of hitting the highway.

We were stopped by the time I awoke. I wasn't sure how long we'd been driving, but the sun was setting, and the first signs of dusk were darkening the sky. Janine was sitting in the passenger seat, humming to Amy Grant and playing softly on the radio. I popped up on my knees to look out of the long rectangular window and saw that we were at a rest stop with a filling station. Henry had just put the hose back onto the pump and stepped inside the RV. He noticed that I was awake.

"We'll be at the campsite soon," he said. "But I don't want you to leave the RV once we get there. You're too sick to do much more than rest this weekend. Do we understand each other?"

I nodded in disappointed compliance, confused as to why they had bothered to bring me. He gave me a cup of rice pudding, two pills from a small orange bottle, and some water. Within 30 minutes, I was asleep again.

When I next rose to consciousness, we had arrived at the campground, and the Hills were busying themselves, setting up for an evening by the campfire. I was given another cup of rice pudding and two more pills and drifted back to sleep.

I awoke a few hours later to the eerie, ritualistic chants of voices outside. The RV was completely dark, and I was the sole occupant. The orange light of a campfire illuminated the cabin against the far wall. As I had never really seen a campfire, I curiously poked my head up to peer out of the window.

There were campfires and five burning crosses in view. They stood high and cast long, dark shadows across the ground. People walked around in cloaks of differing colors: red, white, and black. Some wore tall, pointed hoods pulled over their faces. Inaudible announcements droned from megaphones, and people were socializing happily. The sight scared me. I had seen the atrocities of the KKK portrayed in movies, but what truly terrified me were the personal stories my grandfather had told me. Growing up in South Carolina in the 1930s, he saw his share of the Klan's work. He spoke of their hate for us and how it was a rite of passage for some of them to witness the hanging, dismemberment, burning, or dragging of a Black person behind a vehicle. His chilling descriptions of the horrors he had witnessed were enough to fuel many childhood nightmares.

I placed my small hand over my mouth to muffle my scream and ducked back down below the window to avoid being seen. Tears swelled in my eyes as I pressed my body into the corner of the bunk, trying to become invisible. I had to figure out what to do next.

By then, Henry had figured out how long the pills lasted and returned to the RV about a half-hour after I looked out of the window. I jumped up when he opened the door and ran into the bathroom. I relieved myself, took my time washing my hands, and took some toilet paper to wipe the tears off my face. Henry waited without speaking, but I could hear him pacing. I heard the pill bottle clinking and the kitchen faucet running. When I opened the accordion door of the bathroom, Henry was standing in front of it with a large coat on, holding a glass of water in one hand and two pills in the other.

"You, ok?" he asked. "Your face is all puffy."

"I think I slept wrong on it."

He considered my answer. "Welp, that happens," he said.

He offered me the pills and water. I took both, swallowing the pills down with a large gulp. He ushered me back to my bunk.

"Get some rest," he said softly. "Janine and I will be back shortly." I fought the drowsiness for as long as I could, but the medicine won the night.

The next morning, I awoke to find Henry and Janine busy packing. The announcements still droned on indistinctly outside, but the people's chatter was lower. Henry eventually gave me some jello after a shower. He handed me another pair of pills.

"Take those. We'll be leaving soon."

I woke up a few hours later, and we were still on the road. I rose from the bunk and used the bathroom. As I exited, Henry plastered on a Grinch-like smile that I saw in the rear-view mirror, angled to give him a full view of the back of the vehicle.

"There he is," he forced out a little too cheerfully.

Henry made reflected eye contact, reached behind the passenger front seat, and tapped the chair behind Janine twice to offer me the open chair behind her. I had been intending to return to the bunk and took the seat reluctantly. I peered out of the windshield as Henry spoke.

"So, you got to go camping with us. Sorry, you didn't feel well enough to come out of the RV."

"I didn't feel too bad," I disagreed. "You wouldn't let me. The pills make me sleepy."

"Those pills help you get better after surgery. If I thought you could have handled being busier, you would have been allowed to come out with us."

I frowned, my mind in the turmoil of confusion and wariness. Why bring a sick Black boy to a KKK rally? The implications frightened me.

"Don't you worry; there will be other times for you to get the full experience," he continued in a voice that sent a shiver down my spine. He tapped a knowing hand on Janine's leg, and they shared a silent beat.

Nah, I think I'm good at camping with you two, I thought.

"How long before we get home?" I asked out loud. I desperately wanted the comfort of being with Jacque and Iszel again.

Henry regarded this suspiciously.

"We don't need to tell everyone about our weekend. The other guys will be jealous."

Why? Because I slept in an RV surrounded by white folks who hate Black folks? "I'm just ready to lay in my own bed," I said instead. "The beds back there are a little too hard."

I never told my brothers about the weekend. As much as I longed to share my experiences and fears with Iszel and Jacque, I kept it all to myself. I wanted to carry that burden alone, to protect my brothers from the disturbing truth about the Hills and their affiliations.

I feared what the Hills would do to us. Things in the house were getting worse, and Henry's behavior was increasingly erratic. His temper was even more unpredictable, and we never knew what would set him off. There was always tension in the house, and I walked on eggshells around him. The weekend confirmed my suspicions about what kind of people they were, and I wanted us to stay as far away from them as possible. I made an unspoken promise to myself that I would do whatever it took to shield my brothers from harm. Our bond was stronger than ever, and I couldn't bear the thought of anything happening to them.

I kept a close eye on Henry and Janine, though they never made any other attempts to involve us in their Klan activity. I never did find out why the Hills took me to a KKK meeting. Had they planned something more nefarious and then changed their minds? Did they just want to scare me? Was it on a whim or a dare? It would remain one of the many mysteries of life with the Hills.

CHAPTER 15

Familial Violation

Our first Christmas at the house was uneventful. The Hills were not particularly festive; other than candles on the windowsills, they didn't decorate the house or put up a Christmas tree, and the Hills didn't buy presents for the guys in the house. It didn't bother us; we were used to no fuss. We spent Christmas and the surrounding days at our Aunt Angel's, enjoying the extended family time. We arrived back at the House on the Hill to piles of wrapped donations waiting on our beds. There was a standard variety of socks, t-shirts, and tighty whities, things considered useful by whatever charity they had come from, though nothing personal or exciting amongst the piles. We traded amongst ourselves for sizes that fit us.

Jacque had turned 13 in July, while Iszel and I spent our winter birthdays of 1986 with nothing to mark the occasion other than our age ticking up a year. Fifth grade was going well, though Julio had left for another school, and I missed him. The Hills were just barely tolerable. We did everything in our power to avoid them. Home visits were still a highlight for me and remained so up until the spring of 1986.

It started with one of our bi-monthly home visits to Aunt Angel. Jason met us that night like he usually did, and we returned with him to Aunt Angel's. Jacque, Iszel, and Jason were all goofing around watching TV and playing video games when I started to feel tired. They showed no signs of slowing, but I was done for the night. No one was surprised when I left to arrange my sleeping spot.

As usual, I chose to sleep on a pallet of blankets on the floor. I was mostly asleep but was roused when the rest of them finally joined. I heard them whispering, and Jason plunked himself down next to me in the opposite direction, head-to-foot. I drifted back to sleep.

It was still dark in the room when my eyes flew open a few hours later. I have always been an early riser regardless of what time I went to bed, but this was the middle of the night, and I assessed what might have awakened me. Everything seemed normal. The city was still alive outside, typical for 2 AM on a Saturday. I could hear the engines of the cars driving down Lehigh Avenue, the occasional horn, and the murmur of the night crowd in the many bars, nightclubs, and late-night restaurants open at that hour. I usually didn't mind the city noise, and I welcomed the ambient buzz and the blend of aromas wafting in the open window.

I noticed then that my covers had been pulled aside, and Jason's body pressed close to mine, having flipped his position so he was spooning me. My leg was wet. *Maybe he just turned around in his sleep and peed a little*, I told myself. He was a bedwetter, after all. I wiped the moisture off my leg with a small swath of one of the covers, moved over to give him some space, and fell back to sleep.

I didn't think anything else of it until I woke up the same way the next night. Once again, Jason had flipped his position, so he was pressed along my length. My leg was wet again, but this time my ass was as well.

What the hell, I thought uneasily.

I extricated myself from Jason's spooning and crept to the small bathroom in the hallway. I flicked on the light switch. This was the only floor that was tiled in the whole apartment. There was a heavy, white, lion-foot iron tub and a standard sink with a mirrored medicine cabinet screwed into the wall above it. I looked down at the moisture now running down my leg and dry-heaved. What I felt was not pee. My stomach lurched again. I grabbed wads of toilet paper to furiously clean the sticky stuff off. I wet another wad and wiped it even harder.

I felt sick at the violation and was shaking in fear and anger. On wobbly legs, I collapsed on top of the closed toilet seat, sitting and trembling, trying to make sense of it. I ran the bathtub faucet as hot as I could take and scrubbed myself with the washcloth Angel gave me the night before. I needed to get it off me. I couldn't get the tacky, sticky feel off and out of my mind. It felt like a stain. I felt dirty. *I was dirty,* I thought, and scrubbed my skin harder until it was raw and hurt. The stains never went away.

I stayed in the bathroom for the rest of the night, wrapping my head around what had happened and trying to figure out what to do. I paced from the toilet lid to the edge of the tub and back. Hours later, I heard the house stirring and someone shuffling down the hall. I cracked the door and peeked out. It was Jacque. Relieved, I opened it wider. "You're up early as usual," he remarked. I nodded. He took a closer look at me.

"Yo, you good?" he asked. He squinted and gazed at me, seeming to try to figure out what his brotherly intuition was telling him.

For the briefest of moments, I thought about saying "No" and telling him what had happened, but it was impossible to find the right words. Jacque loved Jason. *How do I tell him this?!* Ever since our mother told him to take care of us that night outside of Aunt Linda's house, he carried the weight of all three of us on his shoulders.

When he was at Aunt Angel's, I saw glimmers of him enjoying himself, of being the kid he still was. No worries about the Hills, the House on the Hill, the racism, or the stress of being separated from our family. I stared up at my older brother and knew I couldn't take that away from him. My heart broke at the thought of doing so. I just...couldn't.

"Nah, I'm good, just a funny stomach; maybe dinner jacked me up last night." I rubbed my stomach and attempted to smile.

He raised his eyebrows and peered over my shoulder into the empty bathroom behind me, concerned. "You blow it up in there? Imma hafta hurt you if you startin' my morning like that," he joked.

"Nah, it's all good, false alarm. Just some bad gas, but it's straight in here. Just hold your nose," I joked back.

I ducked past him and escaped down the hallway back to the bedroom. Jacque's urge to go to the bathroom must have outweighed his fear of what I could have done in the room because the light extinguished when he closed the door. I was in the dark except for the streetlights shining out through Jason's bedroom window.

I stopped at the entrance. Jason was still sleeping, sprawled out in the pile of covers where I had been. Quickly and quietly, I retrieved a change of clothes so I could shower and go about my day, trying hard to pretend that nothing had ever happened. I stayed away from Jason as much as possible. Whenever he approached to deliver a quick jab or headlock, I pushed away. He scowled at me, looking confused by my avoidant behavior. He acted like nothing had happened, like he didn't shatter what I thought our relationship was. *Now, he expects me to act like everything is cool.* I was angry and hurt, and I had no one to tell.

Being back at the House on the Hill was a relief, something I'd never expected to feel. I didn't have to fear falling asleep anymore, but I did have nightmares. What Jason had done had triggered memories of the last time someone tried to sexually assault me at the worst place my brothers and I had ever stayed: Main Campus.

CHAPTER 16

Main Campus

In the world of child welfare, the Department of Human Services (DHS) often entrusts the care of foster and group home children to private agencies. It's a partnership that aims to strike a balance between expertise and personalized care. Picture private agencies as custodians of childhood, offering placement services, case management, and therapeutic interventions tailored to each child's unique needs.

This collaboration, however, is not without its complexities. The motives behind the scenes can sometimes shift the narrative. Private agencies, while tasked with the noble responsibility of child welfare, may grapple with profit-driven motives that can compromise the quality of care.

Additionally, the role of foster parents adds another layer to this delicate arrangement. Some open their homes driven by genuine altruism, while others may be enticed by the monthly stipend, blurring the lines between heartfelt care and financial incentives.

In the midst of this, the DHS assumes the role of overseer, ensuring that the private agencies adhere to standards and prioritize the well-being of the children. It's a delicate dance of coordination, with the DHS striving to maintain a seamless connection between the agencies for the benefit of the children under their care.

Ultimately, the relationship between DHS and private agencies forms a tapestry of care, with each thread contributing to the intricate narrative of fostering and supporting vulnerable children. It's a nuanced dance where the hope is that, despite the challenges, the primary focus remains on providing the best possible environment for those who need it most. Main Campus, and unfortunately, many similar foster facilities, fell well short of that ideal.

Main Campus was a central Hub for "Unparented" or "Fosters" in Philly under the umbrella of a private agency, Baptist Children Services (BCS). It consisted of 10 cottages that housed 30 children each. Main Campus also sourced BCS's eight regional homes in and around the city that housed eight kids each. Four were assigned for girls and four for boys. One of those was located in Avondale.

Main Campus bore witness to the diverse backgrounds that shaped the lives of hundreds of children. It was not a mere collection of buildings; it was a microcosm reflecting the harsh realities of the world we came from. Within its walls, the echoes of varied experiences reverberated, from the struggles of parents with drug problems to the haunting shadows of abuse. The mix of backgrounds brought a raw authenticity to Main Campus, a reflection of the tumultuous lives we had known.

This was the fourth alternative living situation we had lived in 1984 after Aunt Linda's. We arrived in late November, and it was the first time I felt lost in what I came to deem the "Foster Abyss." In this black hole, we no longer had personhood but were numbers and files.

When we arrived, we were ushered into the office of one of the cottages by the case worker. I keenly felt the loss of my last name. Here, the Glover name meant nothing. It didn't instill regard or fear in those we were addressing as it seemed to when we lived in North Philly. I was just another face in the crowd.

Main Campus was the first State-run facility we experienced that year – though not the first in our lives. We had been placed in a foster facility called St. Vincents when I was three years old for two years before our mother was able to care for us again.

We stood in the dimly lit office, illuminated solely by cloudy daylight through an unshaded window. The small space was filled with a heavy-set Black man named Mr. Whitaker. He was a mouth breather with a

Michael Jackson Thriller-styled Gheri curl. The Jacksons had a concert in Philly a few months before, and Mr. Whitaker was clearly a fan.

He sat so far back in a wheeled office chair that it looked like he was lying down. He swiveled from side to side with huge, wide feet planted on the floor. He struggled to move about and opted instead to speak to us from behind a small metal-framed desk where he kept stacks of intake and discharge papers within easy reach.

He rested a bag of potato chips high on his stomach and spoke to us between bites. When he spoke, he had an "S" lisp, pronouncing it with a "TH." "Three brotherth all in one plathe. The oddth of that thaying the thame are thlim to none." I struggled to understand him between the lisp, the mouth breathing, and the chip crunching.

My eyes were drawn to the salty, oily foil of the potato chip bag that rose and fell with every labored breath he took. He licked a salty finger, let out a grunt, and reached for three intake forms, nearly knocking over a small blue bottle of Gheri Curl juice that sat near them. "No oneth gonna want to take in three brotherth even for a thort time. Tho y'all might ath well get uthed to it now."

When I finally parsed what he was saying, I felt cold inside. I hated the idea of being separated from my brothers. Iszel especially. Except for his hospital stay, we were always together, and it felt like we had just got Jacque back after the summer apart while Iszel and I were at Uncle Ricky's, and he was at Aunt Angel's. We exchanged glances and stepped closer to each other, presenting a unified front.

When he wasn't speaking or eating, the tip of his tongue rested just inside his opened mouth. "I'm gonna put you two lil oneth in a dorm with each other in the Childrenth cottage. You older one gonna hafta fend for yourthelf down the hall."

Whitaker completed the intake forms and filed them away in a folder on the desk. "Cordell!" he called out. "Come take theethe boyth to their room athignmenths."

A slim, light-skinned, Black kid came to the doorway. He was dressed in dark jeans, a hoodie, and work boots. He looked to be about 13 and just a little taller than Jacque.

"Ok, Mr. Whitaker."

"Go with him fellath. Welcome to Baptith Childrenth Thervitheth."

We followed Cordell to the corridor that led to the rooms. The place smelled of ammonia, bleach, and Pine Sol. The floors shined, and everything looked clean. When we got far enough away from the office, he strode with a dip.

"Sup, Y'all? I'm kinda tha resident trustee around this piece cuz I've been here tha longest and most often. Moms keep fuckin' up, and I keep endin' up here. I wish they'd just place my ass. Where y'all from?"

"North Philly, 26th and Lehigh," I said.

"I can't stand y'all North Philly Niggas; West is where it's at. That nontalkin' ass Whitaker's from North too. Y'all all sound tha same to me." He said this with a smirk, shaking his head at the idea.

"What evs' man, we ain't got no beef witchu," Jacque said, squashing the turf war.

Cordell stopped in his tracks at this, turned, and stared hard at us.

"If y'all from North and I'm from West, then we got beef. That's the way that shit go." He said this with a raised eyebrow and a nod, agreeing with his own understanding.

He started walking again and stopped at the door for me and Iszel. The room had five beds in it.

"Y'all better watch y'all backs up in here." He stared hard at us again. "Ya lucky I ain't in da mood to be fighting right now."

He took a glance at the three of us, staring hard in return, and realized that he was outnumbered. He cracked a smile when we didn't withdraw. "Nah, man, I'm just fucking witch'all. Just take one of the beds and watch y'all shit. Lotta thieves in this piece. Me and your bro are down the hall just past the bathroom." He nodded in the general direction he was referring to.

They disappeared and walked further down the corridor. "Yo, y'all stay here til I come back," Jacque called to us.

Iszel and I stood in the large room with five single beds, each with its own small footlocker. Two beds were haphazardly made. Someone had taken one across the room, furthest from the door. The other was taken in the middle of the room, out of immediate view of the doorway.

I looked around at the remaining three options. "Yo, which one you want?" I asked, giving him the first choice.

Iszel walked over to the bunk opposite the middle of the room but in front of the door. He sat on it like he was checking its comfort and springiness. This took a minute or two. It wasn't lost on me that this would be one of the rare times in our lives that we didn't have to share a bed. The three of us normally slept on a mattress on the floor together or on a pallet of sheets and covers.

"I like dis one," Iszel said, finally deciding.

I selected the bed just inside the door. For me, it was all strategic. I wanted to avoid the other two kids in the room. Over the last few months, I had become a light sleeper. I figured no one was going to run into the room without me hearing the door opening.

I opened my footlocker and found linens inside. We made our beds and stuffed our belongings into them.

When Jacque and Cordell returned, our slim guide shrugged on a heavy winter coat. "Y'all ain't got no heavier coats than those?" he asked, looking at our thin, worn jackets.

"Nah, but we good," I said, trying to stop him from asking anything further on our lack of proper clothes for the season. We put on our spring jackets. We were dressed in jeans, Pro-Keds sneakers, and long-sleeved shirts. I felt ashamed that we didn't have more seasonally appropriate clothing.

"A'ight," he said, pitching his voice up. "Because the rest of the tour is outside. It's bitin' out there."

We did a brisk campus tour in the wintry weather. Cordell showed us the cafeteria.

"I know y'all niggas prolly like to eat, so get here early for meals, otherwise you gon' be assed out." He laughed at this like there was an inside joke that only he was in on. I didn't get it. He pointed out the library and on-campus day care for young, displaced children and the children of young mothers housed on campus.

He kept asking, "Y'all good?" eyeing our thin clothes, which provided little barrier to the wind and cold. We kept voicing our nonchalant assent, though, by the time we returned to our cottage, we were cold to the bone and welcomed the warmth of the indoors.

Within days of being there, I had my first fight with a kid trying to steal a shirt from one of my plastic bags from my footlocker. We tussled, and I landed a solid punch that sent him running out of the room. My far-side bunkmate watched the whole ordeal and seemed to gain some respect for me for being able to hold my own.

"Yo, if you wanna keep whatchu got, keep your good stuff flat under your mattress."

"What?" I asked, not understanding.

He pulled his mattress up, and the frame was evenly lined with his clothes. "I don't keep much of nothing in that footlocker," he explained. "Ain't no locks. Putting your stuff under the mattress is the only place other kids didn't look for stuff to steal."

"Thanks, man," I replied gratefully.

I didn't get to know him very well. The next day, his bunk was empty. I had a momentary pang of regret, but it was hard to care much anymore. With our nomadic lifestyle, I had become used to getting to know people only to have them abruptly removed from our lives or for us to be yanked from theirs.

A few days later, a kid punched Iszel in the stomach in the rec room. I found out about it happening from a group of "Campus kids" looking to instigate a fight and rushed to see about him. Jacque had heard as well. He was already tending to Iszel, who was keeled over in pain, holding his stomach when I arrived.

Jacque kneeled next to him. "Yo, you good?"

Iszel was grabbing his belly, trying his best not to cry.

"Yeah, that kid over there punched me."

Jacque stood up and beelined towards the dark-skinned youth. Face to face, he was a couple of inches taller than Jacque, stockier, and a year or so older. He had a hard look on his face, but Jacque didn't flinch.

"Yo man, whachu hit my brother for?"

The kid didn't back down. He pointed to a random chair in the large room. "I hit eem because he was sitting in my chair," he said. "Everybody knows not to sit there. I had to teach eem' a lesson. Now he knows, and you do, too. What's up with his face anyways? The kid looks like Frankenstein with those scars." He smirked around at the accumulating circle of boys in the room. A few of them chuckled in agreement.

Jacque punched him hard in the face. "Tha fuck you say 'bout my brother?!"

The kid rubbed his jaw and nodded. *Good punch.* He delivered one back, equally as hard. A sizable group of kids surrounded them and began to excitedly chant.

"Fight, Fight, Fight!"

Hearing this prompted Mr. Whitaker to rise out of his seat in his office to check on the commotion. Jacque was holding his own, but clearly, the other kid had seen more than one fight in his time and was willing to trade blows.

Whitaker's arrival didn't faze the surrounding group of chanting kids.

"Uh, uh Boyth!" he bellowed. He was out of breath from the walk from the office and took a beat to catch it before continuing.

"Y'all gonna hafta take that fightin' shit outthide in cathe thomeone stharths bleeding. I'm not writing no inthident reportth today."

Jacque and the kid stopped fighting and headed to the door. Iszel had picked himself off the ground by this point, still holding his stomach. He glared at his assailant but didn't follow them. I did. We walked into the short corridor that led to the cottage exit. As soon as Jacque opened the heavy, brown-painted metal door, the snow-filled winds blew through with a low-pitched howl. Mr. Whitaker posted himself inside one of the sidelite windows so he could peer out and watch the scrap. I stood just outside, bobbing and weaving along with Jacque during the fight, seeing the angles he should have chosen, the punches he should have thrown, and where he needed to grab and hold to gain the advantage of the kid. *Com' on, Jacque! You got this, man!*

The fight became a wrestling match, and they began rolling around in the eight inches of snow. With this, the kid started getting the better of Jacque. Jacque was a fighter. He slipped, dipped, and even took punches pretty well. But he didn't grapple well at all, and the kid was getting the upper hand. They tussled and rolled into a shoveled mound of snow and ice.

Mr. Whitaker poked his head out of the cottage door and called to me.

"You gonna let him handle your brother like that? You better get out there, boy, or everyone here ith gonna think you're a puththy!" He slammed the door shut when a blast of freezing air flowed through.

I stared at the two struggling on the ground. The kid was mounted on top of Jacque, striking him with punches.

Jacque's losin'!

I raced across the short span of lawn and launched myself into him, knocking him off my brother. He slammed hard against the small dune of ice and snow. Our impact broke a large, jagged chunk of ice from where we hit. I wanted to make sure he was never going to bother any of us again. I grabbed the ice and raised my hand to crush it into his unprotected face.

"No!!" screamed Whitaker from behind me.

The "Fight" chant stopped. I was committed to ending this for good. I swung my fistful of ice toward his temple with everything I could muster. His eyes widened in fear, knowing he was unable to avoid the blow. Just as the ice was about to smash into his head, Jacque tackled me off him, causing me to fall short of my intended mark. Instead, the ice scraped across his forehead, creating a long, deep gash across it as Jacque and I landed in a heap in the snow. The cut on the other kid's face immediately started to gush blood.

Ha! That's gonna leave a mark!! Who's Frankenstein now?

Whitaker stomped across to me and grabbed me by the nape of my shirt. "Tha fuckth wrong with you, boy?! You coulda killed him!! That'th definitely woulda been an inthident report."

I fought and struggled to get out of his grasp.

"Don't make me thit on you out here in thith thnow, cuth I will," he threatened.

He stopped short, looking at the other kids.

"Ain't ch'all got nothing elthe better to do?"

He roughly dragged me towards the cottage. I stared back at Jacque. We met eyes, but he gave me a shake of his head, silently saying, *Bro, you can't do that.* I saw fear in his eyes, not for me, but for the kid. I didn't understand. Main Campus was a place where the mantra was kill or be killed. Perhaps the most shocking thing about the whole encounter was how typical of an occurrence this was in foster care. We would come to experience many times or hear about just how endemic physical and sexual abuse is in group homes and foster families alike. It's one of the failings of a system designed to prevent just that.[15] [16] All I knew or cared about at that time, though, was that no adults were looking out to protect us. All we had was each other.

CHAPTER 17

No Place Safe

The days were tense, with very little time to relax. I have always been an early riser, so at six o'clock one morning, I thought it would be nice to take a shower before everyone else was up to give myself a rare moment of peace. Just as I suspected, I had the bathroom to myself.

The large bathroom was centered in the hallway between the rooms. Brightly lit, it had a row of five sinks and five shower stalls to accommodate the many kids that would need to use it throughout the cottage. I set my water temperature, then hung my towel and change of clothes on the hook just outside of my stall.

I stood under the water and allowed it to run over me for a few minutes, washing away the stress of the past two weeks. I lathered myself, closed my eyes, and finished with my face. Just as I soaped my face, a bucketful of chilly water splashed on my body. I was immediately pulled from my small bit of tranquility. I tried to wipe the soap from my face, but before I could rinse it off, a second icy deluge followed.

I opened my eyes. The soap burned as I reached for my towel. It was missing. Another bucket of chilly water invaded the small space, and I opted to simply jump out of the stall naked, figuring the towel had fallen to the floor. Eyes scrunched shut against the burning; I bent over to pat around for the fallen towel.

I felt a hand squeeze my ass. I smacked it away, stood up straight, wiped my soapy eyes, and tried to see who was there. A kid stood there with his erect dick in one hand. He had it pulled out of the front slit of his boxers. He was taller and heavier than me, maybe twelve years old to my nine. He studied me for a second. I had never seen him before.

His other hand was reaching and grabbing at my nakedness. "Whatchu doin?" I asked angrily, backing up.

My wet feet betrayed me and slipped from under me on the floor. I fell but immediately scrambled upright, being mindful not to get up with my ass in his general direction. I felt him trying to position behind me, pawing at my hips and waist.

"Ged off me!!" I yelled. "Tha' fucks wrong wid you?!"

I hoped someone would hear me. My wet, soapy body slipped from his grasp. I backed away from where he stood. It took me deeper into the shower stall area, backing me into a corner. He stood tall and blocked my passage to the hallway.

He grinned. "Come ere.' Touch this." He poked his member at me.

"Hell naw! Get away from me. What's wrong wid you? I ain't like that."

He took a step towards me. "You ain't gotta be. Touch it, or I'll make you touch it."

Cordell's voice entered the conversation from the hallway. "Whach'all about to get into? Y'all North Philly muthafuckas gay as shit. Jason, man, you gotta stop doin' this."

Jason looked over his shoulder. Seeing who it was, he jammed his erection into his boxers. He quickly glanced over at me with a look that said *This ain't over*. He grabbed his buckets and ran past Cordell out the door. Cordell turned his back to me and kept post at the doorway.

"Hurry up and dry your narrow ass off. I ain't got all day to watch over you."

Jason had put my towel in one of the sinks. I grabbed it, wiped my eyes, and started drying my body off.

I pulled on my underwear. "Thanks, man," I said. "What's wrong with that brotha?!"

"I told y'all to watch y'all backs in this piece. You got lucky this time. I may not be around the next time this shit goes down. Have one of your brothers hang out while y'all are in the shower. He won't go at y'all two against one."

He peered over his shoulder at me, saw that I was dressed enough to get down to my bunk, and walked away from the door.

I ran down the hallway to our room. My heart was pounding with adrenaline, fear, and anger. I threw my towel on my bed and sat at the base of Iszel's. He was still asleep. I suddenly felt drained and exhausted from the whole ordeal. I crawled into his bed and lay next to him, staring at the ceiling until I eventually dozed off.

When Iszel woke up, I told him what happened earlier that morning.

"Yo, there's a kid in here tryna fuck smaller kids up the butt," I told him in a whispered voice. "He almost got me in the shower stall. Cordell stopped him. We gotta watch each other when we're washing."

"Ok. You good?" is all he asked.

"Naw, I ain't good. We gonna have to do something about that kid coming at me. I'm gonna figure out how."

Iszel and I started showering in shifts. One of us would guard while the other showered. About a week later, Iszel and I had just arrived back on campus after school. Iszel had gone off to the bathroom and told me he would meet me downstairs, where we did our assigned daily chores of sweeping and mopping the rec room. I was taking a few moments to sort my schoolbooks while my roommate was on his bed against the far wall, reading his latest comic book acquisition.

As if he had been waiting for Iszel to leave, Jason slid into the doorway of our room only a few minutes later. As soon as I saw him, I jumped to my feet, tensing. His eyes bore into me as he stalked towards me. He carried his Pac-Man handheld arcade game and set it reverently on my footlocker without breaking his gaze.

"Yo man, just leave me alone," I said roughly.

Instead of replying, he shoved me backward, and I sprawled onto the bed.

He tried to fondle me, and I struggled against him, his weight on top of me. I was in a bad position to get in any punches, and he was bigger and stronger than me, but I tried my hardest to push him off or kick him.

"Get off me, man!" I shouted towards the hallway door, hoping someone would hear and come see what was happening to me and scare him off like before. No one showed up. I was on my own.

He had my arms pinned under his knees, and he smiled down at me. I was unable to stop what he was doing. He was too big and too strong, and he knew it. No matter how hard I tried, I couldn't fight him off. I felt completely helpless. My eyes started tearing. Fear, anger, helplessness, embarrassment, spite, weakness; all those emotions jumbled inside me. *Stupid, so stupid!* I was mad at myself for letting my guard down for a minute.

How could I let this happen? I asked myself. Something broke in my mind at that moment. Violence...extreme Violence. I wanted to hurt him like he was hurting me. I wanted to stop him from ever trying to hurt me again. The knot in my stomach flared up and cramped. The pain emitted from the base of my stomach into my chest. My panicking mind, coupled with the weight of his body resting on me, was so oppressive I couldn't breathe. I needed to get him off me, get out of the room to my brothers, and I didn't know how. I wasn't strong enough.

"I'm gonna get Mr. Whittaker!" My roommate called as he ran past us and out the door.

Jason ran one more hand down my struggling frame before straightening abruptly. I sat up and scrambled to the floor on the other side of the bed. He still had the advantage because he was closest to the door, but at least the small, brown-framed twin bed stood between us. I readied myself for his next move. *Come over the bed, and I would run around to the hallway door. Come around the bed, and I go over the bed to the hallway door.* He didn't try either. Instead, he simply smiled at me. Then, whistling as casually as if he'd not done a thing, he grabbed his video game and strutted out of the room. I shivered uncontrollably but felt grateful that, at least this time, I'd had clothes on.

Another week passed, with Iszel and I falling into an uneasy routine of hypervigilance every time we were in the cottage. As usual, after school, we cleaned the rec room. It was a large room, its grey vinyl tiled floors speckled with white. That and the off-white walls combined to create a bland feeling that fitted my mood as I dragged the mop around the room.

We started at the end of the room with a floor model large, 24-inch Zenith TV ensconced in brown wood, drawers at the bottom that only ever held the remote, with each wooden side sporting a panel of brown weave. I glanced at it occasionally as I worked, catching parts of the latest episode of the ABC Afterschool Special. Iszel was sweeping, and once he was far enough ahead, I would follow behind with a yellow industrial mop bucket. I moved the matching mop back and forth, watching as the stringy grey head slid against the floor. We worked our way through the room, past the chair that got Iszel punched in his stomach and past a long grey couch sitting directly across from the TV.

We were a few feet beyond it, not quite to the ping-pong table, when Jason strode in, leaving footprints in the still-drying water on the freshly mopped floor. He barely glanced at us, too absorbed in his Pac-Man game, as he plopped onto the grey couch, legs spread as if he owned the place. I froze my mop mid-slide.

Iszel and I exchanged a look, and that was all we needed to know; we were thinking the same thing. With Iszel there, I felt determination and reassurance that everything would be ok. Jason had to be stopped, and we needed to be the ones to do it. The past had taught us no one else would save us—we had to take care of ourselves. We had to show him it wasn't worth messing with me to deter him from ever harming either one of us again.

In unison, we laid down the mop and broom, and each grabbed a side of the heavy bucket, halfway full of its purple Pine-Sol and bleach solution. Heaving between us, we dumped the entire contents onto Jason's head and slammed the bucket down over his head and shoulders. He let out a surprised chuff, but if he made any other noise, it was lost in the crash of my retrieved mop handle against the bucket, a baseball swing with all the power and fury my 70-pound frame could manage. The weight of the damp mop head added to my swing. It was enough to break the handle when it slammed against his bucketed head.

Jason slumped over, head still under the bucket. His handheld arcade dropped from his hand and clunked into a puddle of sudsy water. I let the mop handle drop, clattering to the ground. My heart was thumping in my ears, and the only other sound now was the buzzing of the TV show and water still dripping from Jason and the couch. Iszel and I walked out of the rec room and never looked back.

We didn't worry about the consequences – we had done what we had to. Though the abandoned bucket, mop, and broom could easily have pointed to us as the culprits, Mr. Whittaker never asked us about it. Nor did we ever find out what happened to Jason. A few days later, we were on our way to the Baptist Children's Services group home for Boys in Avondale.

I didn't like dwelling on my time at Main Campus, but my cousin's actions had stirred up that grim memory. *It must be in the name,* I thought unhappily. I would never name a kid Jason, I decided; the name was cursed.

Jason kept abusing me. Every time we visited and spent the night, I would try to avoid falling asleep before or next to Jason, but he and my brothers would stay up all night, and he would end up right next to me again. I mummified myself in my pallet of covers, but he eventually worked his way through them. He never penetrated me, but I woke up repeatedly with him rubbing against me or with cum on my body.

I kept my clothes on instead of the shorts and T-shirt I normally slept in, and he was less successful. He molested me for two years, starting when I was eleven. I didn't understand why he chose me of the three of us—or any of us at all. I was like a little brother to him. I never had the heart to tell Jacque or Iszel while it was happening. My silence probably emboldened him.

Growing tired of Jason's persistence, I returned to Philly much less often than my brothers. When I did go for visits, it was for the day unless I could stay somewhere else. Eventually, I stopped going altogether. I missed holidays, birthdays, and bi-monthly trips and grew apart from my extended family. They thought my visits had tapered off because I was turning my nose up at them. My brothers would go and come back, talking about the wonderful time they had. All I could think, as they regaled me with their Philly adventures, was how avoiding Jason was worth the chasm that was growing between my family and me.

CHAPTER 18

Early Dismissal

One afternoon shortly after Easter in 1987, I was sitting in science class when I heard my name being called by the office secretary over the classroom loudspeaker.

"Mrs. O'Donnell? Can you send Elliott Glover to the principal's office, please?" All eyes in the classroom turned to me, and there was a collective "Ohh!" throughout the room. I must have been in trouble based on my classmate's reaction. It was one thing to be called to the office, but the principal's office was something else. *No one wants to be called to the principal's office.*

I was a bit of a STEM brat, so Mrs. O'Donnell's Science class was one of my favorites in sixth grade. Having to leave during her astronomy lesson unexpectedly was a bummer. Mrs. O'Donnell, who, despite her Irish-sounding name, was a short, mid-fifties Italian woman, clapped her hands sharply to settle the class.

"Hey, we don't act like that in here," she said, sweeping her gaze around the classroom. The kids quickly snapped back to order.

"Elliott, get your stuff together," she instructed. She pulled her reading glasses up that dangled from a red chain around her neck, pulled out a thick packet, scribbled on the top of the first page, and handed it to me. "Make sure you do the reading and finish these pages for homework tonight."

I grabbed the packet and jammed it into my backpack as I walked out of the door to the hallway. I had already been assigned math and social studies homework for the night. *Was I in college now?* I wondered. My thoughts drifted away from my workload to the probable reason for my summons to the office. I normally knew when there was an appointment but had not been told about one that day.

When I arrived at the main office, Henry was patiently waiting for me but didn't immediately make a move to leave. Iszel showed up shortly after me, which wasn't a good sign. We hadn't done anything to warrant being removed from school, so this was about something else. We never made it into the principal's office. Instead, the principal, Mr. Massaro, stood behind the counter in the main office, silent and concerned, as the school secretary checked us out.

I wasn't surprised when we arrived at the van and saw Jacque through the window, sitting in the second row with a twisted look on his face. Iszel and I took our place in the back row. We all glanced at each other silently, communicating without words our worry. My mind began to race. Were we going to another home? Were we going back to our mom? Had we been adopted? Henry drove quietly back to the house, chain-smoking, as a way to busy himself. The drive was less than fifteen minutes, but he finished three cigarettes by the time we pulled into the driveway.

There was a host of social workers and counselors at the house when we arrived, which only heightened my anxiety. Some stood and seemed to be looking through the windows for us. Others busied themselves with one of the many files they brought in from their cars. The three of us were taken into the office and offered seats. Iszel and I sat, but Jacque opted to stand on the far side of the small room, hands across his chest, preparing himself for the bomb that was about to be dropped on us.

Dr. Frye, the lead Administrative Psychiatrist of BCS, was present to deliver whatever news we were pulled from school for. We had met him before, but he always seemed too busy to be bothered with the specifics of one case or another. Instead, he managed and relied on the social workers to stay on top of their caseloads. He oversaw all of the children at Main Campus and the eight group homes, so it was a big deal that he came out personally to talk to us.

Frye was an impeccably dressed Black man, but despite his outward appearance of sophistication, I detected something unsettling beneath his polished façade. His demeanor hinted at a less-than-savory aspect of his character. It wasn't entirely positive; there was an elusive quality that left me feeling uneasy. His meticulous grooming, refined speech, and confident carriage, while impressive on the surface, exuded an air of artificiality. Dressed in a tailored black suit with a meticulously knotted tie and matching handkerchief, every detail seemed to have been carefully chosen. It was as if every nuance of his appearance and mannerisms had been meticulously studied and rehearsed over the years rather than naturally acquired. There was a sense that the persona he projected was a result of calculated efforts, a mask carefully crafted through years of study and correction, concealing something deeper and more enigmatic.

Frye cleared his throat and said, "Boys, we have to tell you about something that happened to your mother," he began.

This is definitely bad, I thought.

Jacque audibly sucked his teeth, scowled, and shook his head.

"I want you all to know that everyone here today is here to support you all in anything you need," Dr. Frye continued.

In frustration, Jacque interrupted him. "Just tell us what's up. Is she dead or not?!"

His words sucked the air out of the room, and my mind started to race again. *Could she be dead?*

I didn't process loss like others because of the loose bonds I formed with most people other than Iszel and Jacque. I didn't suffer from separation anxiety, even from my mother, so I didn't immediately know how to feel about this. After studying our faces for a moment, Dr. Frye realized that easing us into the news was not helping us, so he delivered the gut punch we needed to begin processing.

"Your mother killed her boyfriend on Easter Sunday, and she's in jail. They decided not to allow her to leave until they sort through everything. Do you guys understand what that means?"

No one answered. Instead, Iszel asked a simple question. "Why'd she do that?" It was the same question I had. We had been on a home visit two weeks prior, and she and Mr. Jim were fine.

I had seen our mother in some tough situations with men. She won or ran with her kids in tow thirty percent of the time, or she was allowed to win or run because she had her kids in tow. Despite her small stature, she could hold her own. MaryAnn had a mouth on her, and her timing was impeccable when she used her intelligence in anger. She could verbally castrate men and cuss people out without using one bad word. When she fell short of dispensing her attacker or talking her way out of the violence, she lost big, many times right in front of the three of us. My brothers and I once witnessed her being thrown through a plate-glass table, landing hard inside the metal frame, bleeding from mini cuts sliced by the shards. She lay there, deciding whether to continue fighting or to accept defeat. But I couldn't picture Mr. Jim doing something like that to her. It was confusing.

Dr. Frye's voice brought me back to the present. "She says she was cooking Easter Dinner, and he came in drunk," he said. "They got into an argument, and he began beating her. She said she stabbed him with the knife she was carving the ham with to stop him from trying to kill her."

I didn't even know Mr. Jim drank. He didn't seem to mind my mother drinking her beer, but I never saw him raise alcohol to his lips.

"So, it was self-defense, right?" I asked. My brothers and I shared a collective sigh of relief.

Dr. Frye's brow furrowed at this, taken a bit aback by my question and our easy acceptance of what he had just told us. It was as if he expected us to be devastated by the tragic possibility of our mother being sent to jail for a long time. What he didn't understand was that we were expecting the worst. With her possible death off the table, we were ok. He also didn't understand that our mentality of self-defense as an acceptable form of violence, even if it resulted in an assailant's death, was taught to us by the very person who had now enacted the lesson by example.

Despite the strong bond between my brothers and me, we had our way of dealing with difficult issues, especially about matters we had no control over. Our mother's situation, though undeniably messed up, fell into that category. We understood that we couldn't change the course of events or influence the legal system's decisions. So, we never really talked much about it after the meeting. It wasn't avoidance; it was a survival strategy, a way to maintain some semblance of normalcy amid the chaos that had defined our lives.

Our mother's situation took a darker turn. She was not only found guilty of second-degree manslaughter, despite her self-defense claims, but was also sentenced to seven to fourteen years in a maximum-security prison in Pennsylvania. To top it off, she was pregnant when she was arrested. She gave birth to my sister in the county jail while awaiting trial, but the heartbreaking part was that the baby was immediately fostered. It saddened me deeply that I was never afforded the chance to meet my baby sister, and I couldn't help but worry that she might be lost in the abyss that foster care and adoption can be, especially for families as splintered as ours.

On the other hand, I was hopeful that my sister might have a different familial experience than I had: one of stability, consistency, love, and freedom from the abuse I suffered. I hoped that the rigors an adoptive couple would have to go through would be greater than the ones for group home parents. My thinking brought little peace when I considered how bad the Hills were.

Although my mother wasn't dead, I didn't know when I would see or speak to her again. My twelve-year-old mind translated her prison sentence into a repeating thought: *You will be nineteen to twenty-six years old when you see your mother again.* This fractured me. I understood that she had to protect herself, but I was mad at her for the choices she made that left us all broken in the first place. That brokenness would define my relationship with my mother.

The angry knot in my stomach that I had first felt in the kitchen at Uncle Ricky's was back. It spread to every cell and settled in my bones. Sometimes, the rage lay dormant, but it was always there. A constant companion that left me with a hair-trigger temper and fueled a violent streak that would rear its ugly head whenever I felt slighted or threatened. I wanted to fight everything and everyone. I didn't have an outlet for it, so I fought Iszel, and Jacque fought me for beating on our little brother, who never fought me back.

CHAPTER 19

Outdoor Ed

Later that spring, Mrs. O'Donnell organized an overnight science weekend for the sixth-grade students, an event she fondly called "Outdoor Education" at the Ashland Nature Center in Hockessin, Delaware. The purpose was simple: to immerse us in the wonders of nature at a local campground close to the school. Mrs. O'Donnell enlisted the help of our beloved gym teacher, Ms. Henry, whose boundless energy and enthusiasm added to the anticipation. A team of student counselors, selected from previous attendees, would be our guides to ensure the weekend flowed smoothly.

I was excited about the upcoming adventure despite my previous 'camping' experience with the Hills. The images of burning crosses and hooded figures still haunted my thoughts. This time, I hoped for an entirely different, more positive experience in the great outdoors. Sleeping in a sleeping bag, spending time with my classmates, and an entire weekend that would be science-focused were all thrilling prospects.

Our journey began with a jovial evening, complete with a barbecue, s'mores, and songs around a crackling campfire. Ms. Henry had thoughtfully prepared a set of flipcharts with campfire songs, most of which involved call-and-response. With the help of our student counselors, we found ourselves singing along merrily under the starlit sky. During the fun, I indulged in a few too many Arnold Palmers and decided to make a quick trip to the restroom in the dimly lit surroundings. As I exited, a lanky white kid with an unkempt, black, mop-top hairstyle stood waiting for me in the passageway leading outside, accompanied by a crew of three others. He leaned against the wall, his leg casually extended far enough in front to potentially trip me if I dared to pass.

It became clear that I had unwittingly become their chosen target for the evening.

"Hey, you black coon you, whatchu doing out here by your lonesome? We ain't gonna have no problems with your coon ass, are we?" the leader asked.

I tensed at the familiar slur. I had been called that dozens of times in this community since living at the House on the Hill for the last two years.

"I don't know who you are to have a problem with you," I replied tersely. "And I ain't no coon." I stepped towards the opening to try to pass.

He stepped forward to block my way. "Name's John. If I say you's a coon, then that's what you are. You be a coon, neeger, and a tree hangin' black speck if I call you one. Where you think you goin' coon? We all got biznez." He spoke like he had watched too many Westerns. I could get over the deliberate cowboy twang, but the racist name-calling was provoking me.

"I'm going back to the campfire," I repeated. Then mocking his ridiculous accent, I said, "And if I'm a coon, you's a redneck, honky. Now, get outta my way."

At this, the rest of his crew stepped into the passageway, further crowding my exit. They were eager to support John's troublemaking, to impress him in some way. He smiled at their loyalty. This emboldened him more, and he stepped closer towards me. "You's a smart mouth nigger ain'tchee?" John said. He had run out of things to say and resorted to tossing slurs at me with extra emphasis on the 'er.' I didn't respond.

The silent stand-off festered for a beat, and everything seemed louder to me. It wasn't fear, but my fight-or-flight reflex made me hyper-aware of every noise. The crickets' leggy mating calls and a small screech owl in the distance were blaring in my head. Ms. Henry was singing an energetic song about a mountaineer yodelin' somewhere. The fallen pine needles that blew into the passageway crunched under our feet as we shifted our weight on taut legs.

I figured I could take on John by himself, but the odds of me escaping unscathed by his crew were slim to none. That meant I had to really hurt John to scare the others out of trying to get involved, and I had to do it quickly. He wasn't the biggest, but he was leading the pack. *Hurt him bad enough, and the others will probably run off. Don't hold back.*

Just as the tension was about to break for this four-against-one standoff, a student-counselor crashed behind them in a rush, dancing and pushing his way through John and his minions, holding his crotch.

"Move guys, you're blocking my way," he said, voice strained, as he ran into where the stalls were, completely oblivious to the standoff. I could hear him sigh in relief behind me. He must have just made it.

I chose flight this time and slowly backed into the stall room as he was finishing washing his hands. I followed him out as he left. John and his friends were still there, but the passageway was now clear.

"You guys can't be hanging around the bathroom all night," the counselor said to them as he passed. "Everyone should be by the campfire right now. Let's go, guys." I followed closely on his heels to avoid John and his friends.

John lumbered behind me. "We ain't done you, black coon," he whispered. "You betta watch ya back." He shoved his shoulder into mine as he and his crew jogged past the counselor and me. The counselor didn't seem to hear the warning, the slur, or witness the shove to the back of my shoulder.

As the weekend rolled around during the camping trip, the tension between John, his crew, and me had been steadily escalating. I'd done my best to avoid them, sticking close to Ms. O'Donnell, Ms. Henry, and the student camp counselors whenever possible. But despite my efforts, John and his group always found a way to target me when we were out of sight and earshot of the adults.

The last day of Outdoor Education was less structured. We gathered for an obstacle course and a friendly game of flag football against the student counselors, followed by a bagged lunch of sandwiches and chips. For a couple of hours afterward, we were free to hang out and socialize with each other. I chose to explore the surrounding trails, for the first time venturing deeper into the woods, away from where the teachers and student counselors were stationed.

It was in a remote clearing that John and his crew found me alone. He immediately began hurling derogatory slurs and racial insults at me, trying to break my spirit. When his efforts didn't elicit the intended response, he ramped up his verbal assault on my family. "Betcha coon daddae left ya nigger mammy soon as she spread dem legs for him. Made you a bastard b'fore you were born, huh?"

Unbeknownst to John, I had been carrying the heavy burden of my mother's legal troubles, and it was still raw and fresh. The weight of that situation hung heavily on my shoulders, and the verbal assaults on my family members pushed me past my breaking point.

The rage that had been building up inside me erupted like a volcano. In a fit of anger, I began pummeling John relentlessly, my fists connecting with his face. He fell to the ground and tried to protect himself with his arms and hands. I relentlessly punched through them. I grabbed his head and began slamming it into the grass. His companions stood frozen in shock, unable to comprehend the level of violence I was inflicting.

It was Danny Wu, a classmate of Taiwanese descent, who found us and intervened. Danny had endured similar verbal attacks from John in the past. He couldn't stand by and watch any longer, fearing I could be in trouble if I injured John badly enough. He courageously tackled me off John, ending the physical confrontation.

John's friends quickly gathered him up, their loyalty overcoming their shock, and they ran back to Mrs. O'Donnell, explaining that John's nose was bleeding. Remarkably, they chose not to tell on me, perhaps realizing they could also be in trouble if the reason behind the fight came to light.

The rest of the camping trip passed without any further incidents. I kept my guard up for their retaliation, but they stayed at bay. As we returned home, something unexpected began to unfold. Danny and I, both survivors of John's hateful words and both defenders of each other, formed a deep bond. We became inseparable best friends who understood the importance of standing up against such prejudice and discrimination.

Mrs. O'Donnell and Ms. Henry recognized the leadership qualities I had displayed during the trip. They selected me to become a student counselor for future Outdoor Education excursions, a role that would allow me to guide and mentor younger students while ensuring that they felt safe and included during their adventures in the great outdoors.

As I looked forward to this new responsibility, I couldn't help but reflect on how far I had come since moving to the House on the Hill. I had not only found a loyal friend in Danny but had also discovered my strength and resilience in the face of racial adversity.

CHAPTER 20

Outdated

After living in the house for over two years, our morning meal had become a boring routine, always consisting of cereal and milk. Derek, who had started to work at the ACME supermarket in Kennett, had developed a habit of checking food expiration dates. On one May morning, he noticed that the expiration date on the gallon jug of milk we were pouring over our cereal was over a year old. He checked a second gallon and found the same thing.

Derek quickly acted. With a furrowed brow, he grabbed our cereal bowls and thrust them into the sink with a clatter, the metal against porcelain creating a jarring noise. He reached for the milk carton and swung it over the sink, emptying the milk into the drain with a forceful gush.

"Why on earth would you give us spoiled milk?!" Derek shouted, raising his voice so the Hills, who were in their apartment area, could hear. His voice was a mix of frustration and anger, his face alight with indignation.

Henry, hearing the commotion, entered the kitchen to investigate. Derek, veins pulsing with emotion, didn't hesitate. He angrily threw one of the empty milk jugs at him. The jug whizzed through the air, narrowly missing Henry's head but hitting the wall with a loud thud. Derek's action showed not only his anger but also his growing disdain for Henry.

"What the fuck is this?!" Derek spat out, his tone laced with irritation.

"What's going on?" Henry asked, confused. I was surprised that Henry didn't reprimand Derek for nearly hitting him with the empty jug or his choice of words. Instead, he maintained a calm facade, keeping his distance from the angry young man.

"You gave us spoiled milk! The expiration date on that milk was from last year!" Derek's voice quivered with a mixture of fury and disbelief.

Finally grasping the cause of the morning's turmoil, Henry offered a placating smile and gently patted the empty air in front of him to symbolize 'calm down.' "Derek, the milk isn't sour. Did it taste bad?"

Derek was incredulous, his face contorted in disbelief. He gestured emphatically towards the milk carton. "Why would I drink that shit?!" Derek's frustration was palpable.

Henry gently shook his head, maintaining his pacifying smile. "It's not spoiled, Derek. Look, I'll show you."

He went to the pantry closet, unlocked it, and retrieved a large blue container of powdered milk. As he walked back to the counter, the pantry's contents came into view, revealing the hidden store of food supplies. The breakfast on the counter included boxes of Cheerios and Rice Krispies, but it was clear that Henry had been serving us generic versions of food while using the branded boxes to keep us in the dark. Derek's outrage had forced Henry to reveal the truth, inadvertently unveiling their concealed budget-saving practices. It was a pivotal moment in our interactions with the Hills, one that made it abundantly clear that we had reached a breaking point. It didn't sit right with us that they would give us cheap food. The frustration and anger in Derek's actions became symbolic of the underlying tension that was reaching a boiling point within the household. I could feel that things were coming to a head, but I wasn't sure how and when.

Growing tired of the Hills' tyranny, Jacque and Derek had become diligent chroniclers of their daily interactions. They filled composition books with accounts of their trials and tribulations, hoping that these written records would eventually serve as our salvation. Altercations, once confined to verbal battles, had escalated into physical confrontations with Henry.

One day, they believed they had collected enough evidence. They provided Kathy, our fresh-faced social worker from BCS, with a brief yet compelling synopsis of their living nightmare. Handing over the journals, they pleaded for help. It was the logical next step in their desperate quest to remove the Hills from the house.

Kathy, initially full of promise and vigor, took possession of the journals with a nod of understanding. She assured them she would act. Months passed, and we anxiously waited for a breakthrough. But each time Jacque and Derek inquired, Kathy had a new excuse, a reason for why progress remained stagnant despite the damning content of the journals. It became clear that Kathy was reluctant to make waves in her new job.

Her failure to help us was a common reflection of what happens in foster care everywhere. Stories of abuse and neglect are often ignored in the foster care system, reported by kids to caseworkers who either bury the reports or send them up the chain to be lost in a facility that oversees itself and hardly wants to act on a grievance that reflects poorly on itself.[17] Caseworkers are also overworked, and the job is so emotionally demanding that there is a high turnover, making it hard for caseworkers and kids to establish any kind of rapport and trust.[18]

Frustration grew, and the boys' desperation deepened. Kathy, in the end, returned the journals with a disheartening declaration—there was nothing that could be done about the Hills without more evidence.

CHAPTER 21

Shoelaces and Showdowns

One early June morning, at the start of an average school day, I waited patiently by the kitchen door for Iszel to join me so we could head to the bus. Henry chose this moment to walk up to me with a disapproving grimace. I eyed him warily. As the other kids in the house were in their teens, Henry challenged them less and less. Instead, he channeled his need for absolute control into his interactions with me and Iszel. I knew, as soon as I saw his face, that he was about to come out with something arbitrary and disapproving.

His glance flicked to my Pumas with New Yorker laces. It was the style then, the intricate threading of laces leaving a short end untied that we often tucked into the shoe itself. I had spent fifteen minutes in my room arranging my laces just right for my day at school, but his gaze gave me an idea of today's manufactured problem.

He positioned himself between me and the door and crossed his arms. "You hafta tie your shoes properly before I'm lettin' ya leave this house," he told me sternly.

I sighed, thinking about how we were only a week away from the end of the school year and had been wearing the same style for months. Not to mention that Derek, Randy, Ron, and Jiggs had just left the house with the same shoelace style. But I dutifully bent to pull out my excess laces and tied a bow on each shoe. I pulled the bottom of my pants up to show them resting on the top of the tongues of my Pumas. It wasn't worth the hassle for me. I knew I'd just be rethreading them back to their proper place once I was on the bus.

Just as Henry began to move aside to let me pass, Iszel showed up, bookbag slung over one shoulder, Jacque not far behind him. Henry slid back in front of the exit.

"I just made your brother lace his sneakers the proper way," he said, locking his eyes on Iszel. "You hafta as well."

"C'mon man, it's the style," Iszel pleaded. Henry was unmoved, standing in front of the door, arms crossed.

"But everyone else just left the house with those same shoelaces," Iszel protested, saying what I had only thought.

"You retie your shoelaces, or you aren't leaving this house," Henry insisted, a hard edge to his voice. He was drawing battle lines. Iszel had that look on his face. That obstinate, stubborn look that I knew immediately did not bode well for the rest of the morning.

"Nah, I ain't doing it," he said.

"Then you're not leaving the house, and you're not getting on that bus," Henry said. "And if you miss the bus, there's no way I'm letting you miss school, so you'll hafta walk."

"Please don't put me in a position to skip school," Iszel responded calmly. "Because I'm not walking to school. But I'm not tying my sneaks either."

On the outside, the two of them couldn't be more different. Henry was a wrinkled, white, angry figure looming in the doorway, and Iszel was a small, skinny, Black kid. But the intensity of their glares was evenly matched. Iszel crossed his arms in mimicry of Henry and settled into his position.

Jacque finally intervened.

'C'mon, Zel, just do it," he said.

Iszel shook his head. "Nope."

Jacque grabbed him by the back of his neck and pushed him down towards his shoes.

"Just retie your damn laces," he said urgently. It made the irony of Jacque's untied laces even more glaring, though Henry, of course, ignored them and his cursing. Iszel or I would have been penalized for saying anything similar.

Grudgingly, Iszel complied. We were cutting it close for the bus's arrival. When Iszel finished, Henry moved aside from the door. I burst out into the cool, crisp air, relieved to be out of the radius of Henry's oppressive energy.

I started towards the cornfield, our shortcut to the bus stop, but Iszel wasn't following. Instead, he slowly walked backward, looking at Henry, who stood watching from the doorway. Deliberately, keeping his eyes trained on Henry, Iszel reached down and untied his shoelaces.

Henry's face reddened in fury. Before he could do anything, Jacque called out, "Zel, let's go! We're gonna miss the bus." We darted towards the cornfield and raced to the bus stop together, agilely dodging the new growth of corn stalks as we went. We just caught the bus as it pulled up. Iszel and I sat next to each other on one of the green vinyl seats. We both replaced our shoes with the proper New Yorker style.

I was relieved to be heading to school, but I couldn't help but replay that thunderous look on Henry's face. I knew there was still a reckoning coming.

When we returned from school that day, Henry was sitting on the porch, waiting for us. He stood as we drew nearer, work boots spread and planted in front of the steps, arms crossed.

"Iszel, you need to hurry up and eat your snack, do your chores, and head straight to your room."

"What for?" Iszel asked, resentment in his voice.

"You know what for," Henry replied disapprovingly.

Iszel brushed past him on his way inside. Henry watched us but didn't follow. Butterscotch Krimpets were laid out for us on the kitchen table, the snack Henry had allotted us before dinner. We stood and ate quietly. I watched Iszel warily, wondering what he would do. Some of the older boys were already outside in the barn, playing a game of basketball. Would he try to join them or listen to Henry?

Both Iszel and I always did our chores immediately following snack time; we agreed it was best to get them out of the way. It was Iszel's turn to set the table; I had to sweep. We continued in silence, each completing our assigned task. Henry, who had been in the kitchen stirring a pot of oyster stew, kept throwing glances our way. It was evident he was waiting for Iszel to try something. When Iszel had laid the last spoon down, he beelined for the porch. Henry immediately followed him to the door. He still held the wooden spoon, which was dripping cheap oyster goo all over the wooden floor. One of us boys would surely be responsible for cleaning that nastiness up later. He jabbed the spoon end towards Iszel, droplets flying.

"Uh uh. Back inside. You're only making matters worse for yourself."

I watched from behind, catching glimpses of Iszel through Henry's bulk. He continued down the steps to the driveway.

"Why? Because I untied my laces? Henry, that's stupid. It's the STYLE." He was earnestly trying for reasonable, but he came out sounding defiant.

"Two weeks, Iszel," Henry said, still waving the spoon around. "That's two weeks in your room for disobeying me. You wanna go for two more?"

I groaned. Iszel would be in solitary confinement for a month if he continued to press his position. The little spark of hatred I had for Henry flared.

"That's not happening," Iszel said, bending over to tie his laces.

"Oh no, It's too late for that now."

Iszel straightened up. "That's not why I tied my laces." He laughed and began to edge away.

"Don't make me come and get you," Henry threatened. He tossed the spoon onto the counter behind him. It clattered, spraying more stew. I jumped out of the way.

"You're not getting me," Iszel retorted, completely confident. Then he made a break for it, darting away with impressive speed.

As soon as Iszel ran, Henry followed at top speed. I immediately followed for a better view. I was surprised at Henry's pace. He was 60-something, but he was giving Iszel a run for his money. Iszel weaved amongst the trees and around the house, once looping around the van. Henry kept pace, though he couldn't gain on him. I wondered, idly, as they ran all over the lawn, what he would do to Iszel if he caught him.

"Come on, Iszel, you got this!" I shouted. The older kids had stopped their game of basketball and had drifted outside to watch the stand-off, cheering him on as well. Our shared contempt for Henry was spilling over.

Iszel continued his zig-zagging up the grade that led to the three-story barn. He slowed for a moment to ensure Henry was following and then sped up again, darting inside. As soon as Henry blew through the sliding barn door, I jogged up to peer in after them. Derek and Jiggs crowded next to me. We had an idea of what Iszel was up to, and this performance was too good to miss.

Instead of running onto the basketball court that comprised the third floor, Iszel had opted to take the stairs to the right that led down to what used to be the second floor, which was now just the joists with large gaps between them. They were uneven; some of them had fallen over, and in our many games of hide and seek in the barn, we had all learned their pattern by heart.

We followed in time to see Iszel chopping his steps across the joists flawlessly, past the bale shoot with its ten-foot drop. Henry, only a few joists in, hesitated a moment. Iszel stood on the other end of the floor, beckoning.

"C'mon old man, whatchu' got? I'm right here, nowhere to go."

Then Iszel looked down as if he might drop through. Henry snarled and tried to run across the joists to stop him, but his left foot landed badly and slipped backward. His leg fell through the slats, taking half his body with him. His right leg was caught on the slat in front, bashing his knee into his head. The tender space between his legs slammed down on the narrow beam of wood. Henry emitted a strangled, animalistic cry of anguish.

I instinctively reached a protective hand over for my own tender parts.

"Ooooh..." I breathed half in sympathy and half in delight. Derek and Jiggs joined in a similar chorus.

Iszel studied him impassively. "Yeah, you stuck, ain't you?"

Henry managed to extricate his right leg, wiggled his way through the gap, hanging from the joist, and then dropped the remaining four feet to land on the ground. He laid himself in a fetal position, still groaning in pain.

Iszel calmly stepped his way back across the joists and brushed past us.

He waved his hands dismissively. "I'm done here."

We followed him out and watched as he jogged across the field and disappeared behind one of the trees, hiding from what would surely be an irate Henry once he could stand up.

After a few minutes of recovery, Henry stormed out of the basement entrance of the barn, his face livid. If thoughts could kill, Iszel would surely have combusted into a pile of ash. Henry stomped up the porch steps, yanked open the door, and slammed it behind him. Moments later, he repeated the reverse, with keys and a file folder in hand. He went straight to the van, slammed the door, and drove off with a squeal of tires and a spray of gravel from the driveway.

Jacque, who had caught the tail end of the drama, watched with Jiggs, Derek, and me in silence until the van disappeared.

"There he go again. He stay goin' to the State Police with a runaway file," Jiggs muttered disapprovingly.

"Henry always be trippin' when he don't get his way," Derek agreed, nodding. "He's mad because he crushed them family jewels."

Jiggs shrugged, grimacing. The two of them headed back to the barn, punching shoulders and laughing about Henry losing the chase.

Jacque, on the other hand, was marching across the field to where Iszel was hiding. He returned moments later, pushing Iszel by the neck. As they drew closer, I could hear Jacque berating him.

"I said you are going to get in that house and go to your room!" he exclaimed, exasperated.

"Listen, man, you don't understand," Iszel protested.

"Yo, man! You showed him those wheels!" I interjected, laughing.

Jacque stopped for a moment to glare at me.

I innocently raised my hands to physically ask, *What'd I do?*

His expression was only slightly less furious than Henry's, but I could tell his anger came from a place of fear, love, and frustration.

Jacque emphasized his next words, so they were each their sentence. "Get. In. The. House. And. Go. To. Your. Room."

"One minute," Iszel said, wriggling out of Jacque's grasp and coming over to me. Jacque shook his head in exasperation.

"Yo man, did you see me?!" he asked, excited. He darted side to side playfully. "I was like Muhammad Ali, float like a butterfly, baby." He did a couple more quick moves, shimmied his shoulders, and threw a few quick jabs around me.

"Yeah, I saw," I said, and I couldn't help smiling. "Caused that man to crush those family jewels. But you know you just floated your way into 30 days of solitary."

Jacque threw his arms out, low and wide, hands spread, as he glared at Iszel. It was a bad sign for my little brother. The lower and broader Jacque's arms, the more dire the situation and his mood.

"Iszel," he said, putting all his authority into the name.

"Yeah, yeah," Iszel muttered. He took slow, dragging steps to the house, taking as long as he could to walk the 100 feet to the porch while still being considered moving. Halfway there, Jacque lost his patience, stalked over to him, and grabbed the back of his neck again to push him the rest of the way.

"Maaaaaaan," Iszel objected. Jacque did not relent.

"Alright, alright, I'm going," Iszel grumbled. "See y'all in 30."

The day was too warm to spend inside, so the rest of us restarted the game of basketball in the barn. It was never my favorite activity, but I'd play or watch occasionally. I walked past the steps that led down to the second-floor joists. The image flashed into my mind of Henry, one leg hanging through the gap, the other knee squashed in his face. I chuckled. At least Iszel would have that memory to keep him company while serving his month-long penance.

Less than an hour later, we heard tires crunching over the drive and stopped our game to pop out of the barn to see who was coming. It was a police cruiser, blue lights flashing. Iszel was sitting on his bedroom windowsill, one leg dangling out of the window, watching it roll up.

He saw me and beckoned me over.

"Yo, some of my photos are missing!" he complained loudly to me. "Why the hell did that honky have to take so many of my pictures?"

I ignored him, turning my attention to the two white state police officers exiting the car. They were dressed in full state police uniform, grey short-sleeved shirts, ties, badges, hats, and black belts, each carrying guns in holsters. I wasn't nervous, but being born Black, I had learned to be sensibly cautious. I held my arms loose at my sides, my hands clearly visible. Every other kid except Iszel did the same. He simply lounged. He rested his elbow on his leg and propped his chin on his fist, knowingly watching everything play out.

The police officers both walked to the edge of the drive and stopped about six feet from us. None of us moved to be closer.

"Hello," said one of the police officers, the burlier of the two.

"Hello, Sir," I replied with a nod.

As the others responded, mostly just with nods, I saw the van hurriedly pulling up the driveway.

"My partner and I are here about a missing person's report," the officer continued. "We've been informed Iszel Glover has run away."

"There's no runaway here," Jacque said. "That's Iszel right there." He pointed up to the window where Iszel managed to make precariously balancing on a window ledge look cool.

"Here I am," called Iszel cheerfully, waving, swinging his dangling leg.

The police officer raised his eyebrows, pulled out a photo, and studied it, then looked up three stories again to scrutinize Iszel.

"That's my photo!" Iszel said. "Can I have my pictures back?"

The police officer ignored this comment. Instead, he turned to Henry, who had just exited his car.

"Sir, is that Iszel Glover in the window over there?"

Henry looked at Iszel, fuming.

"Yes," he barked in a clipped tone.

"Ok, well..." the police officer trailed off and looked at his partner, who shrugged. "I guess that's that. Sorry to trouble you all."

The man nodded in our general direction, and slowly, the two of them walked back to the car, climbed inside, and drove away. Henry waited until they were gone, and he turned back to Iszel.

"You!" He shouted venomously, jabbing his finger towards Iszel. "Get back inside that window! You know that's 30 days in your room! Thirty days, you hear me?!"

"Yeah, yeah," Iszel said, unfazed, sliding back into his room. I thought I heard him mutter, "Yo, you owe me some pictures," but I couldn't be sure.

Henry slunk away into the house, grumbling. Henry's sentence of solitary was completely expected but depressing nonetheless. It was going to be a long and lonely 30 days.

CHAPTER 22

The Soup Standoff

As the summer wore on, the tension between Henry and all of us, but especially Iszel, continued to ramp up. One August evening at dinnertime, I was on table-setting duty. The chestnut oak table filled the dining room, with just enough room for me to squeeze around the chairs as I folded napkins and laid out place settings. The other boys trickled into the dining room, laughing and joking. We all sat and waited until Henry and Janine bustled from the kitchen carrying bowls of soup. They plopped them down in front of us. The other boys also received their salads and entrees, but not Iszel or me.

"Boys, we are gonna teach you how to have a proper meal with manners," Henry said as he sat, looking at Iszel and me. "You hafta finish each course before you get the next. No more of this disgraceful waste."

Henry settled into his place in front of his Hungry Man Salisbury steak meal.

Today's first dish was onion soup. It smelled awful and unappealing to my 12-year-old palate. I held my nose and shoveled the gloppy stuff in as quickly as I could. I was finished before Iszel had taken more than a few spoonfuls. Henry brought me a salad, which I ate drenched in dressing. The final course was an overcooked fish, and I started to eat it in a similar, hasty fashion.

I glanced at my brother, who was still staring grimly at his soup bowl.

"I can't eat this," he said.

Henry's mouth compressed in a thin line. "I've been too easy on you. If you don't eat that, you'll go hungry."

Iszel sighed. He picked his spoon back up and stirred it in the soup, mixing the brown liquid in circles. He took another bite, and I saw him gagging as he tried to swallow it.

"You should appreciate Henry cookin' you such gourmet food," Janine interjected. "He's expandin' your horizons." She took a dainty bite of her Jenny Craig chicken.

Iszel took one more spoonful, and no sooner had he managed to swallow it, then he leaned over his bowl and threw up right back in it.

A chorus of "ughs" and "ewws" came from around the table.

"Yo man, that's nasty," Jiggs said.

The older boys, who had scarfed down whatever bits of food they wanted from all three courses, hastily cleared out from the table.

"You good?" Jacque asked Iszel sympathetically.

He nodded. "I got this."

Jacque looked at Henry. "It's messed up how you be treatin' lil kids."

Janine came to Henry's defense. "It's too late for the likes of you older boys, but we can help these two learn their manners."

"Still don't make it right, and you know it," Jacque retorted. "You just bein' bullies to some kids." He walked away before they could respond. He took his bowl and plate into the kitchen with the rest of the mass exodus. I looked longingly after him, but I hadn't finished my fish and didn't want to leave Iszel alone.

I glanced at Henry, who looked thoroughly annoyed. He crossed his arms and leaned forward, squinting his eyes. He pointed a fork loaded with mashed potatoes at him.

"You threw that food up on purpose, didn't you," he accused.

Iszel had just finished wiping his mouth with the back of his hand and pushed the dish away. He looked paler than his usual dark brown.

"Why would I ever do that on purpose?" Iszel asked incredulously. "I shouldn't be forced to eat something that makes me sick."

Henry stood abruptly and picked up the bowl with the vomit and soup mix. I averted my eyes; I couldn't help but notice that Iszel's puke was the same color and consistency as the soup. I listened to it sloshing and swallowed hard to keep my stomach in check.

Henry walked to the kitchen, and I heard him dump and rinse the bowl, then the slop of more soup as he refilled it. He returned moments later, setting it down in front of Iszel.

"Here you go, a fresh bowl."

Henry took his seat. Janine watched with a little smile on her face. Iszel crossed his arms and settled into the chair's red cushion, staring at Henry.

"You're not getting anything else until you finish that," Henry insisted.

Iszel maintained his gaze, never looking at the soup. "Fine, then, can I be excused? I'll go hungry before trying to eat that stuff again."

Henry regarded him for a few minutes, hoping Iszel's pangs of hunger would get the better of him. They didn't. My stomach had finally settled, so during this little standoff, not wanting to antagonize Henry further, I made a show of holding my nose and shoveled in the rest of the fish, trying hard not to think about or taste it. Henry finally sighed and waved his hand at Iszel, dissatisfied but dismissing him. He had no further recourse – for the moment.

***

Henry and Iszel continued to bump heads almost every night during meals. Henry eventually upped the ante, requiring us to eat all that was served or not leave the table until the plate was clean. To test out the new rule, He served up grilled cheese and tomato soup, knowing that both were on Iszel's most-hated list.

Having been on welfare in Philly, we had eaten plenty of grilled cheese sandwiches when we were younger. One of the monthly welfare items we received was a 5-pound block of bright orange cheese. "Government cheese" tasted like something between Velveeta and American. It came in a large brown box and was wrapped in plastic that imprinted itself into the sheen of its pungent, processed mass. Having no alternative was humiliating for those who could not afford better. We sliced it by hand, which normally resulted in thick, uneven cuts off the block. We came up with the idea to use a potato peeler to achieve thinner slices for cooking our sandwiches. Sometimes, we resorted to putting them in a paper bag and toasting them with an iron when the gas had been turned off due to a bill not being paid. All of this contributed to Iszel's lifelong aversion to grilled cheese.

With Henry's new rule, Iszel spent a lot of time seated at the dining room table, sometimes late into the night when most of the boys had gone to bed. When the Hills settled in for the night or were busying themselves with things that took their attention away from Iszel, Jacque would hasten to the dining room and try to convince him to eat the food.

"Yo man, I need you to take a couple bites of the sandwich. Sitting here all night isn't worth it."

"Naw, I'm good. I didn't like it hot, and I know I won't like it cold." Iszel stirred the thickened red soup with the spoon that was settled in the bowl. "Look at this stuff. No one wants to eat this."

"I know." Jacque lightly smacked him on the back of the head in annoyance, grabbed the cold sandwich, and stuffed it into his mouth in a few large bites. He washed it down with the congealed soup and rushed back out of the dining room to relieve Iszel of further punishment. This went on for a few weeks whenever Iszel ended up at the table past bedtime.

During this period of increasing tensions, one relief for Iszel especially was the start of the new school year, 7th grade for me and 6th for him. It meant that Iszel had another source of food, strengthening his determination not to cave. It didn't stop Henry from trying his hardest.

A few weeks passed, and Henry grew suspicious of Iszel suddenly finishing his food every night during his late-night dining room punishments. Henry upped the ante one night by choosing one of Iszel's least favorites. At dinner, with a tight little grin, he set a gloppy, brown bowl of onion soup in front of each of us. Last time we'd had that, Iszel had vomited into his bowl, so I knew tonight wouldn't go well. I made a show of holding my nose and chugging down the warm onion glop, hoping for once he'd do the same, but Iszel resigned himself to a long night at the table and refused to taste it. "Iszel, you're gonna sit there until you eat that soup. No more supper 'til you do."

Iszel sat back in his chair and began drumming on the dining room table with his two-pointer fingers. "Yup. I don't want the other stuff you're serving anyway."

"Fine," Henry said.

The eleven o'clock hour passed, and Jacque slipped into the dining room for their nightly routine of him attempting to convince Iszel to eat, only to have him steadfastly refuse. Resigned, Jacque reached for the bowl, intending to eat it himself. This time, though, Henry stepped out of a hiding spot in the living room. "Jacque, what are you up to?"

"I'm trying to get him to eat his food."

"No, you were gonna eat it for him. That's not allowed!"

"Iszel, leave the food there and go upstairs to bed," Jacque ordered. He looked at Henry. "You're not gonna keep doin' this to my lil brotha. Old ass man, bullying lil kids. You know he don't like that soup, so stop giving it to him." Iszel stood and turned towards the stairs.

"He hasta learn to eat what's placed before him," Henry insisted, reaching for Iszel. Jacque stepped in front of Henry, smacking his hands away from Iszel and blocking him from advancing.

"Don't touch him!" Jacque, now 15 and having gone through a recent growth spurt, nearly stood eye-to-eye with Henry, and neither was relinquishing his space.

Henry was seething. "There are starving kids all over that can't get a meal, and your brother takes that for granted!"

"You're not gonna keep enforcing rules on him that you don't enforce on all of us," Jacque replied.

Blocked from the stairs, Iszel retreated to the farthest point of the dining room, away from what was about to ensue. The cold bowl of soup still sat on the table. Hearing the raised voices, Henry's wife, Janine, came out of their bedroom, and the other boys started down the steps.

Seeing he and his wife were outnumbered, Henry acquiesced. Jacque stood there defiantly as Iszel ducked behind him and up the stairs. Jacque slowly backed his way up the stairs, never taking his eyes off the old man and his wife, the other boys providing protective, safe passage to the recesses of the 2nd floor.

Once or twice after that, Henry resorted to sitting at the table with Iszel or patrolling the dining room when he had Iszel punished at the table. Each time, Jacque took a bolder stance, cutting off Iszel's punishments earlier and earlier, leaving the food to sit on the table overnight. It would be served for Iszel's breakfast the next morning, which he refused, opting to endure the pangs of hunger until his school's lunchtime.

The food sat there all day and was still there when Iszel returned from school. Henry realized his tactic was now his punishment, too, as he was tasked with cleaning up the disgusting food. He began allowing Iszel to leave the table, hoping Iszel's hunger would get the best of him. Iszel resorted to scoring extra lunch tickets from his classmates, especially his friend Cory. He and Iszel had become close during this time, unexpected allies during the food wars Iszel was enduring with Henry. Cory was the son of a compassionate white couple, Ann Marie and Larry Spencer. He shared Iszel's struggles with his parents. Upon hearing this, Ann Marie decided to send extra food to school with Cory for Iszel. Sometimes, my little brother would arrive at the House on the Hill with his book bag stocked with a sandwich, chips, snacks, and even a box of cereal, all from the Spencers. Through the kindness of his found family, my brother didn't starve.

CHAPTER 23

Lights Out

In the midst of all of this, my eyesight was deteriorating. I could hardly see the blackboard, and it was causing me to struggle at school. One visit to an eye doctor later, and I came home sporting a giant pair of glasses that Henry told me I could 'grow into.' I could hardly process the change, though, so fraught was my home life.

Tussles between the Hills and Jacque and Derek became increasingly frequent. After the setback with Kathy, they began using a Sony Walkman to clandestinely record their interactions with the Hills. Armed with these covert recordings, they decided it was time to rally the others.

On a day not long after, Derek sporting a swollen lip and Jacque a bruised eye, they gathered us to hold a listening session. This was the first "Boys'" meeting we ever had. Jacque pressed play on the cassette, and Henry's angry voice filled the room.

"Don't you tell me what you're not gonna do, you lil' shit! Now, siddown before I make you," Henry bellowed.

"Nah, I'm good with standing," Jacque's voice came through the speakers. "Anything you gotta tell me, you can tell me while I'm over here and you're over there."

Henry's tone escalated. "Boy, this meeting ain't starting until you sit in this chair. Jacque, you're gonna make me have to put you in that seat."

The recording went quiet, and disappointment washed over our faces. Jacque, however, held up a knowing finger, indicating that there was more to come. As the tape resumed, three distinct thumps followed by a cacophony of yelling and screaming filled the room.

"That's him trying to put me in one of those restraint holds," Jacque explained. It was a technique he'd likely learned at one of the training sessions conducted by BCS meant to be used against difficult kids. But it had proven ineffective.

"Ged off 'eem!" Derek's voice suddenly cut through the chaos. The tape continued to capture muffled sounds of a physical fight; presumably Derek jumping in to help Jacque battle against Henry. Despite the injuries they sustained, they assured us that they had prevailed. We gathered around them, nodding, high fives, and hand claps in admiration for their courage in standing up to Henry's oppression.

Rather than entrusting their recordings to the unhelpful social worker, they decided to take a different approach. Carol Smith, a weekend house parent who also served as the high school secretary, became our ally. Derek had established a solid rapport with her, and Jacque had a class with the daughters of the county attendance officer, Ms. Amelie Swendt. They handed the tapes over to them, both of whom were understandably alarmed and promised to do what they could to help us out.

As the physical confrontations in the house escalated, a pervasive sense of dread had taken hold of everyone, leaving us constantly on edge. And then, one fateful Friday afternoon in October, the simmering tensions reached their boiling point. Henry was once again tormenting Iszel about his uneaten dinner, his booming voice echoing through the house. It was loud enough to draw us all from our rooms. Dave and Janine, peeking out from their wing of the house, shared worried glances.

We watched in silence from the railing above as Henry's aggression escalated with each passing moment.

"Boy, this is the last time I'm gonna tell ya to eat your damn dinner!" Henry screamed at Iszel, grabbing his arm and shaking him. "Now sit here and eat!"

"Yo! Get off my brother!" Jacque yelled. I was enough to distract Henry. Iszel, desperate to escape, twisted his arm free and sprinted for the stairs, with Henry hot on his heels.

"Don't you dare run from me!" Henry screamed, his voice echoing through the hallways.

Dave ran up to intervene, closely followed by Janine. "Dad, wait!" he pleaded.

At the top of the stairs, Jacque positioned himself, arms outstretched to protect Iszel, who slipped under his arm. Henry, driven by anger, lunged forward, shoving Jacque in the chest with force. Jacque's back slammed into the wall. The wall bowed and recoiled, shooting Jacque forward back towards Henry. With an inner strength born of desperation and anger, coupled with the energy of the wall, Jacque shoved back, his actions setting off a chain reaction that unfolded in agonizing slow motion.

As if watching a nightmare, we saw Henry, in a state of shock, completely lose his footing. He flew backward and down the flight of stairs, unable to find the wall or banister for support to stop his freefall.

Janine screamed in terror for her husband, "HENRY!!"

The result was a chaotic cascade of bodies as he collided with Dave, who, in turn, crashed into Janine. They all tumbled down the staircase, landing in a bruising heap at the bottom.

There was a collective audible gasp from all of us, but relief washed over us as we heard them groaning and knew all three were still very much alive. The commotion had drawn the rest of the boys to the railing, and eight solemn, determined faces peered down, united by our shared exhaustion from the relentless bullying and petty authoritarianism that had plagued our lives.

Henry's eyes betrayed a mixture of fear and rage as he helped Janine and Dave to their feet. It was clear that they would be sore for days. Without uttering another word to us, Henry ushered the injured pair into their apartment area. The door locked with a loud click.

Exhaling a breath I hadn't realized I'd been holding, I felt a weight lift off my shoulders. The silent exchange of glances among the eight of us spoke volumes. Our moment of accord had arrived. But just as we began to digest the significance of everything that had happened, the lights in the house went out, plunging us into a dimness that mirrored the uncertainty of our future.

The fading evening sunlight was already casting its dwindling glow through the windows, shadows swallowing the rooms and corridors of the house. But it quickly became clear that not all the lights had gone out. A faint strip of light persisted beneath the closed door leading to the Hill's apartment wing. The implication was clear—Henry had selectively cut power to only our part of the house.

Jacque couldn't help but express his frustration. "Ain't that about some shit," he muttered, shaking his head. His sentiment was echoed by a chorus of colorful cussing from us, a collective release of pent-up anger and resentment.

Derek, ever the practical one, suggested moving our group to the basement. He motioned for us to follow him, and we did so willingly.

Descending into the cavernous basement, we sequestered ourselves in the rec room, closing the door. We were in even darker surroundings now, with only two windows near the top of the wall offering a hint of illumination. However, the ample space provided a place to congregate and an escape plan if the Hills decided to come after us, as this room contained an exit to the outside.

As we gathered, ideas and scenarios bounced around the room, some wilder than others. But the prevailing theme was clear—no matter what, we would no longer tolerate the Hills' torment and were prepared to face any threat together. A sense of unity and determination filled the air, much like the teenagers in "Red Dawn," ready to protect each other at any cost.

We had no access to flashlights or candles, relying solely on the faint illumination of the moonlight and one outside light that still had power. By eight o'clock, the room had grown so dark that we could barely make out each other's outlines.

Hunger gnawed at our stomachs, and as the familiar pangs plagued me, I flashed back to my childhood. Hunger had been a constant companion throughout my first decade, a symbol of the helplessness that defined my past. The Hills had made it clear they had no intention of feeding us, as all the food cabinets were locked. The frustration of being unable to eat when we wanted to add to the already complex mix of emotions I was experiencing.

Jacque eventually broke the silence. "Let's pool our money," he suggested. "Derek and I can go to Landhope and buy some food for us."

We all contributed what we could, amassing a modest sum of over 40 dollars. Jacque collected the money and promised to return with dinner. With that, he and Derek opened the basement door, momentarily illuminated by the single working light at the top of the stairs, and then they ventured off to retrieve their bikes from the barn.

After they left, I realized I could no longer ignore my bladder's urgent demands. I announced my intention to go upstairs to relieve myself, and as I left the rec room, the conversation among the other boys shifted to what Derek and Jacque might bring back to eat.

Cautiously, I climbed the stairs, feeling my way in the darkness. At the top, I inched my way down the hallway, feeling along the walls, passing the kitchen. It was then that I froze in the doorway, a chill running down my spine. In the dim moonlight, I could see Henry and Janine silhouetted at the windows, engaged in hushed whispers and peering out. They had a clear view of the basement's outside exit, which meant they had been spying on Jacque and Derek's departure.

The hairs on the back of my neck stood on end as I tried to creep past them. However, fate had other plans. My foot hit a creaky floorboard, producing a loud noise that pierced the silence. The Hills turned to look at me, and before I could react, an indistinct figure lunged at me, growling, pinning me to the hallway wall. In terror, I let out a yelp, feeling warm liquid trickling down my leg—I had peed myself in fear.

It was Wimpy, the Hills' dog. The Hills commanded her to heel, but it was Lady, our house dog, who rushed over, barking and protecting me.

I managed to disentangle myself from the dogs, who were now yapping at each other, and hastily made my way into the bathroom. It was pitch dark inside, but I stood there for a moment, trembling. I sat on the open seat for fear that my aim would be off in the dark and finally began to pee, sighing with relief at the release. Even during such dire circumstances, something as simple as using the bathroom offered a brief but sharp moment of comfort.

After flushing, I briefly wondered if it would refill, and to my relief, both the toilet and sink functioned. At least we had access to water.

Exiting the bathroom, I realized I needed to change my pants. *That Damn Wimpy*, I thought. I couldn't stand that dog. I hurried past the kitchen without looking inside, avoiding the Hills and the dogs. In my room, I changed as quickly as I could in the oppressive darkness, the eerie and unsettling solitude. I moved as fast as I could manage while feeling along walls and descending the stairs holding the banister. I had no further encounters with the Hills or the dogs. Finally, I clicked the basement room door shut behind me, finding solace in the darkened outlines of the other boys waiting on the couches towards the back of the room. I joined them, feeling the strength that came from our numbers.

Before I could relay what had happened, the lights flickered back on. The sudden, unexpected burst of light blinded me, causing me to shield my eyes instinctively and squint against the harsh brightness. Behind the rec room door, we listened intently as Henry descended the stairs. Although no one moved physically, an unmistakable tension drew us closer together.

Henry entered the room, his face adorned with a large, forced smile, holding two plastic bags that emitted the tantalizing aroma of takeout food. The growl of my stomach betrayed my hunger.

"Hey boys, I've got some food here for you," Henry announced with strained cheerfulness. He rested the bags on the pool table. "We saw Jacque and Derek leave," he continued, "We're gonna go ahead and report them to the State police as runaways, but you mustn't let them back in if they return. We'll just keep the doors locked until the police get here. As long as you do that, you can have this." He emphasized his offer by extending the bags of food.

I couldn't help but feel incredulous. Did Henry honestly believe we would side with him over our brother and housemate? I glanced at Iszel, whose expression displayed a mix of hunger and resentment.

"Nah, man!" Jiggs declared, his eyes barely leaving the bags. "We ain't gon' do that to them."

Henry's fake smile disappeared. "You sure about that? None of you are hungry?"

In response, he received six hostile stares.

Henry's face hardened and darkened. "All right, then," he said, his voice cracking. "Enjoy eating nothing." He picked up the bags, turned, and stormed out of the room, slamming the door behind him. A minute later, the lights were extinguished, and darkness enveloped us once more.

Time had a way of stretching when sitting hungry in the dark. We heard the knocking at the basement door that signaled Jacque's and Derek's return. Although it felt like an eternity, it was probably less than an hour. I raced over to let them in. Part of me wished that Henry could see me defying his deceitful offer. Jacque and Derek entered to a warm and excited welcome from the hungry group, eagerly crowding around them.

They had bought rolls, mayo, cheese, and lunchmeat in abundance, intending to make it last for the weekend. My first bite of my sandwich, constructed in near darkness, tasted like heaven.

We ate as much as we dared, carefully setting aside leftovers for the following days. The feeling of fullness eluded us, but our stomachs no longer threatened to consume themselves. Being full was a luxury we often went without.

Derek took the initiative to gather trash, emphasizing the need for us to work together to self-govern. Jacque suggested dividing ourselves into two groups of four for the night, with Iszel and I advised not to go anywhere alone, given the growing threats from the Hills.

As we ascended the stairs in single file, Derek stopped to store the remaining lunchmeat in the now non-functional kitchen fridge, which had little else in it, the majority of the cold foods being stored in a locked fridge and freezer in the off-limits room in the basement. Then, we navigated our way upstairs and collected bedding from various rooms to create makeshift sleeping pallets, including those for Iszel and me.

Settling into the blankets, I recognized that it might not be the most comfortable night's sleep, but the security of having Jacque, Iszel, and Jiggs nearby outweighed the softness of a bed.

CHAPTER 24

A New Day

I woke up the next morning, relieved to find myself bathed in daylight. We hunkered down for the weekend, spending most of our time in the basement together. A few of the older boys managed to use some of their income from their jobs to buy us cereal and snacks. We preserved the lunch meat on ice we'd bought to prevent it from spoiling since the fridge was gradually warming without power.

Throughout the weekend, we saw no sign of the Hills. We lived two separate lives under the same roof; theirs filled with the luxury of electricity and abundant, hot food, ours without either. If Henry believed that starving us or stripping us of conveniences would break us, he clearly didn't understand that he was pushing us further down the well-worn path of survival mode, where our sole aim was to endure.

Monday inevitably arrived, and my internal alarm clock roused me at 6 AM. I carefully untangled myself from the jumble of blankets on the floor and tiptoed to the bathroom. Although I had showered the previous night, I always felt compelled to shower again in the morning to start the day fresh, and luckily, the water heater ran on gas. It was the first time I'd been alone since Wimpy had jumped me, with no one guarding the bathroom door. After finishing in the bathroom, before I opened the door to the hallway, I turned the knob slowly and cautiously, half expecting Henry to be lurking outside, waiting. He had done it before, sneaking around and listening at doors, and it wasn't uncommon to turn down a hallway and unexpectedly encounter him.

When I finally flung open the door, there was nothing but an empty hallway. I dashed back to our bedroom, gently rousing Iszel and trying to wake the others. With the absence of the Hills and working alarms, not all eight of us made it to the bus stop.

School provided a temporary respite: lights, friendly faces, and the promise of food. The last class before lunch was history, taught by Mrs. Hines, one of the few Black teachers at Fred S. Engle Middle School. Mrs. Hines had elevated expectations for her Black students, demanding both Black power and excellence, standards I failed to meet.

She referred to me as Mr. Glover and constantly mispronounced my last name. I was a perpetual disappointment to her, a "lazy Black boy." She never explored anything about my background or current circumstances to understand the nuances of why I was the way I was. I had bigger problems with my basic needs to be overly concerned with the "Black Power" agenda that she was trying to push on me in this racist town.

I always felt a sense of relief when her class was over, but never more so than that Monday when my first hot meal in three days awaited me in the cafeteria. I eagerly stood in line for my chicken patty, shifting from foot to foot, the savory scent of chicken and fries filling the air. Some kids complained about the cafeteria's smell — too greasy, too something — but those people had never gone hungry and couldn't appreciate the value of a guaranteed meal. As I neared the front of the line, I briefly envied those in the money line whose sandwiches were consistently thicker and tastier, with better bread and extra fillings. Nevertheless, I was looking forward to my patty.

After securing my meal, I surveyed the cafeteria, which doubled as an auditorium. It was filled with colorful, round tables. I spotted a group of kids I was friendly with and who usually had extra lunch tickets. I set my tray down on their blue laminate table and was met with warm smiles and friendly greetings.

"It's The Glover!" Matt Martone exclaimed. My fourth-grade last name moniker had stuck. But sometimes, I was referred to as "The Glover," as if I were an object rather than a person. I was known about, but not truly known.

Unlike most students who sat with the same group every day, I floated between different tables as the need or whim took me. I was friendly with everyone, regardless of their popularity. I relished introducing other kids to those with greater social status and forging connections. No one questioned this about me. I had a friendly personality and talents like breakdancing that impressed my peers and kept me high up in the social hierarchy. Consequently, my ability to be accepted into and bridge many groups in school was never questioned. My connections, however, were only ever surface-deep. I often wondered what would become of me if I didn't possess those talents.

Today, though, my focus was on food. The first bite of my chicken patty was heavenly — warm, meaty, and delicious — but it disappeared all too quickly.

"Anyone got any extra tickets?" I inquired.

Matt offered his. "I bought my lunch in the other line today, so I don't need this." He held it up like a golden ticket from Willy Wonka.

"Would you mind getting me another patty?" I asked.

"For The Glover?! Sure!" Matt responded enthusiastically, eager to help. It wasn't the first time I'd shared meals at lunch, and it wouldn't be the last. With locked cabinets at home, none of us were ever getting enough to eat, although this week, the Hills had taken their starvation tactics to new heights. Iszel often complained that the lunch ladies rejected him when he tried to get a second lunch, but he simply didn't know how to work the system.

Matt soon returned with another golden patty, and I savored it, knowing it might be the last meal I ate that day.

When the school bus dropped me and Iszel off later, he was still griping about not managing to score a second lunch.

"This is ridiculous," he muttered, kicking at loose stones on the driveway. I knew he meant more than his failure to grab a second lunch, and I shared his frustration. But what could we do? We had to endure.

We took our time walking up the winding driveway to the house despite the frigid air. Neither of us was eager to return to that looming, unwelcoming monster.

When we finally entered the house, it was silent and dim—no sign of the Hills, no power yet. However, there were Tarts on the counter, an off-brand version of Pop-Tarts, left by the Hills as a snack. It would turn out to be the only food they would give us that night.

Both of us trudged to the basement, waiting for the rest of the house to join us. We diligently completed our homework while daylight still allowed. It was a race against time; the house was dark by six o'clock. We used the bathroom in pairs, and when we grew tired of sitting in the dark in the basement, we all ventured upstairs together to our two bedrooms. The week continued in this fashion, with each morning some of us missing the bus because of our lack of alarms. The Hills remained hidden, occasionally leaving snacks for us. But the power remained off. Finally, Friday morning arrived, and I kept hoping and praying that we would get weekend house parents, who would turn on the lights and feed us.

With so many of the boys from the group home showing up late, Mrs. Schwendt had finally gone by the House on the Hill herself to confirm what Derek and Jacque had been telling her and Carol – the lights were indeed out. Despite insistent pounding, the Hills refused to answer her knocks. She and Carol had called BCS to discuss the reports and tapes that Jacque and Derek had been handing them and the increasingly fraught situation at the House on the Hill. That Friday, Carol met with a representative at the House to discuss the matter. We found out later that they met in the office, and mid-conversation, Janine, casually holding a knife, unexpectedly popped into the room shouting, "Lies, it's all lies!"

It was the final straw. The representative told Carol to pick up the kids and take them home until he could get something sorted out. She was at the House when we arrived after school.

"You're coming home with me for a few days," she informed me, Iszel, and some of the other boys as she packed us into her car. Jacque was headed to Amelie Schwendt's house, and Derek stayed with a friend.

"What happened?" I asked, my heart pounding with anticipation.

"BCS just needs to figure a few things out. Maybe find new house parents to replace the Hills."

My heart leaped at the possibility of escaping our dire situation. Being at Carol's was a reprieve. After the last week, I welcomed regular meals and electricity. Carol situated us as comfortably as she could in her small home. She hadn't been planning for such an overnight. We had dinner and readied ourselves for bed, but the first night of sleeping was rough. We all slept haphazardly around the house on pallets of covers and in sleeping bags, she could find. She spent a little more time tucking Iszel and me in. She hummed and rubbed our backs until we settled down.

Iszel rolled over to look at her in the dimly lit room.

"They said we were going to a better place," he said, his voice small and expressing a rare moment of vulnerability.

"I know, sweety," Carol replied.

"They lied," he whispered.

I saw her lips tremble, though she continued to rub his back soothingly.

"It's going to be o.k. now," she said, her voice not quite steady.

It wasn't until decades later that I learned the whole picture of what had happened to finally get the Hills fired. Though the Hill's behavior had become increasingly unhinged during the years I was at the house, their official reason for being fired was stealing. For the four years they were house parents, they had been submitting false receipts to Baptist Children Services and pocketed the remaining funds. The living room full of antiques was the first thing we noticed confiscated from the house when they were eventually removed. We came to the conclusion that they were investing money they had skimmed into antiques as a way to hide their profits. While we may not have had an exact figure, the extent of these financial irregularities was clear.

One of the grim truths of foster care is that the money assigned to each kid is often at the discretion of the foster parent, and while most spend it appropriately and even invest their own money, there are still countless stories of those who don't, choosing to foster as a source of income. The Hills were performing a form of this by skimping on what they fed and spent on us and keeping the savings for themselves. Even though this was the premise for their removal, rather than the abuse we suffered, which would have reflected poorly on BCS, it was an acceptable outcome for us. Coupled with Carol's journals and the reports of school officials, I had a strong sense that they would never work in another group home again.

We returned to the house after staying at Carol's for a little over a week. It was quiet and had an abandoned air about it. The Hills were gone. The antiques were gone, and their apartment was empty. Despite being late October, Carol opened all the doors and windows, and the warmest breeze gusted through. She told the guys to turn on some music, and it didn't matter what it was as long as there was no bad language.

We did our chores, and the house smelled of lemon and Pine-Sol. She unlocked the pantries and gave us free access to the snacks. She dumped out the powdered milk and eggs and began cooking a meatloaf. We danced and laughed, and for the first time in a long while, the House on the Hill smiled. It had taken a huge exhale with us, and we all felt good.

Amidst the celebration, there was a tinge of sadness. All the animals, including Lady, had been taken by the Hills. Only Mr. Martin remained the wise old cat who had brought solace and comfort to the house. Without the lively presence of the dogs and the other cats, Mr. Martin seemed to wander the empty rooms with a sense of bewilderment. He was a quiet companion, a steadfast reminder of the life we had known.

In addition, the 5th bedroom, which had remained a mystery for almost three years, was now open and empty. Carol informed us that it had been filled with antiques as well, which the Hills had also taken with them. It was almost anticlimactic to see it so vacant and boring after having wondered about it for years.

The Hills were gone, and we celebrated like the munchkins of Oz when they realized the witch would not torment them anymore. Just like them, our elation was short-lived. Their removal left a parental chasm at the house. BCS would have to figure out a way to patch together the shifts of their employee network to keep the house open, or we would have to go back to Main Campus in West Philly.

The insecurity caused by moving from place to place all my life crept back in. In my mind, leaving meant never returning to Avondale. Some of the guys welcomed the idea after what we endured during the Hills' tenure, and there was no assurance that another bad hire would not happen again. I was less certain. For all the racism I had endured, I enjoyed school in Avondale, living with my brothers, and a sense of permanence.

Main Campus had been such a chaotic and challenging experience that the idea of returning stressed me out. Uprooting us also meant that we could eventually end up separated at one of the other three boys' homes in BCS's network. None of them had a good reputation.

The uncertainty was a heavy cloud hanging over our heads, casting a long shadow on the prospect of any stable home life. We had grown accustomed to upheaval, but it didn't make it any easier to accept. We yearned for a place where we could feel safe, where we could build lasting friendships, and where we could finally break free from the cycle of instability that had haunted our lives for so long.

As we contemplated the uncertain future, the memory of the Hills lingered in our minds, a stark reminder of the horrors we had endured. We knew that the world outside could be just as cruel, but we held onto the hope that someday we would find a place where we truly belonged, a place where we could leave behind the nightmares of our past and build a brighter future.

CHAPTER 25

The Golden Age

The departure of the Hills marked the beginning of a revolving door of temporary house parents who seized the opportunity to pick up extra hours while the group home was in a state of parental flux. Many of them strolled around with the blue rule books and the green logs the BCS required, diligently documenting their account of the day. These books dictated strict parameters for meals, bedtimes, and curfews, which felt entirely incompatible with our way of life. After enduring the turmoil imposed by the Hills, the older guys in the house took it upon themselves to repeatedly clarify the situation to these "visiting" house parents: our group didn't conform to the rigid rules outlined in those books. We governed ourselves as a tight-knit unit, well aware of what we should and shouldn't do, with house parents responsible for providing meals and transportation.

Jacque made it his mission to ensure that Iszel and I completed our homework and adhered to a reasonable bedtime. More than that, he kept a close eye on every move any house parent made, especially if they tried to enforce rules that contradicted our established norms. There was no way we were going back to the oppressive regime imposed by the Hills.

Throughout this tumultuous period, Dave Lichter remained a constant presence as a weekend house parent for about a year after the Hills' departure. However, he was our only sense of constancy. Over ten months, the house saw a continuous rotation of over twenty different people who also ushered many temporary group home kids through our core group of guys at the house.

In the summer of 1988, Baptist finally assigned Etwillimae King to be our main house parent at the House on the Hill, giving our lives much-needed stability. Twill had been working for BCS for several years at another group home located in Thornbury, PA. She was a Black, fifty-nine years old, married woman from Philly. She was the matriarch of her large family, which included great-grandchildren. She reminded me of Phylicia Rashad's character, Clair Huxtable of *The Cosby Show*, in both looks and mannerisms. I instantly felt comfortable with her. Unlike many of the temporary house parents, she symbolically threw BCS's blue rule book and guidelines out. She challenged the institutional game plan of providing *three hots and a cot*. Instead, she experimented with the idea of establishing a familial atmosphere in the house, relating to us and treating us like we were eight sons. She included us in the daily goings-on about the house, calling it "ours," which gave us ownership of the home rather than an emotionally unattached abode we happened to live in.

Twill knew that creating a true sense of family required the right team of house parents. She carefully selected individuals who not only had the necessary skills and dedication but also understood the importance of family bonds. One of her first recruits was Paul Brown, an older Black gentleman from Philly, around 60 years old. His presence brought a sense of wisdom and stability to the house, and his being Black was crucial for us to have a male role model.

Another addition to the house was Wilma Staton, a 40-year-old Black woman from Philly who joined as a weekend house parent. Wilma had a teenage son who had recently graduated high school, and she could easily relate to the growing pains of the guys in the house. Her presence felt like a bridge between generations, and her youthful energy kept us on our toes.

Wayne Hill, a 40-year-old Black man with a calm and cool disposition, also became part of our new house-parenting team. Wayne was not only a great mentor but also an amazing cook, which we certainly appreciated after our food battles with the Hills.

THOSE BOYS ON THE HILL

The final piece of the puzzle was an older Black woman named Flora Hector, who lived in the area and worked as a housekeeper for a local family. Ms. Hector had a heart full of love, especially when it came to her cooking. Her meals became a symbol of the care we felt within our newfound family.

Together, this team, under Twill's leadership, ushered in what we fondly call the golden age of the House on the Hill. With Twill's care and attention, the formerly foreboding House metamorphosed into a welcoming home. It was a marked contrast from our time with the Hills. Her recruits wholeheartedly embraced the family mentality that Twill had conceived. We considered them to be the Mt. Rushmore of House Parents, and their presence brought the sense of stability and warmth that we had longed for.

Twill risked her job with her experiment, and it worked. Twill's approach tied us together like never before. We were a patchwork family dynamic, and Twill was a master maternal seamstress. Our connection grew stronger day by day, and we became more than just housemates; we became brothers. The house was ours to care for, and everyone needed to take care of it and everyone inside. My understanding of community was established because of Twill's efforts. She was like an island in the whirlpool of uncertainty that dictated foster care. There was always the chance we would be moved to another house, adopted, returned to our family, and inevitably, we would age out. But while we were with Twill, we were family.

Twill saw beyond our files and learned who we were as individuals. She encouraged us to explore our interests both inside and outside the house. My love for cooking, theater, music, and track and field deepened because Twill not only accepted them but pushed me to "try it." The formerly off-limits living room was now empty, no longer filled with a room full of the Hills' antiques. Left behind were a couple of worn couches and a dusty piano at the back wall. The first couple of times I entered after the Hills had left, the feeling of being an intruder lingered. But the piano intrigued me. I'd never played one before. I tentatively crossed the doorway threshold, walked to the piano, and pressed a few keys, trying to play "Axel F," the *Beverly Hills Cop* theme song. With each note I played by ear, I grew more fascinated. I plopped myself onto the bench and chopped away at other TV theme songs, *Hills Street Blues*, *Chariots of Fire*, and *The Muppets'* "Rainbow Connection." I found if I could whistle the tune, I could rough out a melody on the piano.

Twill noticed my newfound interest and nurtured it. She secured me lessons, and although they only lasted eight months, it was a powerful gesture of support. It wasn't just about the piano; it was about her belief in me and her encouragement to pursue my passions.

With Twill's unwavering encouragement, I found the courage to expand my horizons. No longer content to remain in the shadows, I not only took part in talent shows but also ventured into the world of musicals, plays, and choir. My past experiences, both the painful and the triumphant, provided a deep well of emotions to draw from. It was through these performances that I discovered a powerful outlet for the emotions that had long been bottled up within me. I felt a sense of belonging and acceptance I had never known before. My mother's label of 'Weird Son,' which had haunted me for so long, began to lose its grip on my identity.

Twill also invited us into the group home kitchen. It was now warm and welcoming. The house began transforming into a true home. In her embrace, food was love again, and every meal was a reminder that I was valued and cherished.

Twill understood that many of us had been splintered not only from our parents but from our siblings as well, a norm in the group home industry. We longed for normalcy. Most of the guys wanted to go home to their norms. They preferred the streets because that was what they knew. That was also where their families were.

The combination of my distance from my family because of Jason, Twill's love, and my growing acceptance of myself and my life in Avondale broke the lore of the concrete jungle. For the first time, I truly felt okay with the idea of never returning to my family in Philly.

THOSE BOYS ON THE HILL

Twill leaned on my brothers and me, in particular, to cement the bonds between all the boys in the house. She recognized how special it was to be three brothers living together. We became the home's foundation. She would often talk to the three of us about setting a good example for the other guys. "They will follow your lead, so lead well," she'd always remind us.

Most siblings were split because of available housing dictated placement. Brother and sister pairings almost assured separation. Group homes were rarely co-ed for obvious reasons. Sometimes, a clan of 'troubled' siblings "needed" to be broken up. I never understood that. We were in the system because we all had some form of trouble, mostly with our parents' failings and not our own. Every time a kid would come through the house and mention that they had a brother or sister somewhere else, I counted my blessings. I didn't have to schedule a phone call to talk to my brothers. I knew someone had my back if something went down at home or school. The other boys were on their own.

We knew that the Glover brothers were an exception. Our mother would later tell us that when we were taken from her, she was granted the authority to ensure that we were never separated or adopted. I never believed that. I silently questioned why other parents were not granted the same authority for their kids. No, we were extremely lucky that someone at the main office didn't see anything in our file that called for breaking us up. Because of this, we accepted the responsibility that Twill placed on us. We knew we were fortunate, and it felt good to lead by example.

One of the ways Twill brought us together and treated us like family was by transforming Christmas at the Avondale Group Home for Boys into something special. It was a marked contrast from our time with the Hills, where Christmas passed with little notice. Twill, with her unwavering dedication to her makeshift family, ensured the holiday season was memorable for us. Our first experience with this was in the winter of 1988 when I was 13.

She adorned our living room with a grand Christmas tree that nearly reached the ceiling, and it became a tradition to come together to decorate it, listening to classics like the *Jackson 5 Christmas Album* and *The Temptation's Christmas Card*. Our spirit of togetherness grew stronger with each ornament we placed on the tree and the song we belted out together.

The magic of Christmas Eve was when the tree truly came to life. While we slept, the older guys helped Twill load the gifts under the tree, setting the stage for a morning filled with excitement. The tree, laden with gifts, looked like it defied gravity, almost floating above the ground.

On Christmas day, we would find Twill sitting in the living room, a cup of tea in hand, music softly playing, ready to kick off the festivities. Her expression sparkled with anticipation, mirroring our own. Twill chose thoughtful gifts she carefully selected for each of us. She knew our individual interests and dreams, and her gifts reflected this deep understanding. She bought me my first fishing rod, which became a favored pastime of mine.

For those of us unable to visit our own families during the holidays, Twill ensured that we were not alone. She prepared a lavish dinner featuring ham, mac and cheese, fried cabbage, and all the fixings. We gathered around the table, forming a group bound by appreciation and acceptance. The warmth of our shared laughter and the aroma of the food created a sense of togetherness that rose above our past struggles. After our shared meal, we were free to return for late-night holiday sandwiches or another plate of food. The deliciousness and free access were a testament to just how much better off we were with Twill, someone who nurtured us rather than tried to control us.

It was a time of growth, love, and acceptance that would shape our lives in ways we never imagined. Our house was much better than the other group homes in the system, and people had taken notice. Wilma confided in me that the reports from our social workers and the psychologists we saw were mostly positive. The kids from Avondale seemed less stressed and more cohesive as a group. Most who lived and worked at the house under Twill's tenure bought into her houseparenting style. Those of us who stuck around would always look out for each other. Baptist eventually heralded Twill's family format at the Avondale Group Home for Boys. They even took a little credit for it despite their initial resistance toward her approach. The reputation of the house had changed in the group home community, and it became the place other kids and house parents wanted to go.

CHAPTER 26

Counselling Sessions

One area that Twill was much better at staying on top of than the Hills was ensuring we attended our required counseling sessions. The array of sessions varied depending on the counselor, from quick check-ins with people who would merely skim the surface of our emotions to others who delved deep into the labyrinth of our feelings, meticulously taking notes as we spilled our innermost thoughts. They were a monthly requirement for those of us living in the group home, a mandate set by BCS, but I got the sense Henry often 'forgot' about them because he was afraid that we would confess to our counselors how poorly he treated us.

In contrast, Twill ensured that we met this requirement, recognizing the importance of these appointments in helping us navigate the complex emotional terrain of our lives. The sessions occurred at a mental health facility in West Goshen township, which served both residential and outpatient clients. This facility welcomed visitors seeking counseling, as well as long-term residents and patients who coexisted in shared spaces. There was a distinct quality to the atmosphere that encouraged a sense of camaraderie despite the personal challenges each of us faced. It was an environment that fostered both connections and healthy competition.

The ping pong table, a refuge for many of us, stood as a symbolic centerpiece. Whenever we gathered for our counseling sessions, it was as if the table called out to us, beckoning us to engage in spirited duels of athleticism and strategy. It was a sanctuary where the rhythm of the bouncing ball replaced the drumbeat of our troubles. Iszel assumed the mantle of table tennis champion. His nimble moves and keen eye made him a formidable opponent. He ran the table, only occasionally letting one of us snatch a lucky victory.

As we embarked on these counseling sessions over the years, it often felt like the problems that plagued us remained unresolved. The purpose, in my young mind, was to seek solutions, to mend the tears in our lives. However, the more I took part, the more I realized that the process focused more on unraveling the complex web of thoughts, feelings, and experiences within us and learning how to cope with the emotions they brought up.

One counselor stands out in my memory as different from the rest. Instead of unearthing my problems and dissecting them like a surgeon, he offered me a chessboard. He used the ancient game to build a connection, fostering rapport through strategic battles on the board. His mastery of the chess pieces intrigued me. With every move, he revealed the intricate dance of intellect, and it drew me in. I became a willing student, eager to learn the secrets of the game. Our sessions transformed into a battleground of wits, a war of moves and countermoves. Chess became our language, transcending the need for spoken words. It was a bond built on silent understanding, where every move on the board reflected the unspoken thoughts and feelings within. The counselor helped me realize that sometimes, the most profound connections are formed in the absence of words.

As the months went by, I continued to engage in these counseling sessions. They served as a sounding board, a space where I could pour out the thoughts and emotions that swirled within me. But it wasn't just the chess games that made these appointments unique. The willingness to be open and confront our demons varied among the residents. While I was eager to share and explore my feelings, the older guys in the house were less willing to spend any real amount of time examining their internal landscape. Their reluctance was obvious, as if acknowledging their emotions was a sign of weakness. The ping pong table remained their safe space, an arena for laughter and camaraderie, but counseling sessions were met with resistance.

Although I might not have understood it at the time, these counseling sessions were the stepping stones toward healing. They allowed me to confront my fears, insecurities, and the weight of my past. They became a journey of self-exploration, a path toward understanding the intricate maze of emotions that defined my existence. They were the moments when I learned to put words to my pain, to understand my rage, to face the demons that lurked within. Each session chipped away at the walls I had built, allowing me to embrace vulnerability. In the end, it wasn't about finding easy answers; it was about the process of unraveling and discovering myself and finding a way to cope with difficulties in a healthy manner. It was a journey without a fixed destination, a path that led me toward self-acceptance and the power to navigate the twists and turns of life with resilience.

CHAPTER 27

Behind Bars

Twill kept us out of school one day during the Spring of 1989, my Freshman year, and surprised us with a trip to visit our mother in prison. It had to be a huge undertaking for her to organize the visit, well beyond the scope of what an average house parent would do to keep a family connection intact. Twill would have needed to provide information for all of us to the prison system, and our mother would have had to add all of us to her list to coordinate a visit. My anticipation was high, and my emotions were all over the place. I was happy to soon see her but saddened about where she was at. More than anything, though, I wanted her to be okay.

We set out to visit my mother at State Correctional Institute Muncy, a women's prison in Pennsylvania. I was laden with a mixture of anticipation and trepidation. The facility, nestled three hours away from the House on the Hill, stood as a daunting reminder of the stark realities she faced. As we approached the imposing walls topped with razor wire, my heart carried the weight of the time that had passed since I last saw her as a free woman—over two long years.

The journey itself unfolded through winding roads, a metaphorical path mirroring the twists and turns of our shared destiny. Each mile felt like a poignant marker of the distance between her confinement and my freedom. As I entered the prison gates, a wave of emotions washed over me—sadness, anxiety, and an unspoken yearning for the days when our interactions were not confined by steel bars.

I felt uneasy walking through the prison corridors. The white walls, metal doors, and protocols to get through them were unsettling. When we arrived at the visiting area, it was empty of people, a carpeted room with multi-colored chairs facing each other that were bolted to the floor, serving as the backdrop for our reunion. The harsh fluorescent lights seemed to cast a pallor over the room, further emphasizing the stark reality of the circumstances.

We all paced the room, waiting for her to emerge from behind the large metal door that separated us from the main part of the prison. My fourteen-year-old mind was spinning in overdrive. *There is no way we're going to be able to break her out of this place. There's no reason to be here if she's not coming with us.* I needed to formulate a plan or at least figure out what Twill's was. I eventually stopped pacing and stood focused on the door she was supposed to enter from across the room, trying to catch a glimpse of her through the small, metal-laced window within it.

There was a distant buzzer, and the large metal door was pushed open. Our mother's slight figure emerged, clad in the institutional garb that erased any semblance of personal identity. The contrast between the woman I knew and the prisoner before me was stark. She smiled, but it didn't reach her eyes. She was happy to see us, but I could tell she hated us seeing her like that. We were too overwhelmed to care and nearly tackled her off her feet, hugging her tightly. Twill waited patiently. The guard allowed the family embrace to go on for a couple of minutes but eventually required us to separate. Then, even though they'd never met, our 'mothers' embraced like sisters. They separated and shared an unspoken moment, looking at each other, Twill silently assuring her that we were okay, our mother expressing appreciation to the elder woman for doing so. They embraced again, the second time a bit tighter and longer.

It was a special moment, seeing these two women, who had both played pivotal roles in my life, meeting under such circumstances. Twill had become my protector, my guiding light in this uncertain world, while my biological mother had been absent for so long, imprisoned. They shared a connection that was born from their love for us and their shared responsibility for our well-being.

Our mother's eyes welled up with tears as she looked at us, her children, whom she hadn't seen in years. "You've all grown so much," she whispered, her voice trembling with emotion.

I nodded, struggling to hold back my tears. "We missed you, Mom."

She smiled a fragile but genuine smile and reached out to hold each of our hands. It was a bittersweet reunion, one that held both the joy of seeing our mother again and the harsh reality of the prison bars that separated us. We spent our allotted time as visitors sharing stories, catching up on life, and reassuring her that, thanks to Twill, we were doing well.

As our visiting time ended, the guard signaled for us to prepare to leave. Our mother hugged us tightly once more, her words filled with love and hope for our future. Twill and our mother promised to stay in touch.

Leaving the prison that day was a mixture of emotions. It was heartwarming to have seen our mother, to have hugged her, to hear her voice. But the sadness of leaving her behind in that stark, unforgiving place hung heavy in the air. We walked back through those corridors, the white walls and metal doors a stark reminder of the world she was trapped in. Twill held our hands as we stepped back out into the free world, a world that suddenly felt so much brighter but also filled with the weight of the past and a more keenly felt emptiness in place of where our mother should be.

CHAPTER 28

The Empty Seats

That same spring of my freshman year, I started track and field midway through the season. It was initially just to try out something new and keep busy, but I found myself enjoying it. The adrenaline rush of competition and the physical challenge of running fueled my enjoyment. It offered the perfect blend of necessary determination, exhilarating speed, and the thrill of crossing the finish line. Each track meet presented not just an opportunity to push my limits but also a chance to revel in the camaraderie and shared passion for the sport.

However, I also keenly felt the absence of a parent or a guardian during the season, as almost every other team member had a cheering section in the stands. Ever since elementary school, I faced a constant reminder of my unique situation as a group home kid—the absence of a parental figure in the audience during my pivotal moments. Whether it was performing in a show, competing in track and field, singing in the choir, or receiving awards and accolades like my classmates, I had to navigate these significant moments without the reassuring presence of a loving face in the crowd. The current house parents, as much as they cared for us, couldn't always be there for every event. They had their responsibilities at the house, taking care of seven other guys and their own lives.

It was a challenging reality to accept, and it stung every time I stood on a stage, trackside, or at the front of a classroom, knowing that there wouldn't be a familiar face cheering me on. I remember those nights vividly. The spotlight shining on me as I performed, the adrenaline pumping through my veins as I raced down the track, and the harmonious melodies echoing in the concert hall—all met with a stark emptiness in the seats where my family should have been. It was a void that no amount of applause or accolades could fill.

And we did achieve accolades. We would come home with medals, trophies, and ribbons, tangible proof of our achievements. I would carefully place them in a box, a treasure chest of accomplishments that no parent would ever see. Iszel, I imagined, did the same, his room becoming a shrine to his own successes.

Without the parental presence of congratulations or condolences, Iszel and I became each other's cheerleaders instead. We were a support system born out of necessity. When the final notes of a performance faded or when the last race was run, we didn't have parents waiting in the audience with open arms. Instead, we would find each other amidst the crowd, our faces beaming with pride and our hearts filled with a unique bond that only we could understand. Our presence at each other's events didn't completely erase the sting of the empty seats, but it helped to ease the burden of it. It was just one aspect of our very complex brotherly bond, born of love and trauma and shared understanding. And that, in its own way, made us stronger than any accolade ever could.

CHAPTER 29

Bonds & Breaks

In early June of 1989, one year under Twill's care, she called Iszel and me into the office. Jacque was sitting in the corner, tears flowing from his eyes. She took a sip of her tea and placed a consoling arm around his shoulders.

"Elliott and Iszel, I wanna talk to you about some things that Jacque and I have been discussing."

She gestured to the other two chairs in the office. The space was small, crammed with furniture and a desk with locked filing cabinets in it. It could feel claustrophobic with the wrong people seated inside; it always had with the Hills. Here, with Twill, the space felt warm and comfortable.

"Jacque, you good?" I asked, head nodding in his general direction. "What's up, man?"

"Yo, I'm just tired, y'all. I'm tired of always having to watch y'all's backs. Tired of fighting." He had a ball of tissue in his hand and wiped his wet face. He hated for us to see him cry because he cried ugly. His attempt to control his emotions caused him to hiss instead of moan. His tears flowed and wet his whole face like he was crying from his whole eyes instead of just the inner corners, and his nose ran profusely. It was horrible to see, especially knowing it was my big brother falling apart. It hurt me to see my superhero in pain.

Twill's voice was heavy but reassuring. "Boys, Jacque is tired, but he also feels guilty for wanting a break from the responsibility of looking out for you guys. Do you both understand that?"

THOSE BOYS ON THE HILL

Jacque was a month from 17, finishing his junior year of high school. He had watched over Iszel and me without fail ever since that day outside of Aunt Linda's house when he was 12. Our mother's words were a burden on him. He hadn't had a real childhood, being the oldest of three brothers, watching our backs all those years. I hated seeing him like that. "Man, you know we good now. We're old enough and big enough to take care of ourselves."

Iszel chimed in. "Yeah, and we have Twill now. It's not like it was when the Hills were here. Besides, you know we got each other's backs now."

Jacque's crumpled body heaved when he heard this. Like an invisible yoke being thrown from around his neck. He searched our faces, seeking further reassurance.

"Y'all know I love y'all, right?" he whispered through the large, emotional ball in his throat. His attempts to hold back his tears failed and flowed uncontrollably again.

Iszel and I didn't answer. Instead, we collectively stood up and pulled him into a group hug.

"We know you got us, man," I assured him. "It's all good."

He rested the weight of his body on ours and allowed himself to be supported by us. Twill wrapped her large, delicate wingspan around the three of us. Her motherly touch allowed us to be free with our emotions, and I began to cry along with my brother.

"Y'all be messing up moments with all these damn tears," teased Iszel, who remained poised. Twill allowed the cuss word to pass without scolding him. His comment broke the heaviness of the moment, and we all began to laugh.

"Ikey, you stupid man," Jacque joked. Iszel only allowed a few people to still call him by his childhood nickname.

I looked at my big brother. "Yo, you good man?"

He looked exhausted but relieved and nodded.

"Yeah, man, I'm good," Jacque assured us. And for a while, he genuinely was. After years of tirelessly watching out for us, it was as if a weight had been lifted from his shoulders, and he finally let loose. All too soon, though, a familiar nemesis reared its ugly head and crept back into our lives.

We'd grown up witnessing our mother's struggles with drugs, along with other family members and their acquaintances who spiraled into the same destructive patterns. The memories of those times, of the pain and chaos that drugs had brought into our lives, were etched into our souls.

Signs of Jacque's drug use began to appear, like the occasional dazed look in his eyes and the faint scent of weed lingering on his clothes. It was a stark contrast to the responsible and protective Jacque we had grown used to. One Saturday evening, all of these signals would converge, forever altering my relationship with my older brother.

I found a small bong in the driveway, which, with his change in behavior, I assumed must be Jacque's. He was following in the same dangerous footsteps as my mom. I paced for a while, trying to figure out what to do, and decided to wait up for him.

It was a long wait, extending into the early hours of the morning before he returned from his night of partying with his friend Gavin. When he finally returned home, he looked burnt out and tired.

I stepped down off the porch and held up the bong. "Yo man! What's this?!"

He smiled and grabbed it out of my hand. "Yooo," he exclaimed happily, "I've been looking for this. Where'd you find it?"

"Where did I find it?!" I asked incredulously. "What are you doing with it? When did you start smoking like that?"

"Are you serious right now, man?" he retorted. "You know I smoke weed. I don't hide that from you. I use this to make the high stronger." He shrugged off my concern.

"I can't get down with that," I disagreed. "Not after all the shit drugs did to us. Now you're out here with asshole Gavin doing what our mother did. You look and smell like shit. I can't stand that dude."

Jacque's face hardened. "Get outta' here, man!" he shouted at me. "You ain't gotta like Gavin. You ain't gotta like none of my friends. He's my friend, not yours. You don't tell me who I hang with. I don't know where you found this, but stay the fuck out of my shit."

I flashed back to the many instances I had witnessed drugs being a negative driving force in my life, to the point where they'd taken on a presence of their own, like malevolent spirits lurking in the shadows. Drugs were anathema to me. Jacque's smoking wasn't the first time our family had faced this adversary; rather, it had been a generational problem that stretched back as far as our grandparents. I blamed them for all of my mother's problems, and they were inextricably linked to some of my most traumatizing memories from our time in North Philly.

CHAPTER 30

Childhood Nemesis

When I was four, I saw my mom and her boyfriend bagging weed on his dining table. There were mounds of it all over the place. My mom and her boyfriend were joking with each other, drinking and smoking while they worked, the room filled with the pungent scent of it. They laughed at 3-year-old Iszel, arching on his tippy toes to grab my mom's beer and take a sip. It was entertaining to see my little brother drunkenly stumble around.

Amidst the commotion, with a giant, pungent pile of weed on the table, I couldn't help but feel unhappy at the sight of it. Even then, at such a tender age, I had an innate sense that I didn't like how my mother acted when she smoked and drank. Impulsively, I scooped up a couple of handfuls of the precious weed and bolted through the beaded doorway that separated me from the kitchen, the multicolored bits of plastic clinking together behind me. I raced across the linoleum, my destination, the bathroom.

As I burst through the door, my heart raced with a mix of exhilaration and dread. The sterile tiles offered a moment of reprieve as I swiftly deposited my handfuls into the toilet bowl. My mother's boyfriend, a man entrenched in a world of illicit dealings, was mere inches behind me, desperate to thwart me. His furious voice was a thunderous backdrop as he reached out to stop me, his fingers clawing at my shoulders. He was too late. With a determined press of the lever, the contraband swirled away into oblivion.

I knew, in that moment, that what I had just flushed down the toilet was valuable. I was immediately lifted off my feet, the room spinning in a disorienting whirlwind as he shook me, his rage reverberating through my small frame. The world became a disorienting blur, my vision clouded by panic and disarray. Then, he began to spank me mercilessly with his belt. Each blow slashed across my backside was a painful reminder of my audacity, and I could feel the sting and the warmth of my skin reddening beneath his assault.

Just as I thought I might pass out from the pain and fear, my mother intervened. Her voice, a mixture of anger and concern, cut through my panic. She demanded an end to the violence, and for the first time that day, her presence provided a glimmer of solace. He kept swinging the belt, hitting me for my offense, and landing a couple of slashes on my mother to protect me. He eventually stopped and left us huddled together in the bathroom.

***

That was only the first emotional scar. When I was seven, I witnessed a near overdose of one of my mother's best friends, Aunt Doll. My mother's life had spiraled into a maelstrom of tough times and legal troubles, leaving her with no choice but to arrange for us all to live with one of her closest friends, whom we affectionately called Aunt Doll. Much like our mother, Aunt Doll was ensnared by the clutches of addiction, with her drug of choice being heroin.

One afternoon, my mother asked Aunt Doll to babysit while she ventured out for a good time. We stayed on the first floor, our eyes fixed on the television screen, the volume kept at a hushed level in deference to the possibility that Aunt Doll might be in a drug-induced slumber upstairs. The relative tranquility was shattered by Aunt Doll's piercing screams. Her voice was high-pitched, laced with panic and urgency, calling out our names. We dashed up the stairs, hearts pounding in our chests, and arrived at her closed bedroom door. We knocked, and Jacque called out to her, his voice trembling.

"Aunt Doll, you alright?"

"Boys, help me, please!" she shrieked.

Jacque opened the door timidly. What we saw was fuel for my nightmares: Aunt Doll's partially naked body was contorted into an unnatural position, her fingers clawed, her whole body frozen and rigid. A hypodermic needle protruded from her arm, coupled with a brown belt, still pulled taut around it. Her eyes welled with tears, and she cried out, "Help me!! Elliott, go get your mom!!"

I raced down the stairs and burst through the door, my heart pounding with fear and uncertainty. We had not lived in Aunt Doll's neighborhood long enough for me to be familiar with the surroundings. Panic gripped me as I scanned the unfamiliar streets, desperately searching for where to go. At last, I spotted a bar. Without hesitation, I barged through the entrance, startling the patrons and the bartender. His voice boomed, "Who's fuckin' kid is this? Get him outta here." But I had no time for social niceties. My mother was among the patrons, enjoying the company of her friends. She rose swiftly, her anger obvious as she demanded to know why I had intruded upon her night. Afraid of her wrath, I blurted out, "Aunt Doll is in trouble."

Her anger transformed into urgency as she grabbed me by the shoulders, forcefully turning me towards the exit and pushing me through the door. We hurried back to Aunt Doll's house, where my mother shouted, "Doll?! Doll Baby?!"

Aunt Doll's voice responded, a mix of pain and desperation echoing from upstairs. My mother's face contorted with fear as she rushed towards her girlfriend. "I told you not to get that shit from Johnny. Told you his shit ain't no good," my mother chastised, her voice trembling.

Jacque was on the line with 911, and my mother snatched the phone from his hand. She ordered us to leave the room, and we retreated downstairs.

The wailing sirens of an approaching ambulance heralded the arrival of emergency responders, but Aunt Doll's body remained in a drug-induced muscle rigor. Their attempts to reposition her onto a gurney were met with her agonized screams of pain. They had no choice but to carry her in the contorted state she was in, the brown belt still strapped around her arm, but the needle was now removed.

As the ambulance disappeared into the distance, carrying away the stiff body of Aunt Doll, I couldn't shake the haunting image of her contorted body and the torment she had endured. It was a stark reminder of the devastating toll that addiction had taken on those we loved.

***

The final vivid memory I have that solidified my hatred for drugs happened a few weeks later. It was a scorching summer day in North Philly. Iszel and I were headed to our aunt's house on Bainbridge Street. The sun beat down mercilessly on the cracked pavement, casting long, unforgiving shadows on the worn-out facades of the houses that lined the block.

After Aunt Doll's bad drug experience, we moved into a two-bedroom place of our own. Jacque was visiting our cousin Jason for the day. Iszel and I had been moping around the mostly empty house, our stomachs grumbling from lack of food. It was an all-too-common story for us. Poverty and hunger often took precedence over childhood adventures.

My mother, weary and with nothing but an empty fridge to offer us, sent us on a mission to my Aunt Bubble's house, who had offered to help. She had instructed our mother to send us over to her place to get something to eat, and off we went, eager to comply.

Our hearts racing with anticipation for the meal that awaited us as we turned the corner onto Bainbridge Street. The gritty reality of our surroundings was nothing out of the ordinary. The dilapidated houses bore the scars of time, their once-bright paint now faded and peeling. The streets were littered with discarded wrappers and empty bottles, and the distant hum of sirens was a constant background noise.

What we didn't expect to see was an argument already in full swing between two men, their voices harsh and desperate. We approached cautiously, the air thick with tension.

We deduced that the angry man was a drug dealer and the desperate man, a hopeful client, begging for just one more fix. The dealer's face was a mask of frustration and rage. He yelled, "I told you what would happen if you ain't have my money!"

In the blink of an eye, he pulled out a handgun and shot the man in the head right in front of us. Time seemed to stand still. The deafening roar of the gunshot echoed through the narrow streets, my ears rang, and I could hear nothing for a moment but the whooshing of my own heartbeat.

Then time resumed its normal pace, and the man's body fell to the ground with a sickening thud, twitching. His blood oozed onto the sunbaked concrete, pooling around him.

The drug dealer, his eyes devoid of any remorse, saw Iszel and me frozen in place. He waved us away, screaming at us with his gun hand, his voice a terrifying crescendo of anger and power. "Get outta here, you damn kids!!"

Tears welled up in my eyes as we ran past the drug dealer and the lifeless man's body. Our destination was clear in our minds. We knew that our aunt's house was our refuge, where the promise of food and safety awaited. The street blurred around us, but the image of the murdered man and the echoing gunshot remained etched in my mind. I couldn't help but look back one last time as curiosity battled with fear within me. The drug dealer, now an embodiment of callousness and indifference, was frantically searching the dead man's pockets, the value of his life reduced to whatever he found inside them.

***

I understood objectively by the time I was in high school that drugs were a symptom of the problem of poverty and oppression.

They offered an alluring, if temporary, escape for seemingly inescapable problems. But emotionally, they were the sum total of the enemy, and Jacque had no good reason or excuse to fall into them. Instead, without protest, perhaps even willingly, Jacque had become their latest victim, ensnared by the same demons that had claimed so many in our bloodline and North Philly.

The moment I laid eyes on him, I could see the unmistakable signs that drugs were getting the best of him – his eyes, once bright, had grown spacy and hooded. His speech, once a source of guidance and comfort, was now slow and slurred, as if words themselves were a struggle. When he moved, he was a mere shadow of his former self, leaning and slumping. It was devastating to me. The vibrant spirit that had once defined my older brother, my role model, was now obscured by a suffocating haze of addiction.

I hated drugs with a passion that burned deep within me, and that hate welled up in a sudden rage. Before I even knew what I was doing, I punched Jacque hard in the face. I didn't hold back when I threw it. I didn't see my big brother anymore.

Jacque, who was normally a lot faster than me, may have avoided the hit if not for his inebriation. Instead, he took the full blow to his jaw and went down. Surprised, he scurried back up and punched me back. The blow hurt, but my anger had overtaken me. My stocky 14-year-old frame had just gone through a growth spurt, and except for Jacques' height, we were pretty close in size despite our nearly 3-year age gap.

He was a better fighter than me, so I grabbed him, and we wrestled, rolling around the graveled driveway. I heard the glass bong break in his pocket, and it must have cut him. He yelped and fought me off. He stood up to inspect the cut that was now bleeding.

I was not through and stood to deliver another punch. Twill had descended the porch steps, pajamas flapping, and pushed past him. With no thought for her own safety, she grabbed me in a tackle. We went down in a pile, her thin frame on top of me, pinning me down.

Seeing it was Twill, I didn't fight her off. "Elliott, what's wrong with you?!" she demanded. I didn't answer her. I was done. I just stared past her to Jacque. He looked down at me. "Stay the fuck outta my shit," he warned.

Shocked by his language, Twill chided him. "Jacque!" He turned and walked up the porch steps and into the house.

Twill let me up, and we stood. She rested a hand on my shoulder and asked, "Elliott, what was that all about?" I could feel a lump under my eye where Jacque's punch had landed and started to swell.

"Nothing," I said, shrugging her hand off my shoulder. I dusted myself off and started up the porch stairs.

"Elliott, come back here!" Twill demanded. I couldn't even look at her.

I stood at the top of the porch steps and asked quietly, "Can we talk about it later, Twill? I really don't want to get into it right now."

I didn't wait for her to answer, and she didn't call out. I opened the door and went inside, trudging upstairs to the big bathroom to clean up. Looking in the mirror, I began to cry angrily. I hated drugs! I hated everything they had done to my life.

Gavin's car pulled up the driveway not long thereafter. I could see it out of the bathroom window. Jacque walked out of the house towards the car. I heard Twill call out to him. He stopped for a beat, standing with the car door open in his hand. He didn't look back in the direction of Twill. Instead, he climbed inside, and they drove off down the hill. He was gone for the rest of the weekend. When he did return home, it was for a change of clothes. I lost my big brother, my hero. Drugs fractured us. I didn't see Jacque the same after that.

Jacque graduated from high school that summer and left for boot camp in the Army. The tension between us had never been resolved. It hung over our heads, a silent reminder of the fight in the driveway. I didn't even see him off when he left.

After he left, I felt a mixture of emotions – relief, regret, and a gnawing sense that I should have done more to bridge the gap that had grown between us. The guilt of our unresolved conflict weighed heavy on me, but I didn't know how to mend the rift that had been caused by his drug use and my reaction to it.

In his absence, the memories of that day in the driveway haunted me, and I couldn't help but wonder if I had pushed him further away when he needed support the most. The bond between two brothers, once strong, had been shattered, and I wasn't sure if it could ever be fully repaired.

Iszel found himself caught in the middle of our strained relationship. He stayed neutral, trying to bridge the gap between the two of us, but it was no easy task. Iszel often served as the mediator, the observer of our silent war, navigating the minefield of emotions that surrounded us. He loved us both, and he couldn't bear to see us torn apart. Iszel's presence offered a glimmer of hope that someday, the bonds of brotherhood might be mended.

CHAPTER 31

Bonds in Transition

Throughout the years, foster kids came and went for several reasons: from returning home, being removed for egregiously breaking a rule, being fostered, graduating high school, or aging out and opting to leave the house as an adult before graduation. The revolving door of the group home system remained in full spin, only stopping briefly for the House on the Hill when full, which was eight boys max. Over the nine years that I lived there, I became 'brothers' with 70 or so other guys, not counting Jacque and Iszel. Some people stuck, though, like Bruce and Ray.

Bruce was three years my junior, generally a straight shooter with the occasional wild streak, like when he excitedly ran into the ocean on a trip Dave Lichter took us on to Ocean City, Maryland. Only Bruce couldn't actually swim, and a wave pulled him under. Dave frantically shouted at me, the oldest boy and best swimmer among us, to save him. I managed to haul him out safely, much to Dave's great relief. It was one of the many little moments of comradery that group home kids experience that bonded us.

Ray was six years my junior. He was an easy-going, athletic kid who grew up in the same part of North Philly that I did. In fact, I had been in first grade with one of his older sisters. We hit it off with our shared love of street gymnastics. We used to egg each other on to do increasingly death-defying stunts off our back porch, not as a form of competition, but just to see what we could do.

Ray became close to another of the long-term residents, Tim. Tim was the only white kid in the home but had been there a couple of years and had survived the initial taunts of being so. By then, he was accepted amongst us as one of *Those Boys*. The community and his classmates thought so, too; they treated him as poorly as they treated the Black kids. His association with the house was enough to justify discriminating against him despite his white skin. He was our brother, and we covered him as we did any other living with us.

He was still very connected to his home in the Kensington neighborhood of Philly. His mother and father would drive up to the house to collect him for home visits. Kensington was a bit further away for an 11-year-old to travel on public transportation by himself. It was riddled with drugs, shootings, and murder. That part of the city was constantly on the news.

Tim's parents were trying to kick their drug habit and working closely with his social worker to regain custody of their son. They would come up and look clean, but it was obvious when they fell off. A month or two would go by, and they would be clean again. It was a sad cycle to watch, but they kept trying. Their continued efforts made me a bit envious but happy for him. I had given up on the idea of ever returning home. With my mother in prison and me avoiding home visits because of Jason, there was little hope of me ever returning to the Glovers.

Reunification was always a long shot in foster care, though, anyway.[19] The federal government invests ten times as much in fostering and adopting than they do in reunification, despite it being touted as the goal. Ironically, there is more incentive and money to be made (by private institutions) and less money to be lost (by the government) in fostering and adoption than there is in reunification.[20]

***

Overall, our group home had a good dynamic. It would shift again in the summer of 1990 when Jacque and Derek graduated and aged out, leaving two spots to fill.

Twill called me to the kitchen to an all too familiar scene of two new boys, each holding trash bags full of their possessions.

"Elliott, this is Keith and Reggie; they're joining our house." She looked at the two new guys. "Boys, I want you to meet Elliott. He's the oldest guy in the house." She had a way of saying 'Oldest in the house' that inspired a feeling of responsibility in me.

I gave a cordial nod to them. They both looked to be around 12. "What's up, Fellaz?" I asked, reaching to shake their hands. Keith adjusted his bag from his right to his left to return the courtesy enthusiastically. He was dark-skinned and slight, lanky even. Reggie was light-skinned and stocky. He was too bogged down to return my shake. He had two full, large garbage bags and seemed more concerned about holding onto his belongings than greeting me. I instantly understood his need to cling to them. His whole life was in those bags. Every important thing that tied him back to his home and life experiences. A knick-knack that his mother gave him or a small award he earned and felt proud of. Though my belongings had been hand-me-down clothes, I'd had the same concern for my bags years ago. I withdrew my hand, and we settled on a head nod instead.

"You two brothers or just coming through at the same time?" I asked.

"Naw, we just know each other from around the way and Main Campus. Look at us. He like a Milky Way, and I'm dark chocolate all the way through." Keith laughed at his joke, but it fell flat for the rest of us. Reggie seemed blasé about it, like he'd heard it a thousand times, and gave up on trying to convince Keith to stop telling it.

Twill broke the exchange. She rested her hand on my shoulder and said, "Elliott, I need you to get the boys settled while I start dinner. Grab some linens, towels, and washcloths, and help them get their rooms together." She paused, then said, "Oh! And have them grab some school supplies from the office. Let them choose their favorite colors for the bookbags and books." She was always attuned to stuff like that.

I got them up to speed on the rules, the in-house hierarchy, and the dynamics between the boys and the house parents. They fit in just like most that came through the house. Reggie followed me around like a small duckling to its mother for weeks, taking an interest in everything I did. It grew to be uncomfortable, and I could never put my finger on what was driving it. I eventually told him so, and he eased off. Keith kept to himself mostly, choosing to explore the house, the grounds, and the barn. He and Reggie hung around with each other when we weren't having a meal or doing a houseparent-led activity by Twill, Mr. Brown, Wilma, or Wayne.

***

One cool October afternoon, Ray, Bruce, and I were leaving the barn after playing some basketball and riding bikes. I heard Tim's shrill, high-pitched voice screaming out of the big bathroom window. It was primal and filled with pain. I ran up to see what was happening. I knocked and tried the door handle, which was unlocked. I opened it and walked in, giving him a once over, figuring he must have hurt himself. His face was deep red and moist from tears.

I sat on the radiator facing him. "Yo man, you good?" I inquired.

"No, I ain't good, man. I hate it here." He was still facing the open window, and a cool breeze blew in. It rustled his dirty blond hair, and he rested his hands on the sill, his head falling between his slight shoulders. He shook it like he was trying to sort through tangled thoughts.

"You wanna talk about it, lil bro? I may not be able to change what's up, but I will listen to all you want."

There was a slight knock on the open door, and Twill was standing on the threshold, concern on her face. "You two alright in here?"

I nodded in her direction. *I got this.* I turned my attention back to assessing Tim further. "Yeah, I think we're good," I said. "Just chewin' it up a lil bit."

She nodded with understanding and disappeared out of view, leaving the door slightly ajar.

I waited until I could hear her heading down the step and asked, "Yo, what up, man? You yellin' out the window like that had me ready to come knock somebody around in this piece. You need me to serve someone up some knuckle pie?" The statement drew an appreciative smile and a small chuckle. He knew I was serious.

"Nah, just missing my folks. I don't think they gonna be getting me no time soon. Stuff like that and all." He said the 'And all' like there was a loaded message in it. I wondered what he meant, but I didn't push. He was talking, at least.

I decided to keep prodding gently by joking. "Because you lookin' a bit crazy yelling out this window at no one."

His face darkened, and he peered out of the window again. "I ain't yellin' at *no one*." He burst into angry tears and blurted, "I'm yellin' at God." His whole body shuddered at that. His arms were going to fail him as they buckled a bit.

I stood to steady him, but he waved me off. I sat back on the radiator. "Yeah, I feel you on that one," I said. "I get mad at Him too. Especially when I first got here. What did He do this time?"

"He just let shit happen to me. That ain't the way it's s'posed to go, right? He ain't looking after us like they say He would. Like he forgot about us. Like us, group home kids don't count."

"Man, we're the strongest because we've been through it all. I don't know what the big plan is for kids like us, but we good as long as we stick together. You know I gotcha back, right?" I asked.

"Yeah," he answered.

"We can talk or just hang in silence," I said.

He nodded and wiped his face with his sleeve.

"Now you gonna have dried snot on your shirt. That shit gonna dry up and get hard. Gonna scratch your face the next time you go to wipe one of them heavy tears away." We laughed at the crude joke. "Yo, you're in a bathroom. Just wash your face and come hang with me in the rec room. Cool?" I asked. "And you gotta change that snotty shirt too."

"A'ight," he responded. Tim smiled, walked to the sink, turned it on, and splashed water on his face.

"And if you feel like you wanna scream at God again. Come get me, and we'll do it together so you don't look crazy alone." I walked over to the open window and quietly searched the dark sky, trying to see beyond the stars to the Big Man up there, and said quietly, "Besides, I have some choice words for Him, too."

The next few weeks, Tim chilled with me as much as he could. One evening, as Tim and I were hanging out in my room, he opened up about his feelings again. He had been doing better overall, but the pain of missing his parents still lingered.

"You know, sometimes it's hard," Tim began, his voice soft. "I miss my folks a lot, man. Even though they mess up sometimes, they're still my parents."

I nodded in understanding. "I get that, Tim. It's okay to miss them. We all have our moments."

"Yeah," he sighed, running a hand through his dirty blond hair. "But it's like... I don't know if they'll ever get it together. And what if I never get to live with them again?"

I could see the worry in his eyes, and it tugged at my heart because I knew exactly how that felt. I was going to be at the House on the Hill until I graduated. I wanted to reassure him, to tell him everything would be okay, but I couldn't make promises I couldn't keep. Just then, Mr. Martin, the old cat with seven pads on each paw, entered my room. He must have sensed Tim's need for comfort and solace. Tim reached down to pet him, and Mr. Martin obligingly allowed him to pick him up and settled in his lap, purring softly.

"I can't predict the future, lil bro," I said honestly. "But what I do know is that you're a strong kid, and you've got a lot of people here who care about you. We're like a family here, you know?"

Tim nodded, a small smile playing on his lips. "Yeah, you're right. I'm lucky to have you, Twill, and everyone else here." He paused, then corrected himself. "Well, almost everyone."

"You know how family can be sometimes. You can't choose them, but that's the spirit," I replied, giving him a playful punch on the shoulder.

Tim chuckled, and we continued chatting, sharing stories and laughter. Our bond grew stronger with each passing day, and I was grateful for the friendship we had formed.

As the weeks passed, Tim and I grew closer, spending more time together both at school and at home. We discovered comfort in each other's presence, whether we were fishing by the creek on Indian Run Road or Mr. Pusey's farm, surrounded by the many slow, peaceful cows chewing their cud, as we cast our rods into the large pond on his property. Tim would sometimes watch my track practices, sit in the back of the high school auditorium during musical rehearsals, or simply hang out in my room. Twill would occasionally need to gently remind him of his bedtime, recognizing that he sought and benefited from the support and companionship we had formed.

Life at home wasn't perfect, but having Tim as a friend and "brother" made it a little easier to bear. I hoped that one day, Tim would be reunited with his parents under better circumstances. Until then, we had each other, and that was enough to keep us going.

CHAPTER 32

Inevitable Clash of Paths

By the time my sophomore year rolled around, I had established a reputation as a popular student. My involvement in talent shows, choir, musicals, and especially track and field had earned me recognition not only among my peers but also in local newspapers. The Philadelphia Inquirer had even featured an article about Iszel and me, highlighting our journey from Philly to the Avondale Group Home for Boys and the remarkable achievements we had made in our lives despite our turbulent childhood.

In September, as the school year began, I found myself enrolled in a metal shop class, an unexpected turn of events that took me by surprise. A shop class was a prerequisite requirement for graduation. Unfortunately, the class was taught by none other than John's father, Mr. Taylor. It felt like fate had conspired to bring us face to face. Mr. Taylor's stern gaze bore into me during roll call on the very first day of class. With the way he was glaring at me, he clearly knew who I was.

Class took place standing in a room with concrete floors with tall, metal table workstations. I couldn't help but feel a sense of unease as he assigned me a shop partner. To my dismay, my partner turned out to be Jared Smith, a kid who had once been a part of John's circle. He was one of the kids that backed John when we attended Outdoor Education. Jared was built like a seasoned farmhand with a naturally muscular physique. I felt significantly smaller by comparison and couldn't shake the feeling that this pairing was deliberate, as though I was being set up for trouble.

Mr. Taylor didn't mince words. He approached me under the harsh fluorescent light, his expression angry, his voice low and venomous.

"Mister Elliott Glover, I've been waitin' for this moment for a long time, boy." He emphasized 'Boy' contemptuously, an unspoken threat that 'I better know my place, *boy*.'

I turned to face him. Knowing his son, I wasn't about to back down. "Whatchu want, Mr. Taylor?"

His eyes locked onto mine, his hostility evident. "You remember what happened with my boy, don'tcha? Back in 6th grade? You had no right to do what you did to him."

I maintained eye contact, unflinching. "I did what I had to do," I retorted with as much disdain as he was expressing. "He needs to watch how he talks to people. I bet he knows better now, though." His face flushed red at my audacity. "But I'm guessin' the apple doesn't fall far from the tree, does it, Mr. Taylor? Probably learned that ignorance from the very man standin' in front of me."

We stood toe-to-toe. His eyes squinted, and his lips curled into a knowing smile that seemed to stretch from ear to ear, his face a combination of malice and satisfaction. It was the expression of someone who relished the prospect of causing me daily misery. "You think you can just beat up a kid and get away with it, boy? Well, you won't get away with anything in my class," he hissed in his distinctive drawl. I couldn't help but think that his accent was as ridiculous as I found his son's so many years ago.

The other students in the classroom couldn't hear our words, but they watched our intense confrontation, unsure of what was happening. He looked ready to explode as I glared at him. Aware that the class had noticed us standing there like that, he stepped back and began giving instructions for the first project he would assign for a grade.

I decided on self-preservation. Shortly after he backed off to address the class, I left unexcused and headed straight to the school office. There, I met with Assistant Principal Dave Dickens, who patiently listened to my concerns. I explained the history between the Taylor family and me, expressing my belief that Mr. Taylor was targeting me and that I suspected him of being involved with a hate group like the KKK. Assistant Principal Dickens nodded thoughtfully and, without hesitation, rescheduled me to a study hall for that period. He assured me that I would receive credit for the shop class on my transcript. It was a relief to be out of Mr. Taylor's class, and I never had to endure his presence as a teacher again.

From that point on, I only encountered Mr. Taylor passing in the school hallways. These run-ins were rare, especially during class changes when the hallways were full of students. Every time we crossed paths, he would make a point to stop and stare, his eyes locked onto me with a severe, unwavering gaze. His body language exuded resentment, leaving me with an unsettling feeling that he was biding his time, waiting for the opportunity to retaliate. Each brief encounter was a jolting reminder of the unresolved conflict between us, though as time went on, he gradually backed down until he ignored me completely.

Surprisingly, Jared Smith approached me on one occasion. He looked at me earnestly and began, "Elliott, I wanna talk to you. I just wanna make it clear that I'm not like John. I don't think about colored folks like he does." Seeing he was trying to be solid, I excused the way he referenced Black people. "What happened between you and him was a long time ago, and I'm glad you're not in Mr. Taylor's class anymore."

I nodded, "Thanks, Jared. I appreciate that, man."

"You know, Mr. Taylor, he gotta mean streak in eem' especially when it comes to John," Jared continued, then smiled. "So you know he's got plenty of grudges." We laughed at the joke. "I know he was itching to get to you."

I couldn't help but smile at Jared's honesty. We shook hands and went our separate ways to our classes. Jared's words served as a reminder that not everyone held the same hateful beliefs, and there were individuals like him who saw past bigotry and discrimination or who could, over time, change their beliefs.

***

Around the same time that I was dealing with Mr. Taylor, Iszel was having his own struggles with another student. Unbeknownst to me, Iszel was being hazed by a black senior at school named Mike. Emboldened by his seniority, Mike started with cruel words, but he quickly escalated to physical intimidation. He'd slam Iszel against lockers when they passed each other in the hallway, ensuring every encounter was a torment. If they both found themselves at a party, Mike isolated and alienated Iszel, turning what should have been a time of enjoyment into a nightmarish ordeal.

I'm not sure why Iszel never told me directly. He did regale me with an elaborate scenario he'd concocted in his mind, involving a series of about 30 different people fighting, culminating in me getting into it with another classmate, Shawn Garner, who was much larger than I was. Not understanding the root of Iszel's convoluted succession of fights, I told him there was no way in hell I was getting my ass beat in a tag-team style match that ended with my fighting the most athletic guy in school.

Instead of explaining himself more directly, Iszel eventually confided in Jacque, who had always been his confidant. Our older brother would call the group home regularly to speak with him. I still refused to get on the line with Jacque, the wedge as wide as it could be between us. After Iszel finally shared the horrifying truth about the hazing with Jacque, my older brother requested leave from the Army and was eventually granted a week. He decided to use this precious time to visit our mother in Philly and pay a long-awaited visit to us at the group home.

It had been a little over a year since I'd seen him. As he walked through the door, I was taken aback by the transformation that had taken place. He looked good, clean, clear-eyed, and strong. The Army had molded him into a man who had grown beyond his past. I could see the old Jacque, my hero brother, standing before me, only bigger and stronger. His face was animated, a mix of determination and concern.

In that moment, I knew it would be possible for us to repair our relationship. I could no longer contain the weight of my guilt for the fight and the separation it had caused. I asked, "Yo, you good?" My words were loaded with remorse, seeking forgiveness for my role in our estrangement.

Jacque, understanding the depth behind that simple phrase, nodded and asked back, "Yo, we good?" His hands gestured with sincerity, and we gave each other a firm handshake followed by a hearty clap on the back.

Iszel, standing there, shook his head in amusement, saying, "Y'all ain't gonna start cryin' and shit, are y'all?" We laughed, feeling relieved that the Glover Brothers were on the path to rekindling our bond.

However, Jacque's eyes soon fell upon me, and the concern in his gaze was unmistakable. "Yo, how you lettin' Mike act stupid like that to Zel? You're supposed to have his back." His voice reflected a protective older brother's tone. His eyebrows furrowed slightly, emphasizing his concern.

I responded honestly. "Man, I didn't know that shit was goin' on. Zel didn't even tell me other than tryna get me to fight Shawn Garner for some reason."

"Hey, it was a good plan!" Iszel protested. I shook my head at his convoluted logic.

Jacque's expression grew more serious. "A'ight. I guess I'mma hafta go up to the school and settle that shit."

Iszel, grateful for the support, chimed in, "Yeah, we gotta get that squashed. I'm done with Mike and the way he be actin.' Ain't that many black kids in the school, and he wants to pick on me." He shook his head disapprovingly at the thought.

The next day, we walked into high school, and Jacque found Mike hanging with some of his crew.

He walked up to him, his presence oozing authority and a brother's protectiveness. In a stern voice, he warned, "Yo, if I hear anything more about you bullying my little brother, I'm gonna come back and beat your ass. You got me?" His hand rested on Mike's shoulder, a firm grip that sent a clear message.

Mike, realizing the gravity of the situation and the unity of the Glover brothers, didn't even try to defend himself. He simply looked up at the three of us and nodded in acknowledgment. The unspoken message was clear: "Mess with one of us, and you mess with all of us."

In that moment, the bond we had was reaffirmed, and we stood together, resolute in our support for Iszel and our commitment to ensure that he would no longer suffer bullying from anyone at the school again. It was a turning point where the relationship between Jacque and I began the long road to recovery.

CHAPTER 33

One Last Visit

One brisk December afternoon in my Sophomore year, as I practiced my routine for an upcoming talent show in the echoing emptiness of the auditorium, Iszel approached me with an ashen face. His voice trembled, and tears welled up in his eyes.

"Ell, she's gone," he whispered, his voice barely audible.

I halted my singing and dance routine, looking at him with a furrowed brow. "Who's gone?" I asked, expecting that he was about to mention our imprisoned mother.

"Grandma," he choked out, his tears now flowing freely. "She didn't make it through the surgery."

I blinked, the words taking a moment to sink in. "Grandma? But... I haven't seen her in years."

Iszel nodded, his eyes red from crying. "I know, but she's still our family, man."

Our grandmother had been a heavy smoker, and her addiction had led to esophageal cancer. The surgery, a last-ditch effort to save her, was a gamble with a low success rate. Stage IV throat cancer had spread like wildfire through her esophagus. The doctors predicted that without the surgery, she would only have a few months to live.

"She died on the operating room table," Iszel continued. "Granddad is still in the waiting room with Aunt Terry. He doesn't want to leave the hospital."

The news of her passing brought with it a wave of emotions that I had buried deep within. Our family, the Glovers, had been a breeding ground for generational abuse and addictions, and our grandparents had perpetuated this painful cycle. In my life, marred by the trauma of my past experiences and Jason's abuse, I had distanced myself from our extended family for nearly three years, further isolating myself.

I don't think my grandmother would have even known me if I walked in the door without someone reminding her. Even when we lived with my grandparents, I didn't think she liked me much. She had assigned nicknames for all my cousins and Jacque, and that tradition had skipped me. That hurt. I was the nameless one.

As the day of the funeral approached, I felt an obligation to pay my respects to someone I barely knew anymore. So, for the first time in nearly three years, on the day of the funeral, I returned to North Philly. A neighborhood church served as the backdrop for the gathering. Many cousins, aunts, and uncles were present, yet I kept my distance, feeling like a stranger among my own blood. Jacque had taken bereavement leave to be there. He was chatting animatedly with Iszel and Jason. I opted to avoid Jason's presence, haunted by memories of my past with him.

Amidst the crowd, my cousin Helen approached me with a radiant smile, enveloping me in a warm hug. I stiffened at first, but she wouldn't have it. "You better act like you're gonna give your favorite cousin a hug," she mockingly demanded.

I hugged her back. She gave me a once over and exclaimed, "What's up, cuzzo? Look at you! Got all them young tenders fallin' all over you out there, don't you?"

Helen had been my grandmother's namesake, and secretly, she was one of my favorite cousins. Despite the years of absence, she bridged the gap effortlessly. "It's been a minute," I acknowledged. "I haven't seen any of y'all for a while."

She scowled playfully. "Why you do us like that? You think you're too good for us now?"

I started to defend myself, but she cut in. "Or did you find some young sweetheart out there keeping you busy?" She playfully smacked my shoulder. "That's it, ain't it? Breaking hearts left and right?"

Her joyful energy was infectious, and I couldn't help but laugh. "Cuz, why you so silly all the time?" I shook my head at her energy. We both laughed, momentarily dispelling the somber atmosphere. "It's good to see you, though."

As we shared a hug, Aunt Gwen, her mother, joined us and scolded us for our cheerful reunion on such a solemn day. Gwen sauntered away, her expression stern and disapproving, a subtle frown etched on her face. Her gaze was fixed on some distant point ahead. As she walked away, Helen and I exchanged a look and couldn't help but share in a soft chuckle in the wake of Aunt Gwen's departure.

The church was adorned with flowers, and my grandmother's coffin stood before the altar. It was bright white with gold-painted accents, bathed in the soft glow of overhead spotlights. Her widowed husband, my grandfather, sat in the first pew, closest to his wife, while family members filled the front rows. I gave Helen another squeeze before she went to sit with her mom, and I joined my brothers.

The pastor delivered a moving eulogy, and the choir sang mournful songs chosen to intensify the sorrow in the room. It all felt rehearsed, a scripted performance. I struggled to find genuine mourning within myself, feeling more obligated than connected to the occasion.

When the pastor invited family members to share their thoughts about our departed matriarch, the range of emotions on display was astounding. Love and adoration mixed with bitterness and resentment, highlighting the complexities of our family dynamics. Her death further splintered my already deeply fractured family, and it came pouring out during those small speeches. It brought up years of unresolved, deeply buried hurt and pain for many.

The opportunity came for one last viewing of her before they closed the casket. I gazed down at her lifeless form, searching for the sorrow that engulfed everyone else. But instead, I found myself scrutinizing the funeral home's work. Her appearance was unsettling, as if they had forgotten to place her false teeth. It was a disservice to her memory.

"They made her look so different," I whispered to Iszel, who stood beside me.

Iszel nodded, his voice heavy with grief. "Yeah, it doesn't even look like her."

Her mouth had been sewn into a solemn straight line, devoid of the happiness she once radiated. It left me wondering where the manic energy that once filled her had gone.

In her death, she was even more of a stranger. The person who prepared her body for her final rest had failed to capture her essence. I reached into my pocket, pulled out my Avon Grove high school ID, and placed it gently on her stomach, just under her folded hands. *Maybe it will help you remember my name on the other side,* I thought.

With the casket closed, and the service concluded, I bid farewell to Helen and my brothers, informing them that I wouldn't be attending the burial or the repast at Granddad's house. I left the church, walked to the bus stop, and headed back home to Avondale.

That day marked the end of my home visits to Philly, a chapter in my life that I was eager to leave behind, even as I was still burdened by its unresolved emotions.

CHAPTER 34

Unraveling Harmony

Memorial Day of 1991 started auspiciously, full of sunshine and warmth. Twill, Wilma, Mr. Brown, Wayne, and Ms. Hector had decided to throw a celebration for the eight of us boys, aiming to recreate the comforting sense of normalcy we once had at Philly block parties. I returned from a grueling track practice to the mouthwatering scent of sizzling barbecue wafting through the air. I heard laughter and the chatter of our makeshift family filling the atmosphere, the stereo blaring Teena Marie's "Square Biz."

Everyone seemed to be having a blast, enjoying the delicious barbecue, sharing stories, and bonding over the simple pleasures of life, including a few young kids running around. Ms. Hector, always the nurturing soul, had invited a few of her grandchildren to join in the festivities. Among them was a vibrant 4-year-old granddaughter, Mia, dressed in a pink top, a bright blue skirt, and pristine white stockings. She twirled around the yard, her laughter infectious as she chased butterflies.

After observing the party for a few minutes, I ran into the house and up to my room to change out of my track clothes. As I pulled on a shirt, Bruce burst into my room, his face concerned. "Yo, man, you betta come quick," he said, panting from the rush.

I frowned, slipping on my sneakers. "What's up, man?!"

"Iszel's going at it with Reggie, and it's getting ugly. Nobody else can get 'em apart," he explained, urgency in his voice.

I grabbed my glasses and dashed out the door, my heart pounding. Iszel was the second oldest guy in the house behind me, and Reggie was three years his junior. It was unlike him to pick a fight, especially with someone so young. Whatever had set Iszel off had to be serious. The commotion grew louder as I hurried toward the scene.

When I arrived, I saw Iszel and Reggie locked in a fierce brawl, their fists flying, angry shouts filling the air. It looked more like Reggie was trying to get away from Iszel than fight him. Panic rippled through the onlookers as they struggled to separate the two.

Without hesitation, I lunged forward, my instincts taking over. I managed to grab Iszel 'round the waist and pull him off Reggie. I spun him around by the shoulders, pinning him against a nearby tree. He struggled wildly against my grip, but I held on, my heart pounding in my chest.

"Boys! You all stop this quarreling. We're supposed to be having a good time," I heard Twill shout. I glanced over my shoulder to see her approaching, along with a few other housemates, to help defuse the situation.

I held Iszel in place, my voice steady as I spoke to him. "Yo, calm down, man, it's not worth it. Let Reggie go."

Iszel's breaths began to slow, his muscles gradually relaxing. With a final deep breath, he nodded, and I released my grip. The tension in the air began to dissipate as Reggie stumbled away, bruised but safe. Twill successfully ushered him inside to tend to his busted lip and provide an ice pack for his swollen eye. The other guys in the house returned to the festivities, leaving me and Iszel alone in the backyard.

"Bro, this ain't you. What was that about?" I asked Iszel, confused and concerned. Iszel stared off into the distance for a moment as if he were reliving unsettling memories. Then, he began to describe an incident that had shaken him to the core.

"Yo, I went to go chill in the rec room with my plate of food," Iszel started, his voice heavy with the weight of what he had seen. He shook his head, seemingly trying to forget the horrifying scene he was about to recount. "I saw Reggie push Mia down on the ground, pull her stocking and underwear down, and start to hurt her."

I couldn't hide my shock. "Wait, what?" I asked, my voice rising in disbelief.

Iszel nodded gravely. "Yeah," he confirmed, and his eyes locked onto mine, seeking understanding. "I saw it all happening, man."

My mind raced as I tried to comprehend what Iszel was revealing. "Go on," I urged, my heart pounding.

"I dropped my food and ran to the window," Iszel continued, his voice trembling with frustration. "I started banging on the glass, but those basement windows are so damn thick. Reggie couldn't hear me."

He began to pace back and forth, the distress in his eyes clear. "I grabbed one of the pool table balls and started slamming it into the window. I guess the sound got through to Reggie because he looked at me. He looked right at me!" Iszel clenched his fists at the memory. "I know he saw me because he started hurrying up what he was doing."

"She saw me too, man. She was crying and looked right at me, too. She's 4-years-old, man! And I was too far away to stop Reggie."

The gravity of the situation began to sink in.

"He stopped raping her," Iszel continued, voice quivering with anger. "He was done. He snatched her clothes up and left her there. Then his ass ran. I ran to catch him, and when I did, I wanted to beat the life out of him."

As Iszel recounted the disturbing incident, a storm of emotions raged within me. We had never experienced anything like that in the six years we'd lived there, and it was hard to come to terms with someone in our makeshift family doing something so heinous.

We found Mia with her clothes haphazardly pulled on. We took her to Ms. Hector, her grandmother, and told her and Twill what Reggie had done. She bundled up her other grandchildren and left to take Mia to the hospital. Ms. Hector soon took a hiatus from the house.

Reggie's act should have been enough to have him kicked out, but surprisingly, he remained at the House on the Hill. The rest of us avoided Reggie as much as possible. The only change was that his psychological counseling visits were increased. Leaving him in the home would become yet another major failure of the foster care system to appropriately deal with abuse, and it would have a lasting impact on members of the house and the neighborhood.

***

That November 1991, during my Junior year, the situation with Reggie came to a head. I arrived home after track practice to find a house in tumult. A police cruiser was parked in the driveway with its lights flashing, and an officer was scribbling on a notepad while talking to Wayne. I immediately assumed a casual, non-threatening position, hands visible at my sides as I continued to walk slowly towards the house. The officer reached out and put a halting arm across my chest to stop me from entering. "I need your name, son," he demanded.

Wilma burst out on the porch and said, "Don't you touch him!" She swiped away his hand and followed with, "Whatchu need his name for?! He wasn't even home when all this stuff happened."

"Ma'am, I still need his name," he responded calmly. "I need the names of all the boys living here."

I looked at him and said, "It's Elliott. Elliott Glover." I walked past them and into the kitchen. Wilma followed and hastened me into the office. I hadn't even put my track bag down.

"Elliott, them two boys went down the damn hill and raped two lil boys in the cornfield," she blurted out.

I was confused about what she was referring to or who. "Wait, what?!" I asked. "Two boys from here?! Which two boys?"

"They sayin' Keith and Reggie." She slumped in the office chair and covered her face in disbelief. My mind at once flashed back to what Iszel had seen.

"When did they do that?" I asked.

"Today, they did that nasty shit today," she blurted out through uncontrollable sobs, "And it didn't take long for the police to come up here. Why they messin' with lil boys!" she sat up and shook her head at whatever was going on in her head and followed with, "They gonna be in jail for a long time. They done messed up their lives." She then told me how she feared for the house and what would be coming for the rest of the boys living there. She feared for her and Wayne's jobs because it occurred while they were on duty. She feared the group home would be shut down. I dropped my track and field bag and gave her a hug. I didn't know what was coming next, but I knew it couldn't be good. It was the first time I felt uncertain about the house since Twill started.

About an hour later, our tight-knit group of housemates found ourselves gathering once more, this time in Iszel's room, to confront the unsettling revelations that had surfaced. Our combined anxiety was thick in the air. The events of the past few hours had shattered the illusion of normalcy we had built around our lives in the group home.

Reggie was excluded from the meeting due to his recent troubled history within the house. Keith attended but offered no defense to the accusations against him. Instead, he shared a painful glimpse into his own past, recounting experiences of abuse at the hands of his father and siblings during his time at home from when he was very little.

Keith's history included a father that had violent, serial, adolescent predatory tendencies that he enacted on his sons. They, in turn, performed them on each other. Suffering years of this, by the time 12-year-old Keith arrived at the House on the Hill, he had been nurtured into a violent rapist himself. The revelation left us all stunned, for we had never truly opened up about our personal histories within the group.

The weight of Keith's past hung heavily over us, casting no shadow of a doubt about the allegations. While he hadn't defended himself, we couldn't ignore the possibility that his traumatic history had played a role in his actions, whatever they might have been.

Bruce, normally the most reserved among us, hesitated before speaking. "Guys, I need to tell you something," he began, his voice shaking. "I witnessed something in the basement of the barn."

Silence enveloped the room as we all turned our attention to Bruce, our faces reflecting a mix of curiosity and dread.

Bruce took a deep breath and continued, "I saw Keith having sex with Tim."

Gasps filled the room as the gravity of Bruce's words settled in. Tim, who had been sitting quietly, turned pale, his eyes fixed on the floor as if trying to disappear.

The room was charged with emotions, and Tim finally found his voice. "It wasn't my choice," he confessed, his voice trembling with embarrassment. "Keith forced me."

My heart ached for Tim, and I realized that our newfound friendship had been more than just companionship; it had served as a shield to protect him from Keith's volatile nature and sexual predation. He singled out Tim and began regularly raping him in the hollows of the barn's basement, which most of us avoided or ignored. Tim couldn't fight off Keith and, eventually, simply acquiesced to the assaults to avoid the physical one, immediately followed by the inevitable sexual one. Why suffer a busted lip or a black eye, too?

The room fell silent as we grappled with the implications of what Tim had just disclosed. Unable to bear the weight of the revelation any longer, Tim abruptly stood and fled the room, his steps echoing down the hallway. Ray hurriedly followed him, leaving the rest of us in stunned silence.

As we tried to process the shocking events, I couldn't help but remember Reggie's presence in the house. He had always been different, his actions driven by a need for control. I recalled vague instances of his 'borrowing' another boy's tape deck from his room until he was confronted about it, eventually returning it before it escalated into an altercation.

Reggie had a knack for instigating conflicts between two of the other guys and seemed to derive satisfaction from watching the fallout. He satisfied his need for control by indulging in petty thefts from local stores or even the other guys. He was an opportunist, a street-smart kid who took advantage whenever he could.

All these thoughts swirled in my mind as we struggled with the uncertainty of Reggie's involvement in the recent incident. With what Iszel had seen, it seemed likely he was guilty of the accusations. It became increasingly clear that our house was not as secure as we had once believed and that the events of that day had revealed layers of complexity within our group that we had never anticipated.

Shortly after Tim ran out, the door swung open, and two police officers entered the room, their presence a stark reminder of the escalating situation.

Without a word, they approached Keith, placing handcuffs on him. The sound of them snapping shut echoed in the room, a chilling sound that marked the finality of the situation. Keith's face bore expressions of shock, disbelief, and fear as he was escorted out of the room, leaving us behind in a state of turmoil. I watched from the window as two police officers stoically guided away both Reggie and Keith to their waiting police cruiser.

The rest of us were left to grapple with the sudden upheaval in our lives. We sat in Iszel's room, our minds swirling with unanswered questions and uncertainty about what the future held. The house we had once felt so secure in now felt like a fragile structure teetering on the edge of collapse. With Keith and Reggie taken into custody, our once-cohesive group home felt like a fractured puzzle, each piece shaken loose from its place. We wondered whether our home could ever be the same again. As we looked around at each other, a sense of unease settled in.

The next morning, I went to check in on Tim. I found him in his bedroom, staring out of the window, quietly attempting to process the overwhelming emotions that had erupted in Iszel's room. I couldn't let him face this alone. I went in and gently put my hand on his shoulder. "Yo, you shouldn't try to carry all this on your own," I said softly. "I think you should talk to Twill about what happened to you. She can help you through this."

Tim looked at me, his eyes closed off. "I... I don't know if I can do it," he stammered. "It's too hard to talk about."

I nodded, understanding the immense difficulty of the situation. I was still concealing and struggling with my own experiences of being molested. I couldn't let him struggle through it like I had, not without trying to get him to open up about it.

"I get where you're coming from, but Tim, you need help. I'm gonna have to tell her."

He simply sighed, turned away from me, and refused to talk to me again about it.

I went to Twill feeling all kinds of awful. Haltingly, I explained what had happened to Tim.

I could tell that Twill was tearing up, and her voice quivered as she spoke. "I'm so sorry he went through that. We'll get him extra counseling. There are specialized therapists who can help survivors of abuse."

I fell short of telling her that I needed a specialist, too, that I needed help. I hated feeling helpless, used, powerless, and angry at myself for feeling responsible in some way for what happened to me and at the two Jasons for doing it. I didn't want Tim to feel like I did. But it was easier to try and get Tim's help than to ask for it myself.

The whole house was somber and silent in the days following the arrests of Reggie and Keith. Tim never talked about what happened to him with the rest of us. It was too raw. But he did go to extra counseling, and we worked to support him however we could. I knew from experience that it would be a weight he would have to carry for a long time, possibly for the rest of his life. I could only hope that therapy and the passage of time would help to ease his burden.

CHAPTER 35

Those Boys

In the immediate aftermath, Twill and Mr. Brown were concerned about our safety. They decided it was best to avoid the school bus and the small development near the group home while the incident was still fresh in the community's mind. They tried to coordinate driving the remaining six of us to and from school, but it quickly became apparent that managing our schedules and after-school activities was a logistical challenge. Both Iszel and I were heavily involved in extracurriculars. I was taking part in track & field, acting in a musical production of *Sugar*, and preparing for a choir concert. The demands to drive us around were too much, and we soon persuaded our houseparents to let us hitch rides with friends instead.

After the holidays, the parents of the victims went to the news, and by March, it had spread, reaching regional levels through TV and newspaper coverage. It was during one of the *Sugar* rehearsals that I found myself in an uncomfortable situation. Mrs. Franklin, a school aide and a tailor for the play, was fitting me for my costume as the character Jerry/Daphne, one of the leading roles.

I stood in the school cafeteria's makeshift wardrobe area as she pinned pieces of cloth on me. She began chatting with another adult nearby. At first, I wasn't listening, but then she said something that caught my attention. "You wouldn't believe what Those Boys on the Hill did!" she gossiped, her tone filled with disdain. I became hyper focused on the conversation, Mrs. Franklin oblivious to my sudden attention. Instead, she continued to work on my costume, pinning fabric around my body as she spoke. "They went down the hill and raped two little kids!" I must have stiffened at her words because she paused, looked up at me, and asked if she had accidentally pricked me with one of the pins. I shook my head, signaling that I was fine, but the words she'd just spoken hung heavily in the air.

She went on, adding false accusations about us being a bunch of delinquents who would have ended up in gangs if not for the group home. I couldn't understand why she was being so candid with her gossip, especially in front of me. Prior to this, she had always been friendly. I was friendly and joked around with all three of her children, two of whom were in the musical with me. I was close enough with one of her daughters that I wouldn't have thought twice about asking her to be my date for a school dance. This family genuinely seemed to like me. It was unsettling and demoralizing.

The rehearsal eventually concluded without any further incidents, and I left to bum another ride home. But this was only the beginning of a pattern that I would encounter repeatedly in the coming weeks. I heard similar derogatory comments about "Those Boys on the Hill" at various places in town—Earl's Sub Shop, Perkins' restaurant in Avondale, and even while waiting in line at the ACME grocery store in Kennett. It became clear that this label had stuck, and it defined how people saw me and the other residents of the group home.

In response to the negative perception, BCS went into damage control mode. They tried to paint a more accurate picture of us by giving interviews to local newspapers and *The Philadelphia Inquirer*. They emphasized that we were good kids in need of a second chance due to our troubled families. They made it clear that the two boys involved in the incident were not part of our group.

To change the community's perception of us, someone came up with the idea of an open house at the group home. The plan was to invite the community to see firsthand that we were not delinquents, hooligans, gangsters, or rapists. We would open our doors and let people walk through the house, meet us, and see how we lived. To prepare us for the event, counselors and social workers were sent to the house to provide guidance on what to say and what not to say. The incident itself was to be avoided as a topic of conversation.

THOSE BOYS ON THE HILL

The open house took place on a Saturday, with a PR campaign to promote it. The House was meticulously cleaned, and no home visits were allowed that weekend. Visitors arrived throughout the day, with some genuinely trying to ease their concerns about us while others treated us like a sideshow. It was uncomfortable being on display in my own home. It felt like a violation, as if I were a spectacle to be scrutinized without any choice in the matter. The day changed some relationships, causing tension between my friends and their parents, who attended the open house and realized I was a resident.

Mrs. Franklin eventually arrived. I was in the living room, talking to a group of people about my track career and playing the piano, when I noticed her standing in the dining room, staring at me with her mouth agape. Once the group moved on, she couldn't contain her shock and asked me privately, "What are you doing here?"

"I live here," I replied calmly. Under my breath, mimicking her tone from her gossip session, I added, "I am one of 'THOSE Boys on the Hill."

Her face flushed and turned bright red and then lost all its color. She didn't say anything more and simply turned and left. She remained involved in the musical production but became noticeably stiffer toward me. Her children's disposition didn't change much, but she kept a more watchful eye on them when they were around me.

It was disheartening to realize that, in true Rising Sun form, certain circles replaced the word "Boys" with the word "Niggers." The incident left a lasting mark on our lives, and the negative perceptions surrounding us were challenging to overcome.

CHAPTER 36

Passing The Torch

That same spring, nearly four years had passed since Twill graced the House on the Hill, ushering in what would later be remembered by the long-term residents as the golden age at the group home. Her influence had woven a profound and lasting impact into the very fibers of our lives, binding us together as a tight-knit group of brothers.

The incidents involving Keith and Reggie shook us, but Twill remained a source of guidance. With the way the town had reacted, it felt a bit like the world was closing in on us, but within the walls of the House on the Hill, we refused to let that tear us apart. The houseparents and remaining boys stood in solidarity.

Then came the most heart-wrenching news: Twill's husband had passed away unexpectedly. It added to the house's woes. Although her husband, Earl, had only made a few fleeting appearances during those years, his presence always brought an inexplicable warmth to the house. We might not have known him well, but we respected him as a part of the family we had collectively forged under Twill. The loss of Earl wasn't just a loss to Twill; it was a loss for us all. We felt the absence of her unwavering support during her bereavement leave but understood why she needed the time.

She returned from her bereavement leave, but it wasn't for long. Adding to her burden, Twill was also responsible for her ailing aunt, who needed her daily care. It was an unimaginably difficult decision for her, but she chose to leave the group home. The news of her imminent departure left an ache in the hearts of all of us who had come to see her as their rock and mother figure.

THOSE BOYS ON THE HILL

On the day of her departure, the house was a place of sorrow. We gathered in the living room, the same room where we had shared laughter, stories, and moments of togetherness. Twill addressed us, her voice trembling, struggling to hold back her own tears. "I want you all to know that this is the hardest decision I've ever had to make. You are my boys, my family. But my aunt needs me, and I can't ignore that responsibility. I hope you understand." Tears welled in her eyes, and she reached out to embrace each of us, holding us tightly. The weight of her departure settled in, and the room was filled with a collective sense of profound loss.

Wilma stepped forward with unwavering determination in her eyes. She had witnessed the family mentality that Twill had nurtured. "We'll keep the family mentality alive," she promised, her voice steady. "You've given us a blueprint for love and support, and we won't let it fade away."

It was a promise echoed by the rest of us. Twill's departure marked the end of an era, but we were determined to turn a new page. We hugged her one last time, the embrace heavy with unspoken emotions. As she left the House on the Hill, our world felt emptier without her.

In the days and weeks that followed, the house adjusted to the absence of our matriarch. Wilma stepped up, using what Twill had created to guide us through the challenges we faced. The sense of family remained, a tribute to Twill's enduring influence. Though she was no longer with us in person, Twill's legacy lived on, a reminder that family wasn't just about blood ties; it was about the love, support, and the indomitable spirit that bound us together. The House on the Hill remained a place of warmth, acceptance, and unwavering support.

CHAPTER 37

The Spencer Challenge

In the months following Twill's departure, the House on the Hill underwent significant changes. The loss of our beloved house parent left a void that Wilma had worked tirelessly to fill, but there were aspects of our lives that even her commitment couldn't address.

One of the most significant changes during that time was the increasing presence of the Spencers in our lives. The bond between Cory and Iszel had grown through the years, and the Spencers treated him like one of their own.

But it was a different challenge they embarked on when they decided to become foster parents. Their willingness to foster Iszel wasn't just an act of love; it was a testament to the depth of the friendship they shared with us. They understood that family wasn't determined by the color of one's skin but by the love and connection that bound people together. And yet, their decision would face an obstacle they couldn't predict: Dr. Frye.

Dr. Frye, a Black psychiatric director of Baptist Children's Services, held a personal belief that a white family should not foster a black child. He saw the Spencers' intentions as misguided and their potential parenting as flawed. I never knew exactly why, although being involved in the world of adoption, he'd probably seen many instances of transracial adoption where white parents adopt Black children without fully understanding their unique needs, cultural roots, or the importance of nurturing their identity. His distrust of parents from different racial backgrounds or orientations might stem from deep-seated scars inflicted by historical injustices. His past experiences may have clouded his judgment, making it difficult for him to acknowledge the potential of loving and capable parents like the Spencers.

With the weight of his influence, he portrayed the Spencers as unfit based on factors beyond color, but the racial issue remained at the core of his opposition. It was a frustrating and challenging period for all involved. The emotional toll was immense. Their efforts to foster Iszel faced disappointment, leaving the Spencers devastated. In the end, the system denied a loving and supportive home to a child who needed it, an ironic reversal of its tendency to place Black children with white families that often lacked the tools or desire to help them navigate a race-based society.

After the Spencers' failed battle to foster Iszel, they were left with a bittersweet opportunity: becoming weekend house parents under Wilma's tenure as the main house parent. It wasn't the path they had initially set out on, but it was a chance to make a difference in the lives of children who needed their love and support. As weekend house parents, they brought their warmth and generosity into our lives on a regular basis.

Over the year that they served as weekend house parents, Iszel practically moved in with them, although it went unnoticed by BCS. As they extended their love and care to him, Iszel blossomed in their embrace. The Spencers' home became a sanctuary, a place where he could thrive without judgment or prejudice.

The Spencers remained two of the most influential and loving parents in our lives. They demonstrated that love transcends all boundaries. The Spencers were living proof that family wasn't bound by the color of one's skin or the structure of one's household but by the love and dedication parents poured into their children.

CHAPTER 38

An Early Second Chance

My mother received a good time early release from prison for being a model inmate. She had served five years behind bars, and her transformation from within those walls was nothing short of remarkable. Her dedication and commitment to self-improvement had not only earned her early parole but also equipped her with valuable skills and education essential for the journey of rebuilding her life.

My grandfather, ever the stern figure, agreed to take her in upon her release. This transition came with a set of clear conditions, the most critical of which was her unwavering commitment to a life free of drugs and alcohol. In return, she was tasked with providing care for my grandfather, taking on responsibilities such as cooking, cleaning, and ensuring his well-being.

Our Aunt Terry, who lived just across the street, had been the primary caregiver for my grandfather for years, especially after the passing of our grandmother. While willing to share some of her responsibilities with our mother, she remained a vigilant presence, ensuring that my mother followed the strict parole conditions.

Over time, my mother's place within the family was slowly but steadily restored. She found employment with a company that offered a second chance to ex-offenders, marking a significant step in her reintegration journey. To cope with the challenges of sobriety, she made the courageous choice to substitute alcoholic drinks with their non-alcoholic counterparts, a small but vital step in her commitment to lasting recovery.

THOSE BOYS ON THE HILL

One of the most significant milestones during this period was her visit to the group home where my brother Iszel and I had spent much of our youth. Welcoming her with open arms, Wilma acknowledged the progress my mother had made on her path to rehabilitation. The Spencers extended an invitation for her to spend a weekend at their home.

I vividly recall that weekend when my mother came to visit. It coincided with my performance in *Sugar*. The cast and crew were eager to meet her, and her arrival at the high school where the musical was to take place was met with warmth and admiration. The crew went a step further, presenting her with a unique gift—a pillow crafted from the fabric of all my costumes, symbolizing their acceptance and celebration of her presence.

It was a significant achievement to be one of the leads in the musical as only a Junior. I was elated that she could see my performance, witness my passion, and share in my accomplishments. During my curtain call, the audience seemed to acknowledge her presence by turning towards her while they clapped, adding an extra layer of excitement to the evening. Multiple curtain calls and genuine embraces from everyone in the room marked a moment I will forever cherish. I could see the unmistakable pride in my mother's eyes as she watched me excel. Although I had long moved past feeling like the "Weird Son," now she could, as well, finally understand me in a way she never had before.

However, her release from prison brought a shift in dynamics. She tried to step back into a parental role, an adjustment that I found challenging to accept at 17 years old. One evening, I found myself standing in the kitchen on the phone that hung on the wall, speaking with my mother. She had just finished talking to Iszel and asked to speak to me. I hated her random calls, as they normally interrupted something I was doing otherwise, and most of them ended with me feeling annoyed. I had been weighing my many options regarding leaving the House on the Hill, and although I mentioned to her previously that they were on my mind, I wasn't really seeking her advice about them. Outside of the workforce option, I didn't feel she could really advise about college or the military.

"Hey, Ma." I greeted her.

"Hey Baby." My mother's voice crackled through the line. Her assertive tone echoed through the receiver. "Elliott, I done been through a lot, but I know what's best for you when you leave that House. You need to listen to me, boy."

A mix of frustration and resignation settled within me. Even through the old landline, her unexpected assertions disrupted the peace I had found in my routine.

"Ma, I don't know what you're talking about. How are you gonna start a conversation like that?" I responded. "I've been holding it down for a while now without you. I'm good, and I got people looking out for me. I don't need constant advice from you."

Her response was predictable. "Boy, I'm your mama, and I got some wisdom to drop too. You need to be grateful."

The words echoed in my ears, and I couldn't shake the annoyance that simmered beneath the surface. The life I had built without her was stable, and these unsolicited calls threw me off.

"I respect what you've been through," I asserted, "but things in my life are good right now, and I got things to think about." I didn't hesitate to let her know how I felt. "I got folks looking out for me and a routine that works for me. Stop tryna lord over me, acting like I haven't been doing this without you all this time."

These exchanges underscored the challenge of reintegrating my mother into a life I had built without her presence. Her habit of asserting herself with a "because I told you so" attitude grated on my nerves. A decade had passed since I had last lived with her, and her sudden reentry and the way she carried herself felt undeserved. Her efforts to reclaim a maternal role clashed with my established independence and the relationships I had cultivated in her absence. The unpredictability of these moments added an extra layer of complexity, as her interventions seemed driven more by her own thoughts than any external prompting. This was a period of adjustment for both of us. The foundation of our mother-son relationship remained, but the dynamics had changed, making it a challenge for us to reconnect. I needed to maintain my boundaries and autonomy from her. Finding common ground would be impossible with the way she was trying to do it. I knew deep down it was her way of showing love, but it was hard to accept. Things had been strained and battered for too long for them to go back to the way they were.

CHAPTER 39

The Weight of Aging Out

As my senior year unfolded, the trajectory of my life seemed to be ascending. I had been excelling in high school and had solid friendships. However, amidst the seemingly smooth ride, the shadows of impending adulthood loomed ominously. My eighteenth birthday, a date marked with both anticipation and anxiety, carried the weight of emancipation and the unknown. The secure cocoon of the group home, where rules were familiar and support was constant, was beginning to unravel. As the count to adulthood ticked down, my future appeared as a vast, uncertain landscape, with questions of where to go and what awaited me on the other side. The gravity of the situation grew increasingly oppressive. Living in the group home had brought me into frequent contact with Marsha, our diligent social worker. Unlike many others who danced around the reality of being a ward of the court in a BCS facility, Marsha never minced words. I appreciated that about her.

Marsha bore a striking resemblance to the actress Geena Davis, though less glamorous. She was tall and statuesque, often clad in conservative neck-to-ankle dresses with a buttoned-up blazer designed to conceal her figure. It was a conscious choice, as she aimed to maintain an air of professionalism, especially given her caseload, mostly comprised of young men like me.

About a month before my eighteenth birthday, I received a summons to her office. Inside, she sat with just one file open before her—my file. This was no ordinary meeting. Typically, Department of Human Services social workers juggled multiple cases, yet mine was the sole focus of her attention. This file chronicled every facet of my life since I was a three-year-old. It was thick, dog-eared, and crammed with pages filled with the judgments and assessments of individuals who had observed me since I first arrived at St. Vincent's home in Philly fifteen years prior, alongside my brothers.

I couldn't help but wonder about the words scrawled within those pages – what had people written about me over the years? Did kids in regular homes have files like this? And would I ever lay my hands on it when I finally left the group home?

Marsha interrupted my musings. "Elliott, we need to figure out what happens after February."

I was expecting the question since she didn't sugarcoat things, especially not issues as critical as this. But the truth was that even though I knew I'd have to leave soon, I was still clueless about my destination. After my eighteenth birthday, BCS would no longer be legally obliged to provide for me, and I faced the frightening prospect of homelessness.

"What do you mean by 'happens'?" I asked. "Do I have to leave when I turn eighteen or when I graduate? I still have four months of high school and nowhere to go."

"Well, that's what we have to figure out. Staying here means you have to continue following the house rules until you graduate."

"I've been following the rules for the last nine years," I stated, my irritation stemming more from my situation than her words. "I've been doing this much longer than you've been a social worker. Following the rules for four more months until I graduate won't be hard. Besides, I have NOWHERE else to go." I nearly shouted the last part, the fear and frustration welling up inside me. The reality of my situation was that I had no safety net or fallback once I aged out, and all I could envision on the other side of my birthday was a bleak, unending darkness.

Sensing my agitation, she swiftly moved on. "Then let's assume that's settled. You'll stay at the house until at least graduation." She didn't offer comfort; there were rules to be followed, and I had to navigate my emotions on my own.

"What's the plan after graduation?" she asked calmly, her intention clear: to shift my focus from self-pity to practical considerations.

Staring out of the window, I verbally explored my options, as though discussing them with her might make them more tangible. "I don't know. I could follow Jacque's path and join the military, but it seems like they want to make me disappear." I had taken the Air Force test, but the recruiter had become overly interested in my high recruitment placement score and my status as a group home resident. He even probed about my language-learning abilities and whether anyone would miss me if I were gone for a few years. Given my upbringing in the group home, the only person I could think of was Iszel.

The recruiter called our house relentlessly, trying to meet with me again. My growing fear of his intentions and my desire to avoid him escalated with each call. Somehow, he even tracked down my mother and called her at my grandfather's house. She wasn't pleased and firmly told him never to call her again. I couldn't fathom how he had acquired that number or why he thought she could influence my decision to enlist. He was aware of my group home history and my mother's prison record.

College wasn't a definite for me either. Without parental support, encouragement, or guidance to navigate the college application process, I doubted myself and procrastinated my college applications. My SAT scores were average at best, and though I had a ton of extracurriculars, I had a hard time believing any college would want me. My guidance counselor advised me that West Chester would be the easiest place for me to be accepted, and I finally submitted my application in the nick of time.

"I applied to West Chester University, but they haven't given me an answer yet," I finally said. "I'm not going back to Philly to live on the streets," I added firmly. The Air Force option would be my last resort if I didn't get into West Chester. If I attended college, it would be a big deal. Not only would I be the first in my family, but I would also be the first in BCS's 100-year history. Fosters attend college at less than half the rate of the national average.[21] And only 2-10% ever graduate, one of the many grim statistics facing kids like me aging out of foster care.[22]

Marsha retrieved a page from the folder titled "Independent Living Agreement." "From the month of your eighteenth birthday, until you turn twenty-one, the State is going to provide you with a monthly stipend of four hundred and thirty-five dollars to assist you. I suggest you save it, along with any earnings from your job. It won't cover all your expenses, but it will help. You'll receive the funds as long as you stay out of jail."

The realization hit me that they were reallocating the money that had been sent to Baptist Children's Services every month since my arrival on that cold January day nine years ago. I couldn't help but mentally calculate the amount: nine years, twelve months each at four hundred thirty-five dollars a month, totaling around forty-five thousand dollars. Nevertheless, I recalibrated my expectations for what the State would provide: approximately five thousand dollars a year. It wasn't much, but it was more than I had expected.

"Thanks," I said.

"We'll deposit the money directly into your bank account on the first of each month. Just fill out the banking information and sign the page at the bottom. Your first deposit will be next month. And let's keep our fingers crossed for West Chester."

For a long month, Marsha's words lingered in the back of my mind, casting a shadow over my future, West Chester the one glimmer of hope on the horizon. The prospect of acceptance offered a lifeline—a chance to avoid the military, homelessness, or any other uncertain fate that might await me.

The day the letter arrived from West Chester, I was on edge, restless with anticipation. I ran up to my bedroom, clutching the envelope in trembling hands. This was a momentous occasion, one I had to face alone since, as a group home kid, there were no parents to share in the news. Iszel practically lived at the Spencers by this point and was rarely around anymore. I held the envelope, feeling a moment of intense loneliness.

I hefted the letter, trying to figure out how much paper the school would waste to decline my application, but I couldn't tell either way. I hesitated only for a moment, savoring the suspense, before carefully opening the envelope. My eyes raced through the contents, and there, at the top of the letter, I found it: "Congratulations." The rest of the letter became a blur. That word was all that mattered.

A deep sense of relief washed over me, a feeling of overwhelming happiness. It was as if a massive weight had been lifted from my shoulders, one I hadn't even fully realized I'd been carrying all these years. The stress that had been steadily building within me evaporated, leaving behind an emptiness, but an emptiness that felt lighter and more hopeful.

As I sat on my bed, tears welled up in my eyes, not of sorrow or fear, but of joy and gratitude. It wasn't just about the acceptance; it was about what it represented. It was my ticket out of uncertainty, a ticket to education, independence, and a potential future. In sharp contrast to my happiness, I felt the sting of solitude of being the only one for whom my 'Acceptance' truly mattered. I longed for the presence of family and the warmth of parents who would share in my triumph. Instead, I was alone in that small room, the letter a bittersweet testament to my achievement.

As I sat in my room, overwhelmed by the mix of emotions, I couldn't help but wonder what the journey to West Chester University had in store for me. I faced it with a renewed sense of determination, an emptiness slowly being filled with hope, and a commitment to making the most of the opportunity that had come my way.

***

Another huge weight off my shoulders was when BCS allowed me to stay in the group home until West Chester opened its doors in mid-

THOSE BOYS ON THE HILL

August. This was unusual; most group home kids were booted either when they were 18 or at graduation. It meant I didn't have to suffer a summer of homelessness. My staying at the group home after turning 18 wasn't merely a matter of circumstance—it was a carefully calculated decision orchestrated by BCS. Had I not been a model group home kid, the story might have been different. They needed someone like me to represent them, to be the poster child for their cause.

I remember the discussions vividly. They offered to pay me to make appearances on behalf of BCS, promoting their mission and success stories. It was a win-win situation, they assured me. I agreed, knowing that my presence would help secure funding and housing for myself and support for the organization.

For those critical six months leading up to my departure for college, I found myself featured in monthly foster and group home magazines. They hailed my high school achievements, sports triumphs, and acceptance into a state university. I even delivered 20-minute speeches at various engagements, sharing my personal journey and the impact BCS had on my life.

Marsha played a pivotal role in this endeavor. She bought me a sharp black suit, a few nice ties, and a couple of white shirts. On many occasions, she'd pick me up for fundraising events during the BCS's annual donation drive. We attended galas, BBQs, luncheons, brunches, and dinners with some of the most generous donors around. Over time, the other kids on the circuit and I formed a close-knit group. After mingling with the moneyed individuals, we'd huddle together in a corner, catching our breaths and sharing stories.

The motivation behind it all was too clear: BCS wanted to capitalize on my unique position. They saw me as a trailblazer—the first to be headed off to college in their 100-year history. It was a significant milestone for them, and they had a vested interest in allowing me to stay until I left for college. But as I continued to represent them, I couldn't help but wonder about the true impact of my appearance. What did it mean for the other kids like me? Was this actually improving the lives of other kids or just lining the pockets of the people who ran the agency? And what would my future hold once I stepped out of the spotlight and into the world beyond Baptist Children's Services?

CHAPTER 40

Track and Triumphs

Track and Field was something I looked forward to every year. It started in March and continued until June. Most meets I thoroughly enjoyed. However, I always had mixed feelings about the yearly invitational track meet in Rising Sun, Maryland. Avon Grove's track team was a diverse mix of races, a stark contrast to the predominantly white residents of the small town we were about to visit. From previous years, we knew we were not welcomed there.

As our school bus made its way into Rising Sun, the scene that unfolded yearly was like a page out of a history book, one that depicted how closely our present was tied to a dark and deeply unsettling part of our nation's past. The residents of the small town followed our bus, driving alongside us in their pickup trucks. They displayed shotguns as plain as day, making it abundantly clear that we were unwelcome there.

Coaches Howard and Benson, our dedicated mentors and protectors, believed that the sheer size of our team would deter any potential trouble. We were there to compete in the invitational, and despite the unnerving racial tension that heavily hung in the air every year, the opportunity to run on an all-weather track was something we looked forward to, considering Avon Grove's high school track was like a sand trap. By competing in the Rising Sun invitational, we had a chance to qualify for regionals with just one strong performance instead of two. It was a risk, but the coaches thought it was a risk worth taking.

As we pulled up to the track my Senior year, Coach Benson, a white man, gave us explicit instructions. He was well aware of the tension surrounding us, particularly for those of us who were Black and people of color. He warned that none of us should be alone, and it was especially important for those of us who faced the brunt of racial prejudices.

When we disembarked from the bus, we were met with a sea of angry spectators in the stands, their shouts filled with profanities and racial slurs. The atmosphere was tense and unsettling, but it fueled something deep within us. The nervous energy translated into a fierce determination on the track. We ran our fastest times, threw our longest throws, and jumped our highest leaps. I had four events that day, and the adrenaline was coursing through my veins.

As I prepared for my high jump, I realized that I had time before I needed to be at the pit. I wandered over there alone, lost in my thoughts. It was a moment of absentmindedness that would nearly have dire consequences. I began changing my track shoes to my jumping shoes, and that's when I noticed I was no longer alone. Four white Rising Sun teammates had surrounded me, and their intent was unmistakable: they looked like they were ready to pummel me. I sized up the four of them and determined how to defend myself. Take out the biggest one, and maybe the rest would back off. I was peripherally aware of the vicious energy of the crowd in the bleachers. If a fight broke out, they might all storm the field.

Coach Howard, a Black man, sharp and vigilant, saw the situation escalating. He sprinted across the field, several other Avon Grove runners following closely behind. The four Rising Sun teammates backed off once I had reinforcements, but this only egged on the crowd. People in the stands jeered even louder at me and my teammates, watching the scene play out and hurling an unending stream of racial insults. I watched everything warily, on full alert.

Coach Howard knew he had to intervene to put an end to this potential disaster. He engaged in a heated exchange of words with the pit judge, berating him for failing to manage the Rising Sun teammates and the crowd. The judge, who was from Rising Sun himself, didn't seem to appreciate the tone coming from the animated Howard. The argument escalated quickly, both men vehemently defending their positions. The tension in the air became palpable.

Coach Benson saw that the situation was spiraling out of control. With a firm, commanding presence, he stepped between Coach Howard and the pit judge. He separated the two men and ensured that the focus remained on the competition.

Howard knew he had to put an end to this situation to keep us safe from the escalating dangers. He swiftly asked the judge to report the highest jump of the season by the competing athletes, which was six feet. Then, he made a bold move. He requested the bar to be raised to a daunting height of 6'4" for my jump, 6 inches higher than any jump so far that day.

As they set the bar higher, Coach Benson and Coach Howard pulled me aside. Coach Howard pointed a stern finger at my chest. His eyes bore into mine, a fiery determination reflected in every line on his face. "You feel that?!" he barked, jabbing a finger into my chest. The crowd's roars blurred into white noise as my focus narrowed to his words. "Makes you mad, don't it?!" He asked.

I nodded, my jaw clenched, seething with a mix of frustration and raw determination. "Yeah! Yeah, I'm mad!"

"Good! Use it!" Howard commanded, his voice cutting through the chaos. He pointed fiercely at the bar, now raised to that seemingly impossible 6'4". "They don't believe you belong here. Prove them wrong! Crush it!" His gaze was steadfast, locked onto mine as if willing the fire within me to explode. He was livid. Benson exchanged a glance with Howard, their shared confidence in my ability fueling the flames within me.

Howard stepped practically nose to nose with me, his grip firm on my shoulder. "Get your ass over that bar and shut this thing down. Show them who owns this track so we can get outta here!" His intensity was contagious, a blazing torch passed from coach to athlete.

The crowd's noise reached a fever pitch, the energy electrifying the atmosphere. There was no room for hesitation. The other athletes from Rising Sun stood to the side, arms folded, their smirks fading as they saw the steely resolve in our eyes.

I stretched, taking deep breaths. My teammates stood as a wall of unwavering support. The crowd watched in anticipation. This wasn't just a jump; it was a defiant statement daring anyone to question my place in the arena.

I took my approach, and with every ounce of strength and determination, I launched myself off the ground and executed a flawless Fosbury flop over the bar. The crowd watched in silence, and as I cleared the bar by an inch, a triumphant cheer erupted from our team.

Immediately upon my safe landing in the high jump pit, Howard grabbed me, pounding victoriously on my chest. "I knew you could clear that bar. You showed them. Got them all sitting in those stands quiet now, don't we?" he exclaimed with uncontainable enthusiasm. His words carried a profound weight, validating not just my athletic prowess but also our collective perseverance against the racial hostility that had loomed over the event. Beyond a personal triumph, it was a powerful response to bigotry, the cheers of my teammates, and the silenced stares of the once-hostile crowd composing a sweet symphony of victory that resonated far beyond the track.

Coach Benson grabbed me triumphantly, too, and the Rising Sun athletes, who had been so confident in their intimidation, looked deflated. My jump was enough that no one else on the Rising Sun team could clear it, and after their many failed attempts, it ended the event.

We boarded the bus, our hearts still pounding from the stress of the day. We were followed out of the town by pickup trucks and shotguns, accompanied by chilling warnings never to return. We had faced hate and bigotry head-on, and we had left with our heads held high.

The Rising Sun showdown in my senior year would become a defining moment in our track careers. It was a testament to the support of our coaches, the bond between teammates, and our shared resilience in the face of extreme racial prejudice. This was a memory that would stay with me for a lifetime, a memory that continued to fuel my determination to excel in every challenge I faced.

***

Luckily, Rising Sun wasn't our typical reception. Iszel and I had both enjoyed success on the track, participating in meets on regional and international levels, including the prestigious Penn Relays in Philadelphia. It was with bittersweet anticipation that I approached my last high school track meet ever in mid-May of 1993. The Southern Chester County League Track and Field Championship in Oxford, PA, allowed us to showcase our team's commitment to the sport.

The anticipation was electric as we stood on the cusp of the grand finale of our high school track and field careers. With our coaches, Howard and Benson, guiding us every step of the way, Iszel and I forged a path of excellence throughout our time on the track.

As seniors, the honor of co-captaining the team fell upon me and my teammate, Nate White. Our Avon Grove track and field team had come a long way since my freshman year. Through hard work and solid coaching, we transformed from a small group of 12 athletes into a formidable team of nearly 50. We were no longer underdogs; we were contenders, often viewed as the favorites in the meets we entered.

The event brought together eight schools and hundreds of athletes, creating a competitive atmosphere. The championship spanned two days, with preliminary heats leading to intense final races.

I was a seasoned competitor, poised to face the challenge of the 100-meter sprint. It was a race that demanded nothing less than an all-out sprint, a display of raw speed and power. In past years, the 100-meter finals had always been claimed by senior runners. I was determined to continue that pattern.

My season had been exceptional. I consistently ran the fastest times and remained undefeated in the 100-meter sprint event. However, the competition was fierce. Chris White and Chris Worrell, talented runners from other schools, had the potential to outpace me if my race wasn't executed perfectly.

My Achilles' heel had always been my start, and I knew I needed to improve it to secure victory. I turned to Iszel, who was known for having one of the best starts in the sport. When he raced, he would often have a few meters' lead right out of the starting blocks, and I needed that edge to outpace both Chrises. Iszel took me through a few quick 'Start' drills while I was warming up for the event.

The day leading up to the race dragged on. I occupied my mind with thoughts of my other events, trying to keep my focus sharp. Finally, the time arrived, and we gathered at the starting line.

Nate White would ensure the blocks remained steadfast as I positioned myself for the race. With a final clap of hands, he encouraged me with a resolute, "You got this." The atmosphere was charged with anticipation, and as the starter called out, "Runners, take your marks," I felt a surge of adrenaline.

I settled into my starting blocks, my body in the perfect position to burst forward. The starter's voice echoed, "Set!" I rose, resting my body weight on my arms and shoulders, ready to launch myself out of the blocks with maximum power and precision. The starting gun's deafening report signaled the beginning of the race, and I exploded forward, propelling my body as fast and hard as I could.

I kept my head down, my arms driving with incredible force for the first 40 meters. The sound of cleats striking the asphalt filled my ears, a thunderous rhythm of determination and power. The finish line, approximately 50 meters away, remained my sole focus. I pumped my arms even faster, reaching with every ounce of energy.

In my peripheral vision, I could see Chris White, a fierce competitor, who could outlean me if we crossed the finish line at the same moment. The sight of him ignited a spark within me, and my resolve solidified. I had to surpass him, to remove him from my line of sight. As the race continued, he gradually faded down the last 30 meters, and I could see him no more.

With a triumphant yell, I crossed the finish line and broke the tape with my chest. The rush of victory was unparalleled, a dream achieved after years of effort and commitment.

THOSE BOYS ON THE HILL

I turned to face my coaches, who were exuberantly celebrating, high-fiving my hard-earned victory. Beside them, my mother and Iszel stood side by side, sharing a heartfelt hug, their faces aglow with pride. Iszel raised a triumphant fist in my direction.

The moments following the race were unforgettable. We eagerly awaited the official times and the declaration that I was the winner. It was official—I had secured victory, beating Chris White by a mere 0.01 seconds. After shaking hands with him and acknowledging his exceptional performance, I couldn't help but say, "Great race, man. You almost got me."

In response, Chris White, with a competitive glint in his eye, declared, "That race is mine next year." He had another year of competition ahead of him, and he was determined to claim victory.

I joined my coaches, my mother, and the rest of the team in celebration. Avon Grove had a strong showing, finishing second overall, just behind Unionville. Winning the 100 meters was a highlight of my high school experience, a moment etched into my memory.

CHAPTER 41

A Standing Ovation

As my senior year in high school approached its grand finale, there was one event I had been both anticipating and dreading—the final awards assembly. I sat in the school's auditorium, surrounded by my fellow students and their families, as one by one, my classmates climbed up to the stage to receive their awards. Coaches and teachers gushed over them with endless accolades, and the proud cheers of their families filled the air. It was a bittersweet sight, knowing that I would soon join them on that stage, but my family wouldn't be there to celebrate with me.

I knew what I would be receiving: a varsity letter and certificates for being the president of the choir and SADD (Students Against Drunk Driving) chapter. Iszel, my steadfast brother on this journey, was receiving a varsity letter as well. We had been through so much together, and this was the final moment we could share what we had earned with hard work and dedication. Next year, I would be at West Chester University, and Iszel would become the oldest guy in the house.

Then, it was time for our track and field coaches, Wayne Howard and Carl Benson, to take the stage. As they began to list the letter winners and honors, I listened with a sense of anticipation. Iszel and I were included in their anecdotes, our achievements acknowledged but without the grandeur that some others received. We walked up to collect our awards, a simple nod and handshake, and returned to our seats without much fanfare.

The awards assembly was never-ending, but I couldn't help but smile. It was my last experience of those "empty seats," the final reminder that my path had been different. But I was ready to move on.

THOSE BOYS ON THE HILL

Then came the moment that would forever change how I felt about those empty seats. The last award of the night was "Athlete of the Year." The Athletic Director of the district stepped forward and began to describe the qualities of the student who would receive this prestigious honor. It wasn't about being the fastest or strongest; it was about excelling academically and serving the community. The award was not decided by statistics but by the impact a student had on their peers and the school community.

As he continued, I never expected what came next. He announced, "I am happy to bestow this honor on none other than Elliott Glover." I was completely shocked, frozen in my seat for a moment before Iszel grabbed me and hugged me tightly. He was beaming with pride, and I could feel his happiness radiating.

I walked up to the stage to receive my award, my heart pounding. I shook the hand of the Athletic Director and turned to face the audience, expecting to see those empty seats once again. But to my astonishment, the entire track team, my coaches, and Iszel were walking up on the stage. The auditorium erupted in applause, and the seats were empty, not because there was no one there but because everyone was standing.

I was surrounded by so much love and regard from my fellow athletes, coaches, and friends who had watched me grow up and navigate my scholastic and sports career. It was an overwhelming feeling of acceptance and recognition. In that moment, those empty seats were not a void but a symbol of the support and love that had been with me all along.

As I stood on that stage, enveloped in the warmth of their applause, I knew that I had found a connection in the most unexpected of places, not bound by blood, but by experiences through trials and tribulation. I had people committed to witness my life. They celebrated my wins, mourned my losses, and filled in everything in between. It assured me that my life was just as important to them as it was to me. It was all I wanted. My graduation came and went, but it was that standing ovation, that moment, that would stay with me forever, filling the emptiness with boundless love, joy, and appreciation.

CHAPTER 42

The Brotherhood

As the late July sun began to set on the horizon, casting long shadows across the high school soccer field, the familiar sights of our hometown took on a different hue. Iszel and I stood there among the friends we had come to cherish during our time at the group home, but a realization was settling in. My departure was imminent, and our paths were diverging.

We decided to play a game of football under the twilight sky. Laughter, shouts, and the thud of the ball hitting the ground echoed through the warm evening air. The game was a welcome distraction, an escape from the mounting anxiety that had been shadowing my every thought.

As we wrapped up the game, we made plans to grab some pizza and sandwiches and spend the night at Allen Wu's house. Allen was Danny Wu's younger brother and was in the same grade as Cory and Iszel. The prospect of leaving the group home had been a heavy weight on my mind. The future appeared as vast and unknown as the starry night above us.

Cory made a comment that cut through the banter. "Yo, Ell, I bet you can't wait to get outta here and be on your own at West Chester, huh?"

His words, meant to express excitement about the next chapter, hit me differently. The anticipation of college life was there, but so was the unspoken fear and uncertainty that lingered beneath the surface.

I forced a chuckle, "Yeah, man, it's gonna be a whole new experience."

Cory, still unaware of my conflicting emotions, grinned. "I envy you, man. Freedom, parties, no more rules, and you'll finally be outta that group home."

He continued, oblivious to my growing unease. "But don't worry, we got Iszel's back when you leave, and we'll still be hanging out like we always have."

His well-intentioned assurance hit me differently than he intended. It wasn't just about the freedom of college; it was about the evolving dynamics and the uncharted territory that lay ahead. It was about the uncertainty of my future without any safety net. The fact that I was a senior and they were still in their junior year only heightened the sense of impending change, a forced independence with no fallback.

The clash of emotions was enough to push me over the edge. Counseling was helping me to better understand my emotions, but I still struggled to control my anger once my fuse was lit. Frustration, fear, and a sense of loss all transmuted to rage. Without a clear outlet, I found myself going after Cory, a surge of adrenaline propelling me into a confrontation that he never saw coming. The atmosphere shifted as I lunged at him.

Cory, caught off guard by my sudden aggression, dodged my initial advances. The situation escalated, and the friendly banter turned into a chaotic dance of frustration and confusion.

Allen tried to intervene, realizing that this was more than just a playful scuffle. "Yo, Ell, calm down, man!" He put his hand on my chest to keep me from Cory.

As emotions continued to escalate, Cory, sensing my intensity, bolted towards the cars, fumbling with the keys to unlock it. Panic set in as I pursued him, the lighthearted evening now overshadowed by the confrontation.

Cory managed to reach his car just in time, slamming the door shut and locking himself inside. The dim glow of the car's interior highlighted his wide-eyed uncertainty, and for a moment, we locked eyes through the window.

He yelled at me. "Tha' hell's wrong witchu, man?!"

Iszel, ever the voice of reason, said, "Yo, y'all, bounce. Just leave Ell and me here."

Allen asked, "How're y'all gonna get home?"

Iszel answered, "We'll walk."

Allen hesitated but eventually heeded Iszel's advice. He started his car and drove away, leaving us in the dimly lit parking lot.

As we started our three-mile trek to the group home, Iszel finally asked the question that had been hanging in the air. "Yo, what's up, man?"

I sighed, trying to find the words. "I don't know, man. It's just that, unlike those guys, I have no place to go once I leave the group home."

Iszel nodded in understanding. "You know, none of those guys you were going after are at fault, right?"

"Yeah, I know," I replied, guilt gnawing at me. "I just messed up the whole night."

In the quiet of the night, I finally confided, "I'm gonna be leaving soon, and, honestly, I'm losing it a bit, man. And talking to Marsha messed my head up more."

Iszel's steps echoed in the silence as he spoke. "Yeah, watching what's happening to you has me already thinking about getting things together."

I couldn't help but smile. "You're gonna be fine, Zel; the Spencers will always take you in. I'm not anyone's adopted son like that. I'm gonna be out here on my own. I was feeling pretty good for a while, but it's different being someone's friend and being someone's *family*. Sometimes it feels like I've got no one really looking out for me."

THOSE BOYS ON THE HILL

Iszel paused for a moment, his voice full of reassurance. "Yo, things won't change between us, man. We'll always be close, and we'll always have each other's backs."

The walk turned out to be exactly what I needed. By the time we reached the bottom of the hill, Allen's car pulled up. He teased me, saying, "Ell, you still tryna kill folks? You scared the shit out of Cory." We all laughed, breaking the tension.

"Are you guys coming over to my place or what?" Allen asked.

Iszel replied, "Yessirrr!" as he headed for the passenger side of the car.

But I decided to stay behind. "Nah, I'm gonna head up to the house and chill. I'll catch up with you guys tomorrow."

Iszel paused and looked back at me, concern in his eyes. "Yo, you sure you good?"

I smiled, reassuring my brother. "Yeah, man, I'm good."

Iszel joined them in the car, Allen did a three-point turn, and I watched them drive away into the night. I took my time walking up the hill in the darkness, contemplating my past and the unknown future ahead.

The cornfield that once filled me with dread was now a familiar friend, a sanctuary I had come to cherish. A light summer breeze blew through the tall stalks that towered over me.

I finally reached the top of the hill and cut across the field like we had so many years ago, but now the House on the Hill was a welcome sight. I walked up to the front porch. The house was quiet. The younger guys must have already gone to bed, and the rec room was probably filled with laughter and the glow of a TV from the other guys. It was a warm night, so I sat on the porch for a while, staring down at the small development on the other side of the cornfield, savoring the peace that enveloped me. I had a few weeks left, and the ambiguity of what lay beyond that final chapter was both daunting and exciting.

My unexpected outburst at Cory and the talk with Iszel helped me to process how I was feeling, and for the first time, I let myself embrace the mix of emotions – the fear, the anxiety, the anticipation. I was better able to sit with the uncertainty. After all, nothing in life was ever guaranteed. My brothers and I had always been ok before, no matter what the world threw at us. I sat listening to the chirp of the crickets and the buzz of cicadas. They were sounds that had once been so alien to me and now seemed so familiar, even comforting. The hum of the insects would forever remind me of my time here, which had been an intimidating life change that I had embraced and survived. If there was anything my 18 years had taught me, it was that my brothers and I were survivors. It didn't necessarily make the unknown any easier, but it was an assurance of sorts that I would once again be ok.

CHAPTER 43

Leaving The House on the Hill

On my last night at the group home, everything I was feeling swirled within me, creating a turbulent and restless whirlwind. I carefully set aside the outfit I intended to wear on my departure, then meticulously packed the rest of my belongings. Instead of carrying everything in trash bags, the familiar emblem of group home and foster care kids on the move, I now used two sturdy, large duffel bags containing all my clothes for the journey ahead.

In a corner, a few boxes housed my trophies and awards. Wilma had generously allowed me to store them on the third floor of the house, providing a temporary sanctuary for these mementos that bound me to the past nine years of my life. They were my lifeline to the House on the Hill, and without them, I feared I might lose my connection to the place that had become my home. I knew I'd always be one of "Those Boys," but the reality of no longer being a resident weighed heavily on my heart.

When the van was finally loaded with the essentials, I reentered the house for my goodbyes. Walking through those familiar halls, I shared heartfelt embraces and firm handshakes with the guys who were present, vowing to stay in touch. My farewells reached their poignant climax with Wilma, who displayed a mix of pride and sorrow, her cheeks moistened by tears. I held her close in a comforting embrace until she found her composure.

Iszel wasn't around. He'd practically made a second home at the Spencer's over the past year. It had become customary for him to spend the night there with Cory, particularly after evenings spent with their circle of friends. As I contemplated how best to reach him, I decided instead to call him once I settled in at West Chester University. Our lives were veering down different paths, and there was no need for a prolonged, sentimental farewell; we both understood the depth of our bond.

Leaving the House for the last time, I hesitated for a moment before climbing into the van with Wayne and Marsha. As we slowly drove down the long, winding driveway, I turned and cast a lingering gaze at my former home, allowing a rush of memories to wash over me. I'd spent almost half my life there. It had witnessed my difficulties, sorrows, trials, and triumphs. There was a deep ache in my chest, realizing I was leaving behind the place that had offered me solace. But intertwined with that sadness was a warm blanket of nostalgia.

The House, which had once been vast and imposing, now appeared smaller, like a cherished childhood toy that had shrunk over the years, and in that moment, the years I spent with the Hills seemed far removed. Twill had turned it into a true home, a place of respite instead of conflict, and in that moment, I couldn't help but feel profound gratitude for all the love and support I had received within those walls. I knew I was going to miss the safety and warmth it had provided. I was going to miss it... a lot.

The drive to West Chester University's Sanderson Hall was silent, the weight of my impending departure hanging heavily in the air.

Once we arrived, we began unloading the van, carrying my belongings into the building that would be my home for the next school year. We brought everything inside but left it in the lobby while I checked in with the Resident Attendant. They provided me with my room assignment, and when I returned to the van, I could see on Wayne and Marsha's faces that their part in this journey was ending. There were no plans beyond dropping me off.

"You all checked in?" Wayne asked, his voice cracking with a tinge of sadness he was failing to control.

Wayne reached to his side and pulled out a large grocery bag, handing it to me through the van window. "I packed you a couple of dishes in case they don't season that cafeteria food right."

I nodded, feeling a lump in my throat. "Wayne, you tha' man. Thanks." We shook hands, and then he broke eye contact, blinking away tears. I moved to the other side of the van, where Marsha, maintaining her usual composed demeanor, mirrored the handshake. She pursed her lips and offered a single, silent nod of goodbye.

As they pulled away from the curb, I watched the van recede into the distance. I thought I could see Wayne looking at my reflection in the rearview mirror as they drove away. Left to navigate the unfamiliar terrain of college life on my own, I stood amidst excited families and students, all capturing the first day of this new chapter with photos. The House on the Hill was behind me, and the path ahead was uncertain. Ready or not, I had stepped into the unknown, a tumultuous blend of sadness, gratitude, nostalgia, and anticipation rushing through me as I embarked on this new adventure.

CHAPTER 44
Christmas 1994

I found myself easily settling in my Freshman year. I was majoring in theatre and was involved in related extracurricular activities. I worked a part-time job, earned decent grades, and made a solid group of friends. I spent winter break crashing with a girlfriend, but my luck ran out over the summer when I had to figure out a living situation for three months. I spent a part of it on the floor of Danny Wu's house until his parents decided to sell their home. I had to leave so they could stage and show their home to potential buyers. I slept on the porch of another friend's home who lived with his grandmother for the next week. She would only allow me inside to wash and expected me to be gone during the day. I spent the last month or so sleeping on covered bus stop benches in and around West Chester, waiting for school to finally open back up.

Most of my time was spent in libraries and fast-food restaurants until closing time. I couldn't get a job because I was too transient, and maintaining hygiene was such a struggle. I survived off the monthly stipend BCS deposited into my checking for meals and the occasional room when the weather was bad. It rained a lot during that last month of summer break.

I was hardly alone in my dilemma. Foster care has been referred to as the highway to homelessness. Anywhere from a third to a half of people experience homelessness, like I did, in the first few years of exiting foster care.[23] I hated it. I cursed God for ending up that way. I smelled and looked horrible. I trolled West Chester's campus, looking for some sign that the school was open. I didn't know my return date because my mail was still being sent to the group home.

THOSE BOYS ON THE HILL

It was such a relief once West Chester opened its doors again, and I had a stable place to live for a few months. I continued to earn respectable grades, started working out, and packed on ten pounds of muscle. However, looming over my good times was the impending winter break and another month of potential homelessness.

My mom and I still had a complicated relationship; she wanted to be involved and have a say over my decisions, and I kept her at arm's length. But I was feeling desperate thinking about a month without a place to live or having to couch surf at the mercy of friends and their parents. I decided to call her. I explained my situation, and she invited me to stay with her at my grandfather's house to spend the holidays together—no gifts, no fuss, just cooking and spending time together. We've never been big on giving gifts, mostly because we never had money to afford them. Even today, holidays for my mother and siblings are mostly marked with a phone call to each other.

I would be allowed to stay for as long as I needed, at least until my grandfather grew tired of an extra person in the house, throwing off his precious daytime schedule. With some combination of relief and trepidation, I accepted her invitation.

On the last day of school, my boys, Jeris and Chad, knocked on the door of my dorm room. My dorm mate, Rob, had packed a bag and was doing one last look around before heading out when the other guys showed up.

"Yo man, I'm bouts to bounce," Jeris said when I answered the door. We all interlocked hands, leaned in, and clapped backs.

"See y'all next semester, fellaz," I said. It was the tenth time I'd repeated that phrase in the past few hours, saying so long to my other friends. I was waiting until the last possible minute to leave.

As I didn't own a vehicle, I relied on public transportation to get back to Philly. I took SEPTA's 104 bus from West Chester to the 69th Street terminal, which is connected to the Market-Frankfort Line to 15th and Market, then the Orange Line to Broad and Lehigh. It was my first time going back to the city in four years since my grandmother's funeral. Though it had been a while since I had taken the route, I still knew it like the back of my hand.

I stood in the far corner of the train car so I could have a full view of it. I knew from experience that the holidays brought out some desperate and ruthless people, and I wasn't trying to fall victim to someone's bad intentions. Despite the precaution, I found the familiar rocking, knocking sounds and the occasional flicker of the train lights soothing, lulling me into a sense of nostalgia.

A light dusting of snow lay on the ground by the time I walked up the subway steps and out into the chilly night air on the corner of Broad & Lehigh Avenues around 8 PM. I peered down Broad Street and could see Center City's skyline illuminated in seasonal colors. Neither the snow nor the hour slowed my city. North Philly was bustling.

A car passed by, spraying slush from its tires, music blaring. The bass was turned up so high that it caused the car's panels to rattle. There was a distant siren of an ambulance, fire truck, police car, or all three somewhere within earshot. A couple walked by, holding tightly onto each other, laughing at the shared experience of braving the snow together. I smiled to myself. The chilly, fresh air felt good in my lungs.

The smell of sauteed onions and fried food wafted past me from a corner store somewhere. A nostalgic moment hit me. *Home.* Between Reading Terminal, South Street, Philly's Italian Market, and the Gallery, I knew where to find some of the best food. I missed my city. Visiting again felt like getting back together after a long breakup.

The way I'm feeling, I might have to get Mom and me a cheesesteak tonight, I thought, weighing our dinner options.

I had one more bus to take, the 54, then a five-block walk to arrive at my grandfather's. I was dressed in my "dangerous-part-of-the-city" apparel: laced-up, dark boots, jeans, a hoodie, and a skully pulled low over my head. I settled into a broad stance, quiet but owning my space, trying my best to let everyone know that I was not to be messed with in that dark corner.

A taxi hack approached me, hoping to capitalize on the weather conditions and the late hour. "My mans, lemme give yo' a ride," he cajoled. "Yo' don't wanna be out here this time of night in this weather. I know yo' gotta coupla bucks for me to get yo' home."

He pointed at an old, banged-up car as his means to get me where I needed to go.

"Naw, man," I said in my lowest voice register and flagged him off. "I'm good."

"What? Yo' don't trust me or sumptin?" he asked, offended. "Com' on, man, it's the fuckin' hollydays. Help a brotha out."

He stepped a little too close to me, and the smell of weed and alcohol on him turned my stomach.

"Yo, Ole Head, I'm notcha brotha." I shoved his small frame back, reclaiming my space. "Back up off me. Tha fucks wrong widchu?" I sized him up. He was dressed in an oversized sweatshirt, jeans, and some worn-out boots.

He ain't ready for me.

"You 'bout to get yourself hurt out here ole' head," I warned.

He stopped and raised his hand in innocent regard.

"I don't want no problems, man," he acquiesced. "Jus' tryna make a lil money out here for the hollydays."

He stepped back into the dark towards the car and paced around, trying to keep himself warm or manage his high while waiting to see if anyone else would take him up on his offer.

I considered him for another moment and decided he wasn't much of a threat. He needed a few days of detox, not an ass-whooping.

He just out here, husslin.' I decided.

The 54-bus pulled up. I climbed on, dropped in a token to pay my fare, and took a seat on the sidewalk side of the street. The taxi hack paced out of the dark and into the light side of the corner. I squinted to get a better look at him.

I went numb for a second. It was my Uncle Ricky.

He looked frail, small, and burnt out. A pang of spite in my stomach flared to life, extinguishing the numbness. I stood up and walked to the rear bus door. Heat filled me, making it hard to think of anything but my hatred for the man on the corner.

"Yo, let me back off this piece!" I exclaimed forcefully.

The bus driver saw me focusing on the taxi hack pacing outside and didn't open the door.

"Yo, it ain't worth it, man," he said.

He shook his head at my reflection in the rearview mirror.

"Whatever he did, it ain't worth messing up the holidays for you and your family."

We met eyes in the reflective glass. He kept talking. "Let that shit go, man."

He wore the traditional SEPTA blues uniform and had locs down his back.

"I tell you what," he negotiated. "Let me get you a block down the street. If you still wanna get off and walk back to see if he's still there, I'll let you get off."

I turned and looked at Uncle Ricky, who was still pacing to keep himself warm around the car.

I'm a lot bigger and stronger than I was when you beat on me and locked me in that basement.

I saw the whole thing play out in my head. *I could whup your ass right now, Uncle Ricky!*

I looked back at the driver, and our eyes met again in the mirror. There was a beat of understanding between us. I turned my gaze back to my uncle and fell back down into the seat. I was sweating and tense, my heart racing. I never took my eyes off the man who had tormented me so many years before. He was a shadow of the man I had once feared. His pacing reminded me of Zeus trotting around during that time we spent together in the basement.

I know that dog is smiling from a better place.

The streetlight turned from red to green, highlighting the snow falling on the windshield, and the bus pulled through the intersection. The driver took his time driving down each street, taking me further and further away from Uncle Ricky. He considered me at every corner, silently asking if I was gonna stay on for another block. I don't know if I just didn't want to mess up the bus driver's night with the thought of me hurting someone on his route or if I accepted that I would not get any real satisfaction from hurting Uncle Ricky more than he had already hurt himself. Either way, I stayed on the bus. Eventually, I pulled the cord to signal my stop, stood up, and walked towards the front of the bus.

"Yo, have a good holiday, man," the driver said. He pushed the button to open the door, allowing the icy air to invade the vehicle's cabin.

I stood at the top of the platform that led down the stairs, my back to him.

"Yeah, man, you too... Thanks." I loaded all my genuine appreciation into that last word.

I stepped off the bus and into the snowy air. It was really coming down now. The bus pulled away, and the sound of its engine faded down the next block. I glanced up at the dark sky before tugging my skully further down over my ears, then walked the five blocks to my grandfather's house. I hunched my shoulders to protect myself from the billowing snow and wind.

I fought the idea that somehow God was involved in how it all played out. I was still at odds with the Big Man and wasn't talking to Him. My mind was churning as much as the snow around me, trying to make sense of the series of events. Not recognizing Uncle Ricky sooner, the bus driver not letting me off the bus, and allowing him to take me further away from the pain I wanted to inflict on the man that had hurt me so many years ago.

But my determined anger towards God was wavering. If it wasn't God, then it was an extremely lucky string of coincidences. Whatever the reason, I grew more certain I had made the right choice not to go back. Uncle Ricky's current disposition was worse than any beating he may have suffered from my revenged assault. I took that ball of rage and desire to hurt him and finally, *finally*, let it go. The tightness in my stomach slowly eased with each step I took.

I'd come a long way in the decade since my mother gave us up in 1984. I'd grown and developed so many layers, all aspects of myself, that I would show to different people, but rarely did anyone know the whole picture except my brothers. I thought of myself in my street-smart getup, thinking how few people in Avondale or West Chester would ever see this side of myself.

Who was I at my core? I'd always thought of myself as warm and open-hearted despite some of the things done to me and that I'd seen and done to survive. I had never felt inherently hard, despite what I sometimes displayed. What toughness I developed was born out of necessity: my anger, a response to trauma. I was only as dangerous as the world made me in the hopes of survival, like so many born in the poorest parts of the city. I thought again about the immediate rage at recognizing Uncle Ricky, and the desire for retribution, and then the repeated choice, block by block, to rise above it.

It felt like a growth moment – getting to confront a demon from my past and wrestling control of my anger. I felt proud. People like Uncle Ricky, the Hills, the Jasons of the world, and the racism I faced couldn't break me or strip me of my humanity. I felt strong to have endured and survived, and also lucky – lucky that I'd had my brothers, Twill, and people like Dave Lichter and Carol Smith, or the outcome could have been very different. I felt uplifted by the time I reached my grandfather's. My aunt had moved my grandparents to a house across the street from where she lived about five years before, but I thought about the old house on Oakdale Street. I could never be on that street without thinking of Iszel's car accident, and I was glad my grandfather had moved. I liked this place better. I smiled, thinking of my brother, happy, irreverent, and as determined as ever.

I'd barely knocked on the door when my mother threw it open. She smiled brightly and ushered me in. She looked good – healthy and well. Between her prison time and probation, she had been clean for nine years.

"*Hey baby!*" she exclaimed as she wrapped her arms around my large frame and gave me a big squeeze. Although she had gained a little weight, she still felt small. She stepped back, took me in, smiled approvingly, and hugged me again tighter, pressing her head deep into my chest. For a moment, I let down the protective wall I had built that created a wedge in our relationship so long ago, allowing a break in my hard demeanor, and hugged her back. I gave her a glimpse of my most vulnerable self and felt a moment of connection our defenses so rarely allowed. Instantly, I was her little kid again. We just hugged as mom and son, and all the rest of it, the hurt, the struggle, the sacrifice, the resentment – it also fell away. I let her hold me like that for as long as she wanted. My heart was lighter.

I felt happy to share this moment with her, happy that we had both survived such difficulties and thrived and had this chance to reconnect and enjoy the holidays together. I was so keenly aware of how nothing in life is guaranteed; the space between now and the future is always filled with harsh uncertainties. That, and the chance for new beginnings.

EPILOGUE

Lost & Found

Late one morning in November 2006, my cell phone rang. It was Iszel. I answered with, "Yooo! What's good, man?"

He responded excitedly, "YOOO! Whatever you do, answer the next call you get! That's all I'mma say!" He hung up, leaving me slightly puzzled and intrigued by his cryptic message.

I looked at my phone, shook my head, and laughed at my knuckleheaded brother. He was always so mysterious with his surprises. I had half a mind to call him back and give him a hard time until he told me what was up, but I let it go, allowing him to have his way with whatever he was doing.

Returning to my TV show, I was engrossed in the storyline when my phone rang again a few minutes later. The caller's number wasn't saved in my phone, and their name didn't appear. However, Iszel's earlier message had me on high alert, so I answered the call with a cautious, "Hello?"

A stranger's voice greeted me from the other end, feminine and laced with desperate hope. "Uh, hi," she stammered. "I'm trying to reach Elliott... Elliott Glover." At least she got the pronunciation of my last name right. I'd spent years correcting people, but at thirty-one, I had given up on trying.

"Speaking," I confirmed, my curiosity piqued.

"Hey, Big Bro, it's your Lil Sis, Briana!" Her voice was brimming with excitement, like an overzealous fan talking to her favorite celebrity for the first time.

Her exuberant greeting caught me off guard, and I instinctively pulled the phone away from my ear. "Excuse me?" I asked, trying to make sense of it all. "How did you get this number? Who are you again?"

"It's me, Big Bro! Me?!" she emphasized. "Your Lil Sis, Briana? Mom gave me your number! I just spoke to Iszel; he seems so cool! Jacque didn't answer, so I called you next." The words tumbled out in rapid succession.

I thought about what she'd said. She had pronounced Iszel's name correctly, which struck me as unusual as someone pronouncing our last name correctly.

I didn't answer fast enough, so she kept going, though she tempered her voice for her next statement, offering clarity. "I just turned eighteen, and I want to finally meet you guys, my biological big brothers."

I found myself struggling to process this revelation. Could this really be our long-lost sister, the one who had been a hazy figure in my mind all these years? I quickly did the mental math, realizing that I was nearly thirty-two, which meant she should be around eighteen. The age aligned with what I knew.

Over the years, I had occasionally wondered about her, pondering her whereabouts, experiences, and well-being. She was a lost piece of our family puzzle, left behind in the foster care system. Her voice was the first tangible piece of her identity that I'd encountered.

When I'd thought about her, she sometimes resembled a younger version of my mother. The infinite possibilities of genetics made it difficult to imagine what my mother's and Mr. Jim's child might look like. Neither my brothers nor I resembled our mother, and with different fathers, we barely looked like each other. Iszel and I were the most similar, both of average height with stocky, athletic frames, while Jacque was taller, lanky, and wiry.

And now, this voice on the phone claimed to be her.

"Can you tell me more?" I asked cautiously. I wasn't ready to believe her just yet.

"Bro, I was born in prison and fostered when I was three weeks old," she said. "I was adopted when I was three. I had a good life with my adoptive parents. I've been waiting so long to meet you guys ever since I found out that I was adopted. As soon as I turned eighteen and legally could, I accessed my adoption records. A piece of me needs to connect with you guys. I need to find out where I really come from. I'm asking you all and Mom to meet me and my adoptive family for my birthday. Will you come?" Her voice was brimming with hope. I got the sense she was throwing all this information at me, hoping it would prove her identity and that I would be open to meeting her.

My mind swirled with questions and uncertainty. Was she genuine, or was this some elaborate hoax? Could I trust this sudden revelation and the emotional rollercoaster it had thrust me into?

"You said Mom gave you my number?" I inquired, noting her ease with referring to my mother as "Mom." She had settled in quite quickly, I thought, especially given she had just turned eighteen.

"Yep, she did," she replied. "I want to get to know my biological big brothers. We've missed so much time. Where do you live? Do you live near Philly? That's where I am. Can we all meet for dinner?" Again, a rapid-fire of questions with no space between them for me to answer. An excited whirlwind of thought spilling out all at once.

My suspicion began to rise. I couldn't let my guard down so easily, still harboring the wariness of the city after all these years.

"Yeah, I live around Philly," I answered cautiously.

She squealed happily. "Great, so you're not too far away for dinner with me?!"

As I was contemplating my response, another call beeped in. It was my mother. We hadn't spoken much in years. She had stayed clean and sober until the early 2000s, but once her probation ended, she'd fallen into bad habits again, and our relationship, so painstakingly repaired, fractured again, making it easier not to communicate than to be haunted by watching her addiction consume her again after years of sobriety. But the call added another layer to my swirling emotions. I asked the woman on my line to hold and clicked over.

"Hey, Baby," my mom greeted me, and surprisingly, her voice was clear, lacking the slur that usually accompanied her speech when she was under the influence.

"Hey, Ma. Some girl is on the other..." I started to say, but she cut me off.

"That's your sister, Briana. I was trying to call you before she did," she explained, her voice having a tinge of contrition, a rare tone from her.

A mix of emotions surged through me, and my mother's call added to it. I didn't want to upset her and push her back into her addictive cycle.

"Okay, she's on the other line. You want me to three-way the calls?" I offered.

"Naw, Baby. Just... Just talk to her. She and her foster family, they're good people," she said, her voice carrying a hint of maternal guilt, pain, and remorse as if she were revisiting the circumstances around my sister's birth.

"Okay, I'll call you back after I talk to her," I said, not because I wanted to engage in a lengthy conversation but to check on my mom's well-being. She hung up without saying goodbye.

The call with Briana ended with my assurance that I would check my schedule regarding dinner, but I couldn't promise anything. Iszel, Jacque, and I decided collectively to attend the get-together for our little sister. Iszel planned to collect our mother and bring her.

We walked in together, presenting a united family front. Briana squealed with delight and ran into our gathering for a family hug. She looked like a young, healthy version of our mother – beautiful. I couldn't help but think how my mother would have looked without the drugs affecting her life and looks.

Briana's adoptive mother, Yolanda, joined the family hug, and the tears flowed. Briana wiped her face and stood back. She took us all in and tried to guess who we each were based on some information she must have received from our mother, and surprisingly, she was right. Her adoptive family was wonderful, and the night was exactly what Briana needed. The Glover Brothers added a fourth sibling now that we had our long-lost little sister.

Twenty years after that first meeting, Briana has settled right into the fold, and at times, she feels like the family glue for the rest of us. She is intentional in relating to us. She never forgets a birthday or special occasion and is lovingly referred to as "Auntie Bri" by our children. Where there were once two people I could depend on to have my back, now there are three. Briana hadn't grown up with us, but she slotted into our lives effortlessly, demonstrating through showing us repeatedly that she was in it for the long haul.

Writing this book has been such a time of reflection, of the difficulties and beauty of past and present. For all of the trauma in my life, I was blessed with so much kindness in the form of people who helped along the way, providing spots of hope or a boost of compassion during dark and difficult days. And then there are my siblings, who love me unconditionally. Whether it was through shared struggle or sheer determination, we were bound by more than just blood, but by the bonds of choosing each other over and over.

Iszel and I were talking on the phone a few days ago. I guess he heard something in my tone and asked, "Yo man, you good?" I thought about where we all are and the life I have today despite all that I have seen and been through. It is with gratitude and appreciation that I could truthfully answer, "Yeah, man... I'm good."

The End

Two Sides to Every Story

As I penned this memoir, I felt compelled to be as authentic and accurate as possible in sharing our family's story, including the events that shaped our lives. I had long held onto my recollections of those challenging times, including the account of my mother's experience with the justice system. However, as I continued to write and reflect, I realized that there was another side to the story, a side that had remained hidden from me for far too long.

My mother, a woman of great strength and resilience, had kept many of her experiences and hardships close to her heart. There were aspects of her life that she was understandably not proud of, and she had chosen not to discuss them with me or others. Her silence had led to an incomplete understanding of some key events in our family's history. One of the biggest revelations was that Mr. Jim was not the man she killed; it was someone she started dating after him that I'd never met.

As I delved deeper into our shared past, I had the opportunity to speak with my mother about her side of the story. It was an emotional and cathartic journey for both of us. In those conversations, I learned about the pain and trauma she had carried for years, the details of her life that she had shielded from me to protect my innocence.

It caused me to recognize that her perspective and the truth behind her experiences needed to be acknowledged and included in our family's narrative. This wasn't just about setting the record straight; it was about understanding the layers of our shared history and honoring the depth of my mother's experiences.

In this book, I have strived to honor both our accounts – my recollections and my mother's revelations. It's a testament to the complexity of our lives and the healing power of understanding and forgiveness. By sharing both our perspectives, I hope to provide a more comprehensive picture of our journey, emphasizing that our family's story is a tapestry woven from many threads, each with its own significance.

Through the pages of this memoir, I aim to convey the resilience and strength of my mother, who faced unimaginable challenges with courage. It's a story of redemption and struggle and a testament to the enduring bond between a mother and a child, a bond that can withstand the weight of difficult truths and emerge stronger on the other side. Our family's narrative is an exploration of the human capacity for forgiveness and the healing that can come from confronting the past with honesty and compassion.

MaryAnn's Account – December 2021

Those Boys on the Hill podcast

Episode – Family is Forever

I remember it was a Friday night because we always went out on a Friday. We were in the old neighborhood. I was down near the Uptown Theater, somewhere in that area. It was me and Robert Sproul, who'd been a friend of the family for years but had divorced my mother's cousin from Harrisburg, Pennsylvania.

I had been warned to steer clear of him, but we turned each other on; I was grown enough and thought that he wouldn't do that to me. I wouldn't let him, so it didn't matter.

That particular night, we got off work, and we went out to play some pool. We went to the store on Broad & Lehigh to get something to eat. He had a freakout, slapped and knocked me down, and knocked the food out of my hand. I don't know why; maybe he thought I looked at some dudze; I don't know what his problem was.

We got home, and I was cussing and crying, and he's still acting like an idiot. I said, "Look, that's not gonna happen."

His nephew, who was living there, came down and asked, "What's going on?"

I said he just needs to cool off because he just hit me like that. Robert called me a bunch of names and shit, and I told him don't he dare come at me or attempt to touch me.

He begins to try and beat on me. I walked to the kitchen to try and cool off and get away from him, but he followed me. I happened to see a knife on the top of the fridge; I had no idea why it was there, and I took it down. He was so close that I just stabbed him. I stuck him straight in his chest, in his heart. And he died.

I ran. Real fast. Matter of fact, I stopped some man in the street. I had these white sneakers on, blood all over them and probably on me, too. I told him what happened and that I needed help. He gave me a ride to 24th, where I live. I got down there and didn't tell anybody what happened. I ended up going to the drug house, bought drugs, and went to the corner store on Sterner Street. The police came and got me right then and there because his nephew was in the house and knew exactly where I lived. I paid for the drugs and never did them because the cops arrested me.

Against All Odds

In the face of adversity, the Glover family has not only overcome our challenging upbringings but has also achieved success in our various walks of life. Each member of the family has carved their own path, defying the statistics that often go with group home and foster care experiences.

Jacque

Jacque made his mark through honorable service in the U.S. Army during the Gulf War. His dedication and commitment to his duty resulted in an honorable discharge. Today, he stands as a role model for his two children, regularly attending their sporting events. Jacque's life journey has taken him to Western Pennsylvania, where he has forged a career as a pharmacist. His unwavering dedication to both his family and profession reflects the resilience that has characterized the Glover family.

Iszel

Iszel pursued a path of education and empowerment. Graduating from Lincoln University with a degree in English, he embarked on a journey to share his knowledge with others. Iszel's passion for teaching led him to a career as a high school English teacher, where he influenced the lives of countless students. However, his ambitions didn't stop there. Iszel's entrepreneurial spirit led him to start a personal training company, allowing him to inspire others to lead healthier lives. He conducts boot camp sessions and manages a sub-shop franchise. He is happily married with a child. He maintains strong relationships with many of the guys we grew up with and often spends time traveling with his wife. He now lives in a small town close to the House on the Hill. His dedication to his family, friends, and community reflects the values he holds dear.

Briana

Briana embarked on her own journey to success. Despite the many challenges that being immediately fostered at birth and adopted at an early age may pose, she was fortunate to be adopted by a loving family and thrived. Briana pursued higher education and graduated with a degree in communications from the University of Phoenix. Her commitment to education extended into her professional life, where she found her calling as an elementary school teacher. Briana's impact on the lives of her students and her dedication to her career exemplify the strength of her character.

Moreover, Briana's happiness extends to her personal life, as she is now happily married and has two children of her own. Her commitment to maintaining strong relationships with both her adoptive and biological families is a testament to her ability for love and connection. Residing in Florida with her husband and two children, she has built a quiet, content life, being a beacon of positivity and perseverance.

MaryAnn

Throughout the years, my mother's journey has been a complex one with triumphs and tribulations. Iszel once likened her life's odyssey to navigating a lengthy paper route fraught with challenging potholes and pursued by relentless, menacing dogs. Her story speaks of resilience, love, and the intricate dynamics of family bonds. Despite finding solace in love and marriage, the lingering clutches of addiction have never fully loosened their grip on her.

Amidst the battles, my mother and her late husband managed to create a haven of joy, hosting vibrant BBQ gatherings for family and friends. These occasions became symbolic of their enduring love and the warmth that filled their home.

Her narrative took an unexpected turn with her husband's passing, marking a pivotal moment in her life. Faced with profound loss, she chose to retire, bidding farewell to the bustling city of Philly and embracing the tranquility of a quiet town in South Carolina. This geographical shift was intended to create a protective barrier against the temptations that have long haunted her to usher in a new, serene chapter.

As a grandmother and now a great-grandmother, she holds dear her significant role within the family. The bonds she tirelessly works to nurture over the years remain a continuous pursuit, although the threads connecting us are not as robust as they could be. While she stands as a source of unwavering love for her children and grandchildren, the familial ties are marked by a certain fragility. Life's trials have left us a bit war-torn, but we are always striving to strengthen the bonds.

Her life is one of ongoing struggle and hope.

Return To the House on the Hill

Recently, Iszel and I received an invitation to revisit the House on the Hill three decades after leaving it behind. A group of us ventured there to reminisce about the time that was now so distant. The once-familiar surroundings had transformed significantly. The barn and the cornfield were gone, and many of the trees that lined the driveway had been removed. The house now sat amidst housing developments; its former solitary presence replaced by a community of homes.

The House on the Hill is now privately owned, and the current owner graciously allowed us to explore the space. It had passed through several ownerships over the years, even serving as a convent for a period. Walking through the House, I could hear the echoes of the guys I had lived with during my time there. Iszel and I reflected on the many stories told in this book. The house felt notably smaller, but it remained a symbol of our shared experiences.

As I stood within its walls, I couldn't help but feel a profound sense of nostalgia, a reminder of the challenges and the growth that had transpired during our time there. The journey from the past to the present had taken us on different paths, yet revisiting the House on the Hill was a testament to the enduring connection we shared and the impact it had on our lives.

ELLIOTT GLOVER

About The Author

Elliott Glover is a passionate advocate for change, drawing from his remarkable life experiences to shed light on the often harsh and overlooked realities of the foster and group home systems. His formative and teenage years were spent navigating alternative living situations and group homes alongside his brothers, providing him with unique insights into the challenges faced by those growing up in similar circumstances.

After aging out of the group home system, Elliott embarked on a journey of higher education, earning a bachelor's degree in business from Wilmington University. Fueled by the haunting memories of his past, he felt an irresistible urge to share his family's story with the world. Through his book, he aspires to cast a spotlight on the many hardships endured by individuals and families entangled within the foster and group home systems. His narrative extends beyond the children navigating these systems, reaching out to illuminate the struggles and challenges that ripple through the lives of the many people who are impacted by these multifaceted systems.

Elliott's narrative is just one among many, but he hopes that it can contribute to a broader movement aimed at supporting one of society's most vulnerable and marginalized groups. In pursuit of this mission, he founded the Those Boys on the Hill Foundation, a non-profit organization and scholarship fund dedicated to assisting individuals who age out of or emancipate from the foster and group home systems.

In addition to his written work, Elliott and his brother Iszel launched a podcast under the same name, "Those Boys on the Hill," offering a platform for sharing stories, insights, and discussions related to their experiences and the broader foster care community (thoseboysonthehill.com).

THOSE BOYS ON THE HILL

Today, Elliott lives in Northern Virginia with his wife and family, living a quiet life while continuing to advocate for change and support those in need within the foster and group home systems.

I Once

Iszel felt compelled to pen this poem in June of 2020, in the wake of all the debate surrounding the death of George Floyd. It resonated with me, and so many others of our Black friends, especially those who grew up with us in a predominantly white town, and it deserves a platform.

I Once. . .

By Iszel Glover

I once was called the N-word (actually, probably bout 1000x).

I once was told by a female classmate in middle school that God left me in the oven too long.

I once was told that you are blacker than my crack."

I once was told that "we were nothing but ni@@ers from the home."

I once was told that I only dated white girls.

I once was asked by a cop when pulled over to not say a word as he asked my white girlfriend if she was there against her will.

I once married a black woman.

I once was humiliatingly arrested in a mall in West Virginia bcuz I supposedly was writing stolen bad checks for stereo equipment, so said the three white women that followed me around the mall for 30 minutes (the two white guys I was with were told to go home).

I once was told by Black Africans in my class that they hate that black people in America call themselves African American bcuz we've never been to Africa.

I once was told to go back to Africa if I don't like the way things are done here.

I once thought I had a unique perspective, being from Philly, growing up in a group home in a white country, then to a predominantly white school with a reputation (WVU), and then to an HBCU (Lincoln Univ).

I once was telling a story to my family, and my cousin told me to "talk regular; you're not around your white friends."

I once was told, "I bet if I turn you inside out, I'll see nothing but white."

I once felt that both sides disliked me.

I once chose English as a major bcuz I didn't want to fall into the stereotype that all black men can only be gym teachers.

NOT ONCE did I ever want to trade spots with anyone and be anything but BLACK.

NOT ONCE did I ever want to be light black in hopes of sliding by.

NOT ONCE was I ever rendered speechless, but lately, I've been quiet with not much to say.

NOT ONCE in 44 years have I felt optimistic about this CHANGE that is necessary.

I once was told I had a gift, and I choose to effect change in my own little community.

TODAY, not TOMORROW, but TODAY I ASK, for ONCE, WILL YOU talk to your grandparents that keep the chains on, for ONCE will YOU tell your siblings and aunts and uncles that enough is enough?

For ONCE, will YOU tell your colleague that the off-color joke is offensive and indeed not funny?

ELLIOTT GLOVER

FOR ONCE....PLEASE......because

I ONCE believed in all of us, and right now, I'm a little discouraged because KNEES OR TREES; either way, it's still lynching me.

EDITOR'S NOTE
Fostering Understanding

This note started as a discussion between Elliott and me regarding the Spencer's inability to foster Iszel due to Dr. Frye's prejudice against white people. I thought it prudent to examine why Dr. Frye might have developed that bias. After considerable back and forth, Elliott offered me the space for an Editor's note. I am forever grateful for the opportunity. I know it's a sensitive subject that many are emotionally invested in, so please understand these views are mine.

The Spencers' story is undoubtedly a tragedy – a family wanting to offer a loving home to a foster child denied because of their skin color. Why might Dr. Frye have had such a bias? I cannot know for sure, but one of the reasons may be other cases he'd seen in foster care. There are many accounts of white families adopting Black children and then failing to acknowledge their Blackness. [24] [25] [26] The challenges of transracial adoption are common enough to have a name: the "transracial adoption paradox.[27]" It's defined as the experience of growing up being treated as white and feeling completely unprepared for how the world will treat them as a minority.

This colorblind mentality treats race as if it's not still relevant. That would be great if it were true, but unfortunately, it's not. Pretty much every racial statistic created by valid sources emphasizes the inequalities in American society regarding race systemically: in government, corporations, healthcare, economics, and policing.[28] [29] [30] [31] [32] [33] [34] [35] [36] [37] Therefore, acting colorblind (pretending we're equal without addressing existing inequalities) allows racism to continue unacknowledged and unchecked.[38] When white families treat Black children like they're white, they are leaving kids unprepared for some basic realities that Black kids face, such as encounters with racism, whether it's personal, systemic, or institutional. Some white families completely divorce their Black children from their cultural and familial roots, which can cause feelings of alienation. Some kids are gaslit about their own experiences of racism by parents who dismiss it as something else. Many live in predominately white areas, where no one looks like them and with no easy way to connect with their Blackness.

For those who do foster and adopt, it's a call to be educated and keep an open mind about race, to keep kids connected to their roots, and to always work towards transcending the boundaries of bias and prejudice. There are still plenty of loving white families who are aware of and successfully navigate these challenges with their Black foster or adopted children. But I thought it worth noting that Dr. Frye's prejudice did not form in a vacuum.

Prejudice takes many forms. Today, LGBTQ+ adults who are keen to adopt or foster also face obstacles.[39] Anytime we allow such biases to impact the system, we are doing a disservice to the children within it. The pressing issue is that thousands of children are still waiting to find their Forever families. According to recent statistics, there are over 391,000 children in the foster care system,[40] with approximately 20,000 of them a year aging out of the system without ever finding a permanent home.[41]

As mentioned in this book, though reunification is theoretically the goal of foster care, there is very little incentive for this to occur. It accounts for only a fraction of the budget allotted to foster care, and the system is structured in such a way that fostering and adoption are financially prioritized over successful reunification. Fewer resources are given to families post-reunification than to foster parents or adopted parents, and almost all that is invested is in the short term.[42] Research suggests that longer-term investments would help keep kids out of foster care.[43]

Black children, in particular, are more likely to experience foster care than their non-Black counterparts,[44] often due to over-policing of Black communities and racial stereotyping.[45] One example of many:

Black women are more likely to be screened for drug use and reported to child welfare authorities after delivery.[46] Another issue is poverty. Due to segregation and a long history of racist policies in America, Black people are more likely to be poor and live in poorer communities.[47] Only 17% of children are taken from their parents because of abuse; mostly, they are removed because of neglect charges related to poverty.[48] Furthermore, though children are often taken from their parents to theoretically offer them a better life, they enter a system that exposes them to physical and sexual abuse. The current structure of the system gives kids in foster care very little voice. Caseworkers are overworked and underpaid, and many reports of abuse simply get buried or ignored.

The challenge becomes how to prioritize the well-being of children in a system that is overwhelmed and dubiously structured. Grim statistics face adults who were children in the foster care system. Teens who age out often experience homelessness, and only a small percentage ever finish college. This multi-faceted issue serves as a call to action, highlighting the pressing need for legislative change. Elliott formed Those Boys on the Hill Foundation as a way to work towards legislative change (and offer funds to teens), specifically as it relates to aging out of the foster care system. There are many other avenues out there that people can support to effect improvements in foster care. Educating yourself is the first step, which you've already started by reading this book. Supporting charities aimed at changing legislation and improving outcomes is another (such as Elliott's, but you can find a lot of great options online, depending on what area you're most passionate about). Being informed and helping to change public opinion, such as increasing awareness of the potential benefits of long-term reunification support, is another. Basically, educate yourself and find the people who are trying to effect positive change (like Elliott) and then help them!

I'd like to end this Editor's Note by thanking Elliott for putting up with me. It's been three years, three thousand comments, a pile of my disorganized notes, my convoluted effort to create a timeline and list of people appearing in this book (think ball of string), repeated requests for him to relay the same information to me that he'd JUST given the day before, a wide range of emotions on all the topics in this book (some *hard* talks), and a lot of disbelief and then deep, enduring admiration as to how much Elliott's been through while still turning out so amazing (the disbelief was all mine because of course he lived it, I think the only thing Elliott couldn't believe was just how bad my memory really is). A significant number of ramblings, overly long explanations, tangents, passionate diatribes, the occasional discussion of the zombie apocalypse, and a lot of minion gifs later, and we've reached the end of this thing.

Elliott has laid himself on the line. He's displayed courage beyond my capacity to comprehend. He's been to hell and back and somehow came out whole. Elliott's basically a unicorn. The fact that he's doing so well after all of the trauma he endured is a testament to a strength inside of him that most people don't have (including myself). It's what gives me so much sympathy for other people who are broken by their circumstances. Because no one should have to endure what he did. Rising from poverty and abuse should not be the American Dream. The American Dream should be that abject poverty doesn't exist in the first place, that we dismantle systems of oppression, and that places like foster care that are designed to help, actually benefit the children within their custody. The only way to go about making that a reality is to change people's minds so that we can change legislation. Elliott wanted to tell his story, no matter how vulnerable it made him, in the hopes of shedding that light. In the hopes of making an impact. In solidarity with others who have experienced similar situations. To give voice to the voiceless. I think he's done all of that. What an honor and a privilege.

BREAKING THE CYCLE

Empowering Foster Youth for a Brighter Future

The statistics of foster kids aging out of the system in the United States are a stark reminder of the challenges faced by these vulnerable young individuals. Many find themselves at a crossroads, lacking the necessary support and resources to transition into adulthood successfully. The statistics are disheartening. I established the Those Boys on the Hill Foundation and Scholarship Fund, which is aimed at addressing this critical issue and providing hope to those who have aged out of the foster care system.

A Rocky Transition to Adulthood:

- *A Growing Number of Youth Aged Out*: Almost 20,000 children age out of the US foster care system each year.[49]

- *The Harsh Reality of Homelessness*: After aging out of the system, 31%-46% of foster children face homelessness by the time they turn 26.[50]

- *The Employment Challenge*: In a California study, only half of youth aging out of foster care will have gainful employment by the time they turn 23. 60% will have an annual income below the poverty rate.[51]

- *Education Dreams Deferred*: The odds of former foster children earning a college degree are dishearteningly low. Former foster children enter college at less than half the national average, and only an estimated 2-10% will ever graduate.[52]

- *Teen Pregnancy and Its Impact*: A study done in the Midwest shows that 7 out of 10 girls who age out of the foster care system will become pregnant before turning 21.[53]

- *The Lingering Effects of PTSD*: An alarming 25% of children who age out of the foster care system continue to suffer from the direct effects of post-traumatic stress disorder.[54]

The Foster Care to Prison Pipeline:

- *Involvement with the Justice System*: The "foster care to prison" pipeline statistics are staggering, with close to one-fifth of the US prison population comprising former foster children.[55]

- Approximately 70% of youth who exit foster care as legal adults are arrested at least once by age 26.[56]

The Those Boys on the Hill Foundation and Scholarship Fund:

- The Those Boys on the Hill Foundation is a non-profit organization and scholarship fund dedicated to addressing the challenges faced by those aging out of foster care.

- *Comprehensive Support*: Advocating for more comprehensive support systems, including initiatives like Delaware's HB123 bill. Collaborating with colleges, universities, and technical schools to provide room and board for attending students who aged out of foster care during holiday breaks.

- *Empowering Through Education and Training*: Partnering with social workers, state and private foster care and group home agencies, and local unions to offer training programs in various trades for working-age teens.

- *Scholarship Opportunities*: Establishing a scholarship fund for individuals who graduate high school or achieve a G.E.D., offering a lifeline to higher education and career advancement.

While the statistics regarding foster kids aging out of the system are disheartening, the Those Boys on the Hill Foundation serves as a beacon of hope. Through advocacy, collaboration, and scholarship opportunities, this non-profit organization is striving to break the cycle and provide a brighter future for those who have experienced the foster care system's challenges. With dedication and support, we can empower these young adults and offer them the opportunities they deserve to lead fulfilling lives.

To support our efforts, go to:

thoseboysonthehill.com

tbothfoundation.org

thoseboysonthehillfoundation.org

ACKNOWLEDGMENTS

I extend my heartfelt gratitude to the extraordinary individuals who have made sharing "Those Boys on the Hill" possible:

First and foremost, to my incredible wife, La Shawn, your love, unwavering support, encouragement, and boundless patience have been my anchor and a blessing throughout the entire TBOTH journey. I thank God for you every day.

To my children for loving and supporting me through this process. My hope is to show you that the challenges in life are here to make you stronger. Believe that God has a plan.

To my dear mother, MaryAnn, and my cherished siblings, Jacque, Iszel, and Briana, your enduring love and unwavering belief in me to tell our story have been a source of strength and inspiration.

To the exceptional house parents at the Avondale Group Home who shaped our lives in countless ways: Etwillamae King, Paul Brown, Dave Lichter, Wilma Staton, Flora Hector, Cindy Johnson, Carol Smith, Wayne Hill—your dedication to our well-being will never be forgotten. You are the Mt. Rushmore of house parents.

To Jeanelle Dech (MAWW), your unwavering belief and support in our ability to tell our story has been a driving force behind this project.

To Casey Dech and the Man, the Myth, the Legend Felix Agosto Jr., your talents and dedication shone brightly during our podcast and brought our story to life for thousands to experience.

To the Those Boys on the Hill Podcast Guests and Hosts: Your contributions enriched our narrative.

To Jennifer Allain, thank you for adding your time and talents to help edit this work.

A special heartfelt thanks to Leah Gallo. Your extraordinary talents, patience, vision, research, unwavering support, and encouragement have been amazing. There truly are no words to fully express what your help has meant to me. I can never thank you enough for your tireless efforts in making this project a reality and for pushing me to keep going. It is so much better than anything I could have dreamed it could be. In short, you are amazing!

To Mr. Derek Frey for allowing me to take up so much of your wonderful wife's, Leah Gallo, time to help me with this project, and thank you for answering the late call to give this manuscript a solid read before it went to final proofing. Your insights and suggestions made this book so much better.

To the many educators who provided more than just scholastic lessons. For offering empathy, guidance, a listening ear, and a shoulder to cry on, especially Wayne Howard, Carl Benson, and Amelie Schwendt—you made a lasting impact on my journey. There are too many others to name.

To the many families who opened their hearts and homes to me, including the Knoll, the Spencer, the Craig, the Maccombie, the Jones, the Rivera, and the Wu families—your love has been a constant source of comfort and belonging.

To the unnamed circle of friends, families, and teachers who have embraced us as their own over the past four decades, your love, guidance, and acceptance have made TBOTH infinitely stronger.

With the Deepest Gratitude,

Elliott Glover

Endnotes

[1] Erin Blakemore, "How the GI Bill's Promise Was Denied to a Million WWII Veterans," *History*, 21 June 2019, accessed 15 December 2023, https://www.history.com/news/gi-bill-black-wwii-veterans-benefits.

[2] Jake Blumgart, "How redlining segregated Philadelphia," *WHYY*, 10 December 2017, accessed 13 December 2023, https://whyy.org/segments/redlining-segregated-philadelphia/.

[3] "Employment for African Americans in the 1940s and 1950s: Hartford's G. Fox Department Store," *CT.GOV*, 1948, accessed 8 December 2023, https://portal.ct.gov/SDE/Publications/Labor/Employment-for-African-Americans-in-the-1940s-and-1950s-Hartfords-G-Fox-Department-Store/Documents.

[4] Valerie Wilson, "Understanding black-white disparities in labor market outcomes requires models that account for persistent discrimination and unequal bargaining power," *Economic Policy Institute*, 25 March 2022, accessed 8 December 2022, https://www.epi.org/unequalpower/publications/understanding-black-white-disparities-in-labor-market-outcomes/.

[5] Lisa Durán, "Caring for Each Other: Philanthropy In Communities Of Color," *Grassroots Fundraising Journal*, (September/October 2001), accessed 15 December 2023, https://coco-net.org/wp-content/uploads/2012/08/20_5_PhilCommOfColor.pdf.

[6] Isabel Wilkerson, *Caste: The Origins of Our Discontents*, (New York, Random House, 2020).

[7] Jake Blumgart, "Integrating Whitman," *Shelterforce*, 4 May 2016, accessed 15 December, 2023, https://shelterforce.org/2016/05/04/integrating-whitman/.

[8] Timothy J. Lombardo, "Civil Rights and the Rise of Frank Rizzo in 1960s Philadelphia," *Pennsylvania Legacies 18:2 (2018)*, accessed on 15 December 2023, https://hsp.org/blogs/fondly-pennsylvania/civil-rights-and-rise-frank-rizzo-1960s-philadelphia.

[9] David Gambacorta and Barbara Laker, "Frank Rizzo leaves a legacy of unchecked police brutality and division in Philadelphia," *The Philadelphia Inquirer*, 3 June 2020, accessed 11 December 2023, https://www.inquirer.com/news/philadelphia-frank-rizzo-police-violence-legacy-shootings-20200603.html.

[10] Gambacorta and Laker, "Frank Rizzo leaves a legacy."

[11] "Children In Single-Parent Families By Race And Ethnicity In United States," *The Annie E. Casey Foundation*, Data from 2011-2021, accessed 8December 2023, https://datacenter.aecf.org/data/tables/107-children-in-single-parent-families-by-race-and-ethnicity#detailed/1/any/false/2048,1729,37,871,870,573,869,36,868,867/10,11,9,12,1,185,13/432,431.

[12] "Statistics," *Adoption Connection, PA*, 2018 & 2019 Data, accessed on 8 December 2023, https://adoptionconnectionpa.org/statisitics/.

[13] ACLU of Pennsylvania, "PA Officials Routinely Deny Federally Mandated Aid To Relatives Acting as Foster Parents," *ACLU*, 16 August 2000, accessed 7 December 2023, https://www.aclu.org/press-releases/pa-officials-routinely-deny-federally-mandated-aid-relatives-acting-foster-parents.

[14] Alice Liu, "Case: Anderson v. Houstoun 2:00-cv-04148 | U.S. District Court for the Eastern District of Pennsylvania," *Civil Rights Litigation Clearinghouse*, 1 January 2013, accessed 7 December 2023, https://clearinghouse.net/case/5505/.

[15] Christina K. Sorenson, Esq., "Screaming Into The Void: Youth Voice In Institutional Placements," *Juvenile Law Center*, 3 February, 2023, accessed 7 December 2023, https://jlc.org/resources/screaming-void-youth-voice-institutional-placements.

[16] Christina Sorenson, "I was in foster care. Now I fight for kids like me," *The Philadelphia Inquirer*, 19 October 2023, accessed 7 December 2023, https://www.inquirer.com/opinion/commentary/foster-care-institution-abuse-protection-20231019.html.

[17] Sorenson, "Screaming Into The Void."

[18] Steve Volk and Julie Christie, "Crushing caseloads and low wages drive out foster care workers, but children pay the price," *The Philadelphia Inquirer*, 3 November 2022, accessed 7 December 2023, https://www.inquirer.com/news/philadelphia-foster-care-caseloads-worker-turnover-dhs-hope-jones-20221103.html.

[19] Annie E. Casey Foundation, "Child Welfare and Foster Care Statistics," *AECF Blog*, 16 May 2022, accessed 15 December 2023, https://www.aecf.org/blog/child-welfare-and-foster-care-statistics#:~:text=Children%20Exiting%20Foster%20Care,down%20from%2057%25%20in%202000.

[20] Elizabeth Brico, "The Government Spends 10 Times More on Foster Care and Adoption Than Reuniting Families," *Talk Poverty*, 23 August 2019, accessed 29 November 2023, https://talkpoverty.org/2019/08/23/government-more-foster-adoption-reuniting/index.html.

21 "Lyss Welding, "College Enrollment Statistics in the U.S.," *Best Colleges*, 8 August 2023, accessed 8 December 2023, https://www.bestcolleges.com/research/college-enrollment-statistics/#:~:text=What%20percent%20of%20students%20go,the%20rate%20was%20the%20same.

22 ABA Center on Children and the Law, "Fast Facts: Foster Care and Education Data at a Glance," *Legal Center for Foster Care and Education*, (January 2022), accessed, 8 December 2023, https://docs.fostercareandeducation.org/OurWork/NationalDatasheet 2022.aspx.

23 Amy Dworsky, PhD, Laura Napolitano, PhD, and Mark Courtney, PhD, "Homelessness During the Transition From Foster Care to Adulthood," *Am J Public Health* 103:2 (December 2013); S318–S323, doi: 10.2105/AJPH.2013.301455.

24 Rachel Hatzipanagos, "Adoption across races: 'I know my parents love me, but they don't love my people'," *The Seattle Times*, 13 December 2021, accessed 15 December 2023, https://www.seattletimes.com/nation-world/nation/adoption-across-races-i-know-my-parents-love-me-but-they-dont-love-my-people/.

25 Gina Miranda Samuels and Ralph LaRossa, "'Being Raised by White People': Navigating Racial Difference among Adopted Multiracial Adults," *Journal of Marriage and Family* 71:1 (February 2009): 80-94, *JSTOR*,https://www.jstor.org/stable/40262860.

26 Karen Valby, "The Realities of Raising a Kid of a Different Race," *Time*, accessed 15 December 2023, https://time.com/the-realities-of-raising-a-kid-of-a-different-race/.

27 Richard M. Lee, "The Transracial Adoption Paradox," *The Counseling Psychologist* 31:6 (December 2003): 711-744, doi: 10.1177/0011000003258087.

28 Shayanne Gal, Andy Kiersz, Michelle Mark, Marguerite Ward, Katie Balevic, Yoonji Han, and Annie Fu, "25 simple charts to show friends and family who aren't convinced racism is still a problem in America," *Business Insider*, 31 December 2022, accessed 15 December 2023, www.businessinsider.com/us-systemic-racism-in-charts-graphs-data-2020-6.

29 Bureau of Labor Statistics, "Usual Weekly Earnings of Wage and Salary Workers Third Quarter 2023," *US Department of Labor*, 18 October 2023, accessed 15 December 2023, https://www.bls.gov/news.release/pdf/wkyeng.pdf.

30 Sean Collins, "The systemic racism black Americans face, explained in 9 charts," *Vox*, 17 June 2020, accessed 15 December 2023, www.vox.com/2020/6/17/21284527/systemic-racism-black-americans-9-charts-explained.

31 Latoya Hill, Nambi Ndugga and Samantha Artiga, "Key Data on Health and Health Care by Race and Ethnicity," *KFF,* 15 March 2023, accessed 15 December 2023, https://www.kff.org/racial-equity-and-health-policy/report/key-data-on-health-and-health-care-by-race-and-ethnicity/#:~:text=Back%20to%20top)-,Health%20Status%2C%20Outcomes%2C%20and%20Behaviors,data%20available%20(Figure%2013).

32 Bureau of Labor Statistics, "Usual Weekly Earnings."

33 Celine McNicholas and Margaret Poydock, "Who are essential workers? A comprehensive look at their wages, demographics and unionization rates," *Economic Policy Institute,* 19 May 2020, accessed 15 December 2023, https://www.epi.org/blog/who-are-essential-workers-a-comprehensive-look-at their-wages-demographics-and-unionization-rates/.

34 "DFA: Distributional Financial Accounts: Distribution of Household Wealth in the U.S. Since 1989," *Board of Governors of the Federal Reserve System,* accessed 15 December 2023, https://www.federalreserve.gov/releases/z1/dataviz/dfa/distribute/chart/#quarter:121;series:Net%20worth;demographic:race;population:1,3,5,7;units:shares.

35 Curtis Bunn, "Report: Black people are still killed by police at a higher rate than other groups," *NBC News,* 3 March 2022, accessed 15 December 2023, https://www.nbcnews.com/news/nbcblk/report-black-people-are-still-killed-police-higher-rate-groups-rcna17169#.

36 Emma Pierson, Camelia Simoiu, Jan Overgoor, et al., "A large-scale analysis of racial disparities in police stops across the United States," *Nature Human Behaviour* 4 (2020): 736–745, doi: https://doi.org/10.1038/s41562-020-0858-1.

37 Stephan A. Schwartz, "Police brutality and racism in America," *Explore (NY)* 16:5 (September-October 2020): 280–282, accessed 15 December 2023, doi: 10.1016/j.explore.2020.06.010.

38 Adia Harvey Wingfield, "Color Blindness Is Counterproductive," *The Atlantic,* 13 September 2015, accessed 15 December 2013, www.theatlantic.com/politics/archive/2015/09/color-blindness-is-counterproductive/405037/.

39 Julie Moreau, "LGBTQ parents face 'state-sanctioned discrimination,' American Bar Association says," *NBC News,* 6 February 2019, accessed 15 December 2015, https://www.nbcnews.com/feature/nbc-out/lgbtq-parents-face-state-sanctioned-discrimination-american-bar-association-says-n968456.

⁴⁰ USAFacts Team, "How Many Kids Are in Foster Care?" *USA Facts*, updated 23 August 2023, accessed 15 December 2023, https://usafacts.org/articles/how-many-kids-are-in-foster-care/#:~:text=2021%20data%20shows%20a%2030,a%20single%20day%20was%20414%2C863.

⁴¹ Kids Count Data Center, "Children Exiting Foster Care by Exit Reason in United States," *The Annie E. Casey Foundation*, 2013-2021 data, accessed 10 January 2024, https://datacenter.aecf.org/data/tables/6277-children-exiting-foster-care-by-exit-reason?loc=1&loct=2#detailed/2/2-53/false/2048,574,1729,37,871,870,573,869,36,868/2632/13050,13051.

⁴² Child Trends and ZERO TO THREE Policy Center, *Changing the course for infants and toddlers: A survey of state child welfare policies and initiatives,* Child Trends (2013): 5 & 32, accessed 15 December 2023, https://cms.childtrends.org/wp-content/uploads/2013/09/changing-the-course-for-infants-and-toddlers-FINAL-1.pdf.

43 Catherine A. LaBrenz, Rowena Fong and Catherine Cubbin, "The road to reunification: Family- and state system-factors associated with successful reunification for children ages zero-to-five," *Child Abuse Neglect* 99 (January 2020): 104252, doi: https://doi.org/10.1016/j.chiabu.2019.104252.

⁴⁴ AECF Blog, "Black Children Continue To Be Disproportionately Represented In Foster Care," *The Annie E Casey Foundation*, 13 April 2020, accessed 15 December 2023, https://www.aecf.org/blog/us-foster-care-population-by-race-and-ethnicity.

⁴⁵ Edwin Rios, "'Family policing system': how the US criminalizes Black parenting," *The Guardian,* 14 April 2023, accessed 15 December 2023, https://www.theguardian.com/world/2023/apr/14/family-policing-system-black-childcare.

⁴⁶ Kathi L. H. Harp and Amanda M. Bunting, "The Racialized Nature of Child Welfare Policies and the Social Control of Black Bodies," *Social Politics* 27:2 (June 2020): 258–281, accessed 15 December 2023, doi: https://doi.org/10.1093%2Fsp%2Fjxz039.

⁴⁷ Calvin Schermerhorn, "Why the racial wealth gap persists, more than 150 years after emancipation," *The Washington Post.* 19 June 2019, accessed 15 December 2023, https://www.washingtonpost.com/outlook/2019/06/19/why-racial-wealth-gap-persists-more-than-years-after-emancipation/.

⁴⁸ Janell Ross, "One in Ten Black Children in America Are Separated From Their Parents by the Child-Welfare System. A New Book Argues That's No Accident," *Time*, 20 April 2022, accessed 15 December 2023, https://time.com/6168354/child-welfare-system-dorothy-roberts/.

⁴⁹ Kids Count Data Center, "Children Exiting Foster Care."

50 Amy Dworsky, PhD, Laura Napolitano, PhD, and Mark Courtney, PhD, "Homelessness During the Transition from Foster Care to Adulthood," *Am J Public Health* 103:2 (December 2013), S318-S323, doi: 10.2105/AJPH.2013.301455.

51 Mark E. Courtney, Nathanael J. Okpych, Justin Harty, et al., *Findings from the California Youth Transitions to Adulthood Study (CalYOUTH): Conditions of Youth at Age 23*, (Chicago: Chapin Hall at the University of Chicago, 2020), 47-53, accessed 10 January 2024, www.chapinhall.org/wp-content/uploads/CY_YT_RE1020.pdf.

52 ABA Center on Children and the Law, "Fast Facts: Foster Care and Education."

53 Mark E. Courtney, Amy Lynn Dworsky, Gretchen Ruth Cusick, et al. *Midwest Evaluation of the Adult Functioning of Former Foster Youth: outcomes at age 21*, (Chicago: Chapin Hall Center for Children, 2007), 50-53, accessed 10 January 2024, https://pdxscholar.library.pdx.edu/cgi/viewcontent.cgi?referer=https://scholar.google.com/&httpsredir=1&article=1059&context=socwork_fac.

54 Peter J. Pecora, Ronald C. Kessler, Jason Williams, et al., *Improving Family Foster Care: Findings from the Northwest Foster Care Alumni Study*, (Seattle: Casey Family Programs, 2005), 1, accessed 10 January 2024, https://www.casey.org/media/AlumniStudies_NW_Report_FR.pdf.

55 Lauren G. Beatty and Tracy L. Snell (BJS Statisticians), "*Survey of prison inmates*," *Bureau of Justice Statistics (BJS)*, (2016), date created 8 January, 2019, accessed 10 January 2024, https://bjs.ojp.gov/data-collection/survey-prison-inmates-spi.

56 Mark E. Courtney, Amy Lynn Dworsky, Gretchen Ruth Cusick, et al. *Midwest Evaluation*.

Made in the USA
Monee, IL
27 May 2025

18258698R00174